Institutional Microeconomics of Development

CESifo Seminar Series
Edited by Hans-Werner Sinn

Prospects for Monetary Unions after the Euro
Paul De Grauwe and Jacques Mélitz, editors

Structural Unemployment in Western Europe: Reasons and Remedies
Martin Werding, editor

Institutions, Development, and Economic Growth
Theo S. Eicher and Cecilia García-Peñalosa, editors

Competitive Failures in Insurance Markets: Theory and Policy Implications
Pierre-André Chiappori and Christian Gollier, editors

Japan's Great Stagnation: Financial and Monetary Policy Lessons for Advanced Economies
Michael M. Hutchison and Frank Westermann, editors

Tax Policy and Labor Market Performance
Jonas Agell and Peter Birch Sørensen, editors

Privatization Experiences in the European Union
Marko Köthenbürger, Hans-Werner Sinn, and John Whalley, editors

Recent Developments in Antitrust: Theory and Evidence
Jay Pil Choi, editor

Schools and the Equal Opportunity Problem
Ludger Woessmann and Paul E. Peterson, editors

Economics and Psychology: A Promising New Field
Bruno S. Frey and Alois Stutzer, editors

Institutions and Norms in Economic Development
Mark Gradstein and Kai A. Konrad, editors

Pension Strategies in Europe and the United States
Robert Fenge, Georges de Ménil, and Pierre Pestieau, editors

Foreign Direct Investment and the Multinational Enterprise
Steven Brakman and Harry Garretsen, editors

Sustainability of Public Debt
Reinhard Neck and Jan-Egbert Sturm, editors

The Design of Climate Policy
Roger Guesnerie and Henry Tulkens, editors

Poverty, Inequality, and Policy in Latin America
Stephan Klasen and Felicitas Nowak-Lehmann, editors

Guns and Butter: The Economic Laws and Consequences of Conflict
Gregory D. Hess, editor

Institutional Microeconomics of Development
Timothy Besley and Rajshri Jayaraman, editors

See http://mitpress.mit.edu for a complete list of titles in this series.

Institutional Microeconomics of Development

Edited by Timothy Besley and Rajshri Jayaraman

CESifo Seminar Series

The MIT Press
Cambridge, Massachusetts
London, England

For information about special quantity discounts, please email special_sales@mitpress.mit.edu

This book was set in Palatino on 3B2 by Asco Typesetters, Hong Kong.
Printed and bound in the United States of America.

Library of Congress Cataloging-in-Publication Data

Institutional microeconomics of development / edited by Timothy Besley and Rajshri Jayaraman.
p. cm.—(CESifo seminar series)
Includes bibliographical references and index.
ISBN 978-0-262-01406-9 (hardcover : alk. paper)
1. Institutional economics—Case studies. 2. Economic policy—Case studies.
3. Organizational change—Case studies. I. Besley, Timothy. II. Jayaraman, Rajshri.
HB99.5.I575 2010
338.9—dc22 2009048456

10 9 8 7 6 5 4 3 2 1

Contents

Series Foreword

This book is part of the CESifo Seminar Series. The series aims to cover topical policy issues in economics from a largely European perspective. The books in this series are the products of the papers and intensive debates that took place during the seminars hosted by CESifo, an international research network of renowned economists organized jointly by the Center for Economic Studies at Ludwig-Maximilians-Universität, Munich, and the Ifo Institute for Economic Research. All publications in this series have been carefully selected and refereed.

Contributors

Manuela Angelucci Department of Economics, University of Arizona (USA)

Oriana Bandiera London School of Economics (UK)

Pranab Bardhan Department of Economics, University of California, Berkeley (USA)

Timothy Besley Department of Economics and STICERD, London School of Economics (UK)

Martina Björkman IGIER, Bocconi University (Italy)

Robin Burgess Department of Economics and STICERD, London School of Economics (UK)

Giacomo De Giorgi Department of Economics, Stanford University (USA)

Stefan Dercon Department of Economics, University of Oxford (UK)

Marcel Fafchamps Department of Economics, University of Oxford (UK)

Rajshri Jayaraman ESMT Berlin (Germany)

Pramila Krishnan Department of Economics, University of Cambridge (UK)

Eliana La Ferrara IGIER, Bocconi University (Italy)

Gilat Levy Department of Economics, London School of Economics (UK)

Marcos A. Rangel Harris School of Public Policy, University of Chicago (USA)

Imran Rasul Department of Economics, University College London (UK)

Ritva Reinikka World Bank

Jakob Svensson IIES, Stockholm University (Sweden)

Institutional Microeconomics of Development

Introduction

Timothy Besley and Rajshri Jayaraman

Motivation

The narrative of development economics is now infused with discussions of institutions. From an analytic point of view, game-theoretic tools are now routinely brought to bear in understanding how institutions shape incentives. Empirically, institutions are given a central role in accounts of the forces that shape development and growth. Recent research has taken measurement in exciting new directions, enabling researchers and policymakers to better appreciate how institutions and institutional change matter.

This book brings together a collection of microeconomic perspectives on institutions from a group of leading scholars in development economics.[1] The role of institutions in economic development is the unifying theme.

The microeconomics of institutions has a long history. The focus of the earlier literature, with notable collections of essays compiled in Bardhan (1989) and Hoff, Braverman and Stiglitz (1993), was on agrarian institutions. Some of it was empirical, but its key insights came from incorporating game theory and contract theory into our understanding of how institutions work. Arrangements that seemed inexplicable to an earlier generation of researchers could be seen as rational responses to information constraints, transaction costs, and enforcement difficulties.

A good illustration of how institutional economics has taken root in microeconomic analyses of development concerns our appreciation of an institution like sharecropping. In spite of its prevalence, Marshall had dismissed it as economically inefficient, making its existence and apparent robustness a puzzle from an economic point of view. However, Stiglitz (1974) and subsequent contributors showed that a persuasive rationale lay in the trade-off between risk sharing and incentives when information is limited and hence monitoring, difficult.

The literature on sharecropping and agricultural contracts more generally blossomed and showed how modern economic theory had a role to play in understanding nonmarket arrangements as well as markets. It also laid bare the kinds of imperfections and inefficiencies that are now appreciated to be prevalent in low-income economies. Traditional institutions could be understood through this lens, but there was no need to romanticize them.

In the last fifteen years or so, institutions have featured prominently in macroeconomic thinking, particularly in trying to explain the persistence of inequality between nations. This takes up the challenge from earlier work in economic history by Douglass North. At the center of such debates has been the role of institutions in protecting private property, in particular by checking the arbitrary authority of rulers. In England, for example, it was argued that beginning with the Magna Carta, there had been a progression toward a system of government that limited the power of the king and created an environment where incentives to invest could be maintained.

The most influential contributions in recent debates have been those of Acemoglu, Johnson, and Robinson (2001) and Engerman and Sokoloff (1997; 2002). Acemoglu and colleagues observed a strong correlation between historical patterns of settler mortality and modern-day development. They argued that this effect is mediated through the protection of property rights. Their narrative is compelling. Places where settlers could not survive led to short-termism, where states were extractive. However, in places where settlers were able to survive, they created institutions oriented toward long-term development goals, which are conducive to prosperity.

The work of Acemoglu and co-workers has reignited debate among mainstream economists, bringing institutions back to center stage in thinking about issues in economic development. The main focus of this debate is whether institutions or something else altogether—geography, culture, or religion—is central to development. Sachs (2003), for example, found that malaria ecology has a direct impact on economic growth, and Hibbs and Olsson (2004) found that climate, latitude, and East-West orientation matter even after controlling for institutional quality.

Quite apart from this debate are two important by-products of Acemoglu, Johnson, and Robinson's work. The first is that researchers in institutional economics have been challenged to think seriously about identifying the causal effect of institutions on economic development. The second is that a greater interest has arisen in exploring historical data and looking at economic development over an extended window of time. Nunn (2008), for example, used painstakingly gathered data from historical documents and shipping records to make a convincing case that the slave trades had an adverse effect on development in Africa.

The macroeconomic institutions literature has demonstrated the importance of both political and legal institutions in promoting development. Countries with better rule of law, more private property rights, smoother bureaucracies, and better functioning financial institutions have, on average, grown faster. At the same time, there is clearly a great deal of heterogeneity in institutions as well as in outcomes associated with a given institutional metric. A microeconomic perspective is well equipped to grasp this heterogeneity.

Take the new political economy literature, for example, which has focused on understanding how policymaking and implementation work. There is a very wide range of institutional arrangements for making policy decisions; despite an increase in the number of democratic countries using the standard POLITY IV definition, a large number of nondemocracies remain. In looking at economic performance in its broadest terms, the heterogeneity among democracies and autocracies is striking.

This makes it clear that it is necessary to get behind the labels in order to understand how incentive structures work. Persson and Tabellini (2003), for instance, argued that it is not democracy per se that matters for the kinds of policies that get chosen, but the form of democracy. At the national level, however, countries have only one form of democracy, for instance, presidential or parliamentary systems, or majoritarian or proportional representation. This makes it difficult to appreciate the nuances of incentive structures using macroeconomic data.

Given that many countries have decentralized political systems, there is scope for looking at variation within countries for understanding how political institutions work. In contrast to cross-country studies, it is typically feasible to control for a number of sources of heterogeneity, which will tend to be fixed within a country. A number of prominent recent papers have exploited intercountry variation at the state, municipal, or even village level to explore how heterogeneity mediates outcomes in the context of democratic politics.

For example, using randomized gender assignment in council leadership across Indian villages, Chattopadhyay and Duflo (2004) found that village council heads invest more in the types of infrastructure favored by members of their own gender. The authors concluded from this that mandated representation, in this case of women, has important ramifications for policy decisions. Ferraz and Finan (2008) explored the effect of randomized audits of expenditures of federally transferred funds to Brazilian municipalities on electoral outcomes. They found that the dissemination of information regarding corruption of public officials reduced incumbents' likelihood of reelection.

The recent interest in institutions has also emphasized the importance of understanding legal institutions. Shleifer and co-authors argued at a macroeconomic level that colonial legal origins are a strong predictor of financial development as well as banking, firm entry, labor markets, and so on (see La Porta, Lopez-de-Silanes and Shleifer (2007) for a review). In each of these spheres, civil law is associated with more government ownership and regulation than common law. A natural way to proceed in pushing this agenda further is also to move to within-country variation and a microeconomic focus.

While the work of Shleifer, Acemoglu, and others on legal institutions has emphasized constraining mechanisms, market-supporting mechanisms are clearly also important. As Greif (1994) described in his classic study on Mahgribi traders, cultural influences and social networks play a key role in the organic development of different institutions, by shaping contract enforcement. Moreover, constraining as well as enabling institutions often interact to form evolving market and political institutions.

This Book

This book examines political, legal, social, and market institutions through a microeconomics lens. The microeconomic perspective confers a number of advantages. First, it permits an examination of de facto rather than de jure institutions and in the empirical analyses allows for a large variety of controls, which helps to minimize the problems of omitted variables bias and measurement error to which coarser cross-country measures are sometimes vulnerable. Second, it is a natural context in which to examine heterogeneity in outcomes, in particular the distributional consequences of a given set of institutions as well as potential interactions between different types of institutions.

The book contains eight chapters. The first two are introductory chapters written by Pranab Bardhan and Marcel Fafchamps. They present a comprehensive overview of the state of the study of institutions in development thinking.

The remaining six chapters examine institutions from the perspective of a variety of actors—industries, families, and local communities—drawing from a wide array of data sources and empirical methods. They seek to understand the role that institutions play in development. Each of these chapters presents original empirical research, exploring data from more than six developing countries spanning three continents: Angola, Ethiopia and Uganda, Indonesia and India, and Mexico.

Pranab Bardhan was writing about agrarian institutions in the 1980s, well before institutions entered mainstream thinking in development. As such, he is uniquely placed to reflect upon the state of the study of institutions in economic development. As he notes in chapter 1, his early work was part of a body of contributions toward understanding the role of institutions in a (predominantly rural) development setting.

This work on microeconomic institutions in the 1980s presented earnest examinations of the specific channels through which institutions affected economic outcomes, for example, how tenancy or land rights affected agricultural productivity. That this literature is largely overlooked today may be accounted for by its failure to pay closer attention to identification. This book essentially picks up where the earlier literature left off, by examining specific channels through which institutions affect outcomes while being careful about identification.

After reviewing the microeconomic literature on institutions, Bardhan argues that our understanding of institutions would be enriched by broadening the discussion beyond the current preoccupation with property rights. With regard to the impact on economic development, his first important point is that where one stands regarding the desirability of a given set of institutions depends on where one sits. Different social groups care about different types of property rights; the impact of any given institutional setting is likely to vary with individuals' socioeconomic status, and institutional change is likely to produce its set of winners and losers. This is not captured in a monolithic view of institutions, in which the outcomes of interest are restricted to *average* income or *aggregate* growth.

North (1981) famously defined economic institutions as "a set of rules, compliance procedures and moral and ethical behavioral norms designed to constrain the behavior of individuals in the interests of maximizing the wealth or utility of the principals" (201–202). Bardhan's second argument in favor of broadening our view is that institutions need not be restricted to *constraining* functions. They also serve in an important *enabling* or *coordinating* capacity. There are three main actors in this: the state, local communities, and the market. Various chapters in this book look at each of these actors.

In the second half of chapter 1, Bardhan reflects upon what is one of the big unresolved questions in the field: Why do dysfunctional institutions persist for a long time? He argues that the answer may lie less in the problem of political commitment, which has been the focus of the macroeconomic literature, than in the fact that there exist underlying distributive conflicts. Although no other chapters in this book directly address the dynamics of institutions, they do find that institutional change is far from distribution-neutral. There exist sometimes surprising winners and losers, and understanding how such outcomes are mediated promises to enhance our understanding of the dynamics of institutions.

Most of us take the existence of markets for goods and services for granted. We fail to realize that in order to be willing to trade, buyers and sellers need to have a great many assurances. Buyers want to receive the good, sellers want to receive payment, and so forth. The presence of market institutions provides the bedrock for these assurances.

Marcel Fafchamps has published important work on the role of the formal and informal institutions that enable exchange between firms and within households and communities. Drawing from his decades-long research in Africa and Asia, he formulates in chapter 2 an original analytic framework within which to think about such institutions. Emphasizing the central role of contract enforcement, he explores the ways in which, in the absence of formal institutions, informal institutions that foster trust, reputation, information sharing, and (statistical) discrimination mediate market exchange.

One could argue that the poor remain poor precisely because of the preponderance of informal institutions. For example, as Fafchamps points out, markets characterized by relational contracting tend to be inimical to entry, and this hurts competition and growth. But, he argues, there is a limit to what formal legal systems (judges and courts) can do to remedy this because many transactions in the developing world tend to be small and take place between agents who do not have much by way of assets that can be seized in the event of contract breach.

This does not mean there is no room for formal institutional support. Fafchamps emphasizes that there is a role for legal institutions in enforcing large transactions, particularly in the context of foreign direct investment (FDI), and a strong case to be made for increasing support to extant legal systems in order to increase their efficacy in law enforcement and stamping out corruption.

Fafchamps echoes Bardhan's point on the role of the market as a key enabling and coordinating institution. He argues that perhaps even more important than formal legal institutions are formal market support institutions like franchises, quality certification, and external auditing. He emphasizes the role of the private sector in creating such market support functions by leveraging brand names or formal legal support or oversight from a third country where such institutions function better.

The remaining six chapters are empirical. Each examines a particular set of institutions in a unique setting. Chapters dealing with institutional change at the macroeconomic level start with an extensive review of the macroeconomic literature and discuss the advantages of a microeconomic focus. Chapters using unfamiliar methods are careful to spell out their empirical models. After presenting original empirical evidence, each chapter outlines economic policy implications that might be drawn by understanding the microeconomics of the institutions in question.

Sub-Saharan Africa has grown at a snail's pace over the last two decades, and today it is the poorest region in the world. There is a large macroeconomic literature exploring why this is the case, and Collier and Gunning (1999) provide a fine review of the cross-country evidence. One of the three broad explanations for this is weak institutions, a dramatic correlate of which is conflict. Not only is Africa poor, it is also one of the most conflict-ridden places on earth. In chapter 3, Eliana La Ferrara provides an extensive review of the literature on the causes and consequences of violent conflict. As she points out, a major drawback of most of this literature based on cross-country evidence is its failure to establish a *causal* effect in one or the other direction.

Whereas at a country level national income and conflict may be endogenously determined, from firms' perspective conflict can typically be regarded as exogenous. It is with this basic insight that La Ferrara is able to exploit stock market data to assess the impact of conflict on firms investing or operating in these countries. She does so using an event study methodology. This tool, a workhorse in finance, is relatively unexploited in economics, and La Ferrara explains the empirical model in careful detail.

The macroeconomic evidence suggests that conflict is closely associated with underdevelopment, and a natural conclusion from this would seem to be that events pointing to a cessation of conflict would be a good thing for the economy. La Ferrara's work makes it evident that at the microeconomic level, there are also losers. In one of the two event studies she presents she finds, for instance, that the cumulative abnormal stock market returns for diamond mining companies operating in Angola were *negative* following news of Jonas Savimbi's death as well as the signing of a cease-fire agreement. In other words, events that were presented in policy press circles as heralding a new era of peace and prosperity in Angola were viewed by financial investors as bad news.

La Ferrara's work is among only a handful of examples that effectively tackle the issue of identification in the context of conflict. Her empirical results highlight the distributional tension inherent in any given change in the policy environment, even when the change is widely regarded as a change for the better. This is made possible by allowing for different stakeholders, in this case, individual companies with different vested interests. Recognizing that there may be winners and losers in the process of institutional change, and identifying who these may be, brings us closer to understanding what Pranab Bardhan views as the central question in the institutional economics of development: why seemingly desirable institutional change is so difficult to procure.

If Africa's meager growth performance is due to weak or dysfunctional institutions, then a lack of accountability bears much of the blame. This is especially true in service delivery. Of course, it is one thing to recognize that good governance is important, and quite another to go about creating systems of accountability. In chapter 6, Martina Björkman, Ritva Reinikka, and Jakob Svensson discuss some reasons why it is so difficult to hold public service providers accountable. One reason is clearly inadequate rule of law. But these authors point out that even a well-functioning legal system may be unable to tackle the complexity and overcome the informational asymmetries inherent in public service provision. These problems are only exacerbated by the fact that providers tend to be a coherent, well-organized interest group whereas service recipients represent diffuse interests.

Björkman and colleagues use recent evidence from a relatively novel institutional mechanism through which to strengthen providers' accountability to citizen-clients, namely, a citizen report card instituted in Uganda. Under this intervention users (and potential users) provided feedback regarding public services. This information was aggregated and then disseminated to communities, allowing them to compare the quality of their services to those in other communities.

The community monitoring project studied by Björkman and coauthors had two important elements. First, it focused on a carefully constructed mechanism aimed at improving information dissemination. This enabled examination of *whether* a given institutional structure affects outcomes and *how* it does so. Second, it used randomized assignment to aid identification. This type of study design, possible only in a microeconomic setting, is extremely important from a policy perspective given the monumental failure of service delivery in developing countries and in particular for the poor in these countries.

Information dissemination is one way to promote public service delivery. The devolution of decision-making authority is often touted as another. While recent microeconomic evidence suggests that giving a voice to weaker groups through decentralized democratic institutions typically increases service delivery to these groups, a number of studies have also found that community-based projects may be subject to local capture.

That decentralized governance may lead to undesirable outcomes is, in and of itself, not a novel finding. It has long been recognized in the political economy literature that the political process may lead to inefficient public goods provision and that local governments may be subject to elite capture. The interesting question in this context is, Under what circumstances do local democratic institutions foster the interests of the poor?

Intuitively (where the poor constitute a majority) the answer is likely to be, When the poor are able to act cohesively as a group. But there are many reasons why the poor may not act cohesively. Conflicting interests on the basis of ethnicity is one, and this is the focus of Oriana Bandiera and Gilat Levy in chapter 5. They argue that when the poor are divided along the lines of ethnicity, they are less likely to act as a cohesive class. Under such circumstances, public finance is more likely to succumb to elite capture under democratic institutions. Another way of seeing this is that with more ethnic diversity, public goods provision under democratic local governance is likely to resemble that under political systems (oligarchies, for example) in which power is concentrated among the elites.

In order to test this using microeconomic data, one would need to find a country with comparable democratic and oligarchic local governments as well as ethnic heterogeneity. Indonesia fits this bill. Using village survey data, Bandiera and Levy found evidence of elite capture associated with ethnic diversity. In particular, they found that public policy outcomes in democratically governed villages characterized by ethnic diversity closely resembled outcomes in villages governed by oligarchies.

There is by now a considerable body of empirical evidence showing that ethnic diversity is negatively correlated with economic development. In their seminal paper Easterly and Levine (1997) showed, for example, that this explained 30 percent of the growth differential between the countries of Africa and East Asia. From a policy perspective, it is difficult to know what to take away from this. By analyzing the *channels* through which ethnic diversity may matter, Bandiera and Levy's microeconomic approach, both theoretical and empirical, sheds light on how institutions may (or, in their case, may not) alleviate the negative consequences associated with ethnic diversity.

Of all the pillars of the Washington Consensus, the merits of trade liberalization is one of the most hotly contested. Supporters have argued that access to larger markets and increased exposure to competition is good for growth. Detractors have pointed out that liberalization may stifle infant industries as well as learning by doing. Empirical evidence based on cross-country data is mixed at best.

Robin Burgess in chapter 4 presents a nuanced view of the merits of this macroeconomic policy change by examining how its effects are tempered by local variations in institutional environment. Using industry-level data, Burgess analyzes how nationwide industrial delicensing reforms interacted with investment climate in different Indian states, which exhibited considerable heterogeneity in institutional environment. This microeconomic approach has a distinct advantage over a cross-country approach in that it allows for *heterogeneous treatment effects* of a homogeneous policy change based on local differences in *comparable* institutions.

Burgess's key finding is that liberalization magnifies policy and institutional disadvantages. Those states with a poor investment climate are relatively worse off after liberalization, and states with better investment climates are better off. This insight enhances our understanding of institutions on two counts. First, it highlights the role of complementary local institutions in economic development. The fact that local institutions play this mediating role in economic growth is important for policy purposes because (unlike, say, geography) local institutions may be more amenable to manipulation.

Second, in demonstrating that this macroeconomic policy reform has not been distribution-neutral, it fosters a better understanding of why the process of economic liberalization is so controversial. In the Indian context Burgess's findings suggest one explanation for why the loudest regional dissenters are often the most "backward" states, and why this is likely to persist.

Economists have long recognized the importance of social institutions in economic development, and the oldest and most resilient of these is families. There are at least three ways in which families mediate economic outcomes. The first is through insurance or redistribution, the second, through learning. Individuals acquire information and update their beliefs and expectations based on the experience of other members of their family network. Third, family members influence the marital bargaining positions of husbands and wives.

Economists since Gary Becker have recognized these functions by focusing on households rather than individuals as their primary unit of analysis.

Households, however, typically operate within the context of extended families, and particularly in developing countries these extended family networks have a profound influence on their decision making. Yet, we know relatively little about extended family structures.

In chapter 7, Manuela Angelucci, Giacomo de Giorgi, Marcos Rangel, and Imran Rasul take a step toward filling this gap. Exploiting the patronymic naming convention in Mexico, they used household data to map and analyze extended family structures across 506 Mexican villages. Understanding the structure of extended family networks is important if one is to understand how this particular institution mediates households' policy responses. This is especially relevant if targeted programs are to reach their intended beneficiaries.

For example, the authors (in a companion piece) find that households' response to Progresa, a social assistance program in rural Mexico, differs according to the presence and type of extended family ties. A failure to understand the rules of the game at the family level in this context can lead to serious errors of commission and omission in targeted programs such as these, which lie at the heart of many developing countries' poverty alleviation strategies.

While many economists have been critical of the seeming preoccupation of the macroeconomic institutions literature with property rights, few would claim that these are unimportant. Chapter 8 presents a microeconomic perspective on property rights. The book therefore closes with a chapter that brings together the old development microeconomic institutions literature, with its focus on agrarian institutions, and the new macroeconomic institutions literature.

In chapter 8, Stefan Dercon and Pramila Krishnan examine what some meaningful measures of land rights may be, what determines land rights, and what bearing land rights may have on microeconomic investment decisions. They use household data from Ethiopia, one of the poorest countries in sub-Saharan Africa. While identification remains tricky, their approach highlights three strengths of a microeconomic approach to property rights. First, the relative homogeneity of the institutional and economic environment within a country reduces the problem of unobserved heterogeneity. Second, heterogeneous treatment effects at the household level can be permitted. Third, a more subtle understanding of de facto land rights can be developed.

Basic Insights

A major challenge that remains is to join up microeconomic insights to the macroeconomic level, thereby merging insights from these two vibrant traditions of institutional analysis. Some useful basic insights emerge on this from the chapters in this book.

One is to be reminded of the remarkable heterogeneity of institutions. Institutions of accountability are found in citizen report cards and decentralized governance. Policy change is mediated through local market institutions, state government–established institutions, and families. From a policy perspective, this speaks against a top-down view of a globally unique set of best practice institutions. That there is there is no monolithic path to development finds ample corroborative evidence when one looks at the staggering variety of historical development experiences.

While confirming that institutional design really is a tricky business, there is an inherently positive message for policymakers that economic prosperity that builds from the historical context can potentially lead to successful development.

Second, the ingenuity in terms of data as well as methodology adopted by these researchers in an effort to establish a causal link between institutions and development-relevant outcomes suggests that identification, while challenging, is not a hopeless task. Taking identification concerns to bear on the study of institutions is a major task, and it can pay dividends. It can also proceed in a way that is complementary with our theoretical understanding of how institutions work. Theory can shape our view of what to measure and in understanding the heterogeneous impact of institutional arrangements.

Allied to this last point, the microeconomic approach presented in this book highlights the immense heterogeneity in responses to institutional rules. This heterogeneity may arise from a number of different sources. One possibility is that it arises from differences in the socioeconomic characteristics of microeconomic actors—individuals, firms, households. Another possibility is that heterogeneity arises from interactions of extant formal or informal institutions with (often top-down) institutional change. Some of these interactions are complementary. Burgess's local investment climate and liberalization is one such example. Others, such as family-based transfer mechanisms and government social programs, may be substitutes.

Accounting for and studying heterogeneity in responses should give policymakers the kind of sure-footed knowledge that is needed to cultivate a better understanding of why seemingly sound policy prescriptions do not necessarily translate into good outcomes. This is important in the design and implementation of both first-generation policy reforms of the Washington Consensus variety and second generation institutional reforms that are the currency of current policy debates.

Moreover, understanding why institutions are embraced or rejected and by whom provides important input into answering some of the big unresolved questions in the institutional economics of development. For example, it helps to clarify why we don't always observe positive selection in institutions and why dysfunctional institutions tend to persist.

Note

1. The collection of essays edited by Helpman (2008) shares a similar ambition.

References

Acemoglu, D., S. Johnson, and J. A. Robinson. 2001. The Colonial Origins of Comparative Development: An Empirical Investigation. *American Economic Review* 91 (5): 1369–1401.

———. 2005. Institutions as a Fundamental Cause of Long-Run Growth. In *Handbook of Economic Growth*, ed. P. Aghion and S. Durlauf, vol. 1A, 385–472. Amsterdam: North-Holland.

Bardhan, P., ed. 1989. *The Economic Theory of Agrarian Institutions*. Oxford: Clarendon Press.

Chattopadhyay, R., and E. Duflo. 2004. Women as Policy Makers: Evidence from a Randomized Policy Experiment in India. *Econometrica* 42 (5): 1409–1443.

Collier, P., and J. W. Gunning. 1999. Why Has Africa Grown Slowly? *Journal of Economic Perspectives* 13 (3): 3–22.

Easterly, W., and R. Levine. 1997. Africa's Growth Tragedy: Policies and Ethnic Divisions. *Quarterly Journal of Economics* 112 (4): 1203–1250.

Engerman, S. L., and K. L. Sokoloff. 1997. Factor Endowments, Institutions and Differential Paths of Growth among New World Economies: A View from Economic Historians of the United States. In *How Latin America Fell Behind*, ed. S. Haber. Stanford, Calif.: Stanford University Press.

———. 2002. Factor Endowments, Inequality and Paths of Development among New World Economies. *Economia* 3 (1): 41–88.

Ferraz, C., and F. Finan. 2008. Exposing Corrupt Politicians: The Effect of Brazil's Publicly Released Audits on Electoral Outcomes. *Quarterly Journal of Economics* 123 (2): 703–745.

Greif, A. 1994. Cultural Beliefs and the Organization of Society: A Historical and Theoretical Reflection on Collectivist and Individualistic Societies. *Journal of Political Economy* 102 (5): 912–950.

Helpman, E. 2008. *Institutions and Economic Performance*. Cambridge, Mass.: Harvard University Press.

Hibbs, D., Jr., and O. Olsson. 2004. Geography, Biogeography, and Why Some Countries Are Rich and Others Are Poor. *Proceedings of the National Academy of Sciences* 101 (10): 3715–3720.

Hoff, K., A. Braverman, and J. E. Stiglitz, eds. 1993. *The Economics of Rural Organization*. New York: Oxford University Press.

La Porta, R., F. Lopez-de-Silanes, and A. Shleifer. 2007. The Economic Consequences of Legal Origins. NBER working paper 13608.

North, D. 1981. *Structure and Change in Economic History*. New York: W.W. Norton.

Nunn, N. 2008. The Long-Term Effects of Africa's Slave Trades. *Quarterly Journal of Economics* 123 (1): 139–176.

Pande, R., and C. Udry. 2006. Institutions and Development: A View from Below. Working paper 928. Economic Growth Center, Yale University.

Persson, T., and G. Tabellini. 2003. *The Economic Effects of Constitutions*. Cambridge, Mass.: MIT Press.

Sachs, J. D. 2003. Institutions Don't Rule: Direct Effects of Geography on Per Capita Income. NBER working paper 9490.

Stiglitz, J. E. 1974. Incentives and Risk Sharing in Sharecropping. *Review of Economic Studies* 41 (2): 219–255.

1 Institutional Economics of Development: Some General Reflections

Pranab Bardhan

Institutional economics is now a thriving subject in development, as it should be, because the major difference between the economics of rich and poor countries is arguably in the different institutional frameworks we implicitly or explicitly use in understanding or analyzing them. Other substantial differences, say, in geography or culture or history, also work sometimes through institutional differences. Because institutional economics of development is a vast subject, in this chapter I confine myself to a subset of institutional issues, still keeping the range rather broad, broader than most of the other chapters in this book.

After a brief foray into the history of economic thought regarding institutions particularly in development economics, I try to (1) unbundle the complex of generic institutions important for development, going beyond the narrow focus of the current institutional economics literature on security of property rights; (2) speculate on the processes of institutional change (or lack of change), in particular on what should be a central question of institutional economics of development—why do dysfunctional institutions persist over long periods of time?—and focus on the impact of distributive conflicts in this context; and (3) identify a central dilemma in governance institutions and some suggestions for future research. The focus throughout is on the role of distributive conflicts in shaping institutions.

Most recent papers on institutional economics start with North (1990), or at most with Williamson (1985), ignoring a long tradition of institutionalist literature going back to the German Historical School in the latter part of the nineteenth century, and the role played by Marxist economics (as a major discourse on how economic institutions are shaped by technology and changed by collective action) and by the American institutionalists (like Veblen) in the early part of the twentieth century. In the field of development economics, most discussion of institutions also starts with North and then jumps to the cross-country empirical literature, most widely cited of which is Acemoglu, Johnson, and Robinson (2001). Professional memory or attention span in economics is always rather short, but most remarkably so in this case, because North (1990) was immediately preceded by at least two decades of vigorous economic analysis of institutional arrangements in developing countries. It started with the literature on sharecropping, followed by a proliferation of analyses of institutions in rural land, labor, credit, insurance, and some general interlinked markets. By the early 1990s two multiauthor volumes of essays on rural institutions, *The Economic Theory of Agrarian Institutions* (Bardhan 1989b) and *The Economics of Rural Organization* (Hoff, Braverman, and Stiglitz 1993), put together and extended the results of the rich literature on rural institutions in developing countries that had come up in the preceding two decades. Another collection of essays, *The New Institutional Economics and Development* (Nabli and Nugent 1989), put together various applications of transaction cost analysis with problems of development, both rural and urban (with application to case studies in Tunisia).[1] There is hardly any trace of this literature in the recent outpourings on the institutional economics of development.

There may be two reasons for this. One is that North's Nobel prize in institutional economics deflected attention away from the microeconomic analysis of the earlier literature to large macroeconomic institutions in trying to explain why historically some countries have developed and others not, quickly buttressed by the massive amounts of cross-country regressions on the basis of the easily downloadable international data that became available in the last decade or so. The second reason is that while the earlier literature was to a large extent theoretical, the recent dominant trend is in the empirical direction. Yet, the earlier microeconomic literature was also significantly empirical; there were many attempts to quantify the impact of institutions or the determination of institutional choice. For example, the impact of land tenure on farm productivity was carefully estimated in the articles by Bell (1977) and Shaban (1987), testing the competing models of sharecropping with Indian microeconomic data. Variations in forms, contractual terms, and extent of tenancy were empirically examined by Matoussi and Nugent (1989) with Tunisian household-level data; Bardhan (1984) with Indian household-level, farm-level, region-level, and state-level data; Morooka and Hayami (1989) with plot-level data in a village in western Java; and Otsuka (1991) and Roumasset (1984), both with farm-level data for the Philippines. Variations in farm labor institutions (including labor-tying arrangements) were analyzed by Bardhan (1983) with Indian region-level and household-level data; the impact of ownership security on investment was analyzed by Feder and Onchan (1987) with farm-level data in Thailand; the impact of indigenous land rights on agricultural productivity was analyzed by Migot-Adholla, Hazell, and Place (1991) with farm household data in sub-Saharan Africa; the impact of changes in rules of credit access on productivity was estimated by Carter (1989) with farm-level data in Nicaragua; the role of credit arrangements in risk pooling was analyzed by Udry (1990) with household-level data in northern Nigeria; the impact of reform of collective rights on productivity and resource allocation was empirically analyzed by Carter (1984) with farm-level data for Peruvian agriculture and by Lin (1987) with province-level data for China. And so on.

Some of these empirical attempts did not pay as scrupulous attention to the identifying strategy in econometric estimation as we do today, but they represented a considerable amount of advance. For that matter, much of the recent macroeconomic empirical literature on institutions on the basis of cross-country regressions is also flawed, largely on account of unobserved heterogeneity, use of necessarily coarse instrument variables, and poor data quality and cross-country comparability.[2] As Pande and Udry (2005) pointed out in their survey,[3] the cross-country empirical strategy cannot disentangle the specific institutional channels through which an outcome is affected or the impact of institutional changes on it.

Beyond Private Property Rights

Following the leadership of North, the recent literature has shown how important secure property rights are in encouraging investment and innovations, allowing for the investor and the innovator to reap the harvest of their efforts.[4] There is, however, a general impression that if one can get the rule of law that protects property rights (preferably, laws that are supposed to protect minority shareholders against insider abuse in the corporate sector), the market will take care of much of the rest. This preoccupation with the institution of security of property rights, often to the exclusion of other important institutional issues, severely limits our understanding of the development process. Different social groups may be interested in different types of property rights;

for example, the poor may care more for simple land titles or relief from the usual harassments by local goons or government inspectors, whereas rich investors may care more for protection of their corporate shareholder rights against insider abuses or for banking regulations, and a general rule-of-law (or legal origin) variable is too crude to capture these differences. In general, as Pande and Udry (2005) pointed out with an example from Ghana, the incentives provided by a given institutional setting often vary with individuals' economic and political status.

Second, in history securing property rights for some has often meant dispossessing others. For example, the rights of enclosure in England eliminated the traditional land use rights of many poor villagers; in the nineteenth-century United States ensuring the security of property rights superseded communal tribal rights in land traditionally enjoyed by Native Americans; in recent years in Africa land-titling programs have sometimes dispossessed women of their traditional farming rights. In South America, in contrast with many parts of North America, property rights in land were often bestowed on people who were politically influential but not necessarily good farmers. This led to polarization and conflicts with poor peasants, which served neither efficiency nor equity.

In general, when contracts are incomplete, attempts to enforce private property rights may weaken the mechanisms of prior cooperation among resource users (e.g., of previously common or weakly defined property). In particular, a central characteristic of most private property rights is their tradability, and tradability (particularly to outsiders) may undermine the reliability of a long-term relationship among users of a resource.[5] Similarly, the market-enhancing features of securing rights in one market (say, credit) may undermine implicit contracts in related transactions where markets are weak (say, insurance). Kranton and Swamy (1999) gave an example of how the British introduction of court enforcement of contracts in agricultural credit markets of the Bombay Deccan in the nineteenth century reduced lenders' incentives to subsidize farmers' investments in times of crisis, leaving them more vulnerable in bad times with formal insurance markets largely absent.

Third, in the fast growth of the last three decades in East Asian countries, particularly China and Indonesia, prudent (though corrupt and tyrannical) rulers, more than formal rule of law and guaranteed security of property rights (which were often rather weak), succeeded in providing for a predictable and durable contractual environment for private business to thrive. In the East Asian business environment (e.g., among Chinese business families in southeast Asia) the transactions between private parties were governed less by court-enforced private property rights than by implicit relational contracts and reputational incentives. But the relation-based systems of governance become weaker as the scale of economic activity expands.

Fourth, institutions in the standard view have mainly a *constraining* role, constraining the state or other parties from intervening with property rights. But there are many cases of *enabling* institutions that have a somewhat different role: a community or a state institution may enable common people to do things they could not do by themselves in isolation. Social networks, community organizations, networks of government extension services and local experimental stations, a national innovation system that facilitates training and technology absorption are a few examples of many such enabling institutions. This distinction between constraining and enabling resembles the distinction philosophers make between negative and positive liberty, discussed in depth in the literature relating to the famous essay by Isaiah Berlin (1969). In one strand of this literature, a third concept of liberty was introduced (see Skinner 2002) that emphasizes the need for democratic institutions that promote civic participation. Consistent with (though not always aware of) this literature, many economists emphasize the importance of participatory institutions (as opposed to merely constraining institutions), particularly in the management of local environmental resources (like forests, fishery, irrigation) or in worker participation in firm management, or in maintaining ethnic networks of trade and long-distance credit (e.g., the community responsibility system discussed by Greif (1997), preserving multilateral reputation mechanisms in late medieval commerce around the Mediterranean).

Fifth, historically the way the various *coordinating institutions* in a society function made a big difference in development. In general, economies at early stages of development are beset with coordination failures of various kinds. Alternative coordination mechanisms—the state, the market, the community organizations—all play different roles, sometimes conflicting and sometimes complementary, in overcoming these coordination failures, and these will remain important even if private property rights were to be made fully secure. Also, these roles change in various stages of development in highly context-specific and path-dependent ways. To proclaim the universal superiority of one coordination mechanism over another is naive, futile, and ahistorical.

Markets are superb coordination mechanisms in harmonizing numerous noncooperative interactions and in disciplining inefficiency and rewarding high-valued performance. But when incentives and control rights are misaligned (e.g., because of initial asset ownership differences constraining contractual opportunities), and there are important strategic complementarities in long-term investment decisions, markets fail to coordinate efficiently. The implications of imperfections in, or the nonexistence of, credit and insurance markets are severe for the poor, sharply reducing a society's potential for productive investment, innovation, and human resource development. The state can provide leadership for (and put selective incentives and pressure on) individuals interacting cooperatively in situations where noncooperative interactions are inefficient. But state officials may have neither the information nor the motivation to carry out this role; they may be inept or corrupt, and the political accountability mechanisms are often much too weak to discipline them. In the context of these pervasive market and government failures it is often pointed out that a local community organization, if it has stable membership and well-developed mechanisms of transmitting private information and enforcing social norms among its members, has the potential to provide more efficient coordination than either the state or the market. But community organizations fail, too, when they are captured by elite (or sectarian) interests or are hamstrung by the secession of the rich and the talented from local communities, and they may face covariate risks and costs of small scale.

Thus all three types of coordination mechanisms have their strengths and weaknesses, and they sometimes work in mutually conflicting ways. State versus market is, of course, the staple of traditional left-right debates. And bureaucratic as well as market processes may encroach upon or weaken the viability of traditional community management, say, of environmental resources, based on peer monitoring in proximate groups. But it is also important to keep in mind that these relationships need not be adversarial, that these three types may have institutional complementarities in many situations. There are many cases of public-private partnerships (e.g., joint venture industrial or trading firms, collaborative research in crops, vaccines, and drugs), of community organizations using market processes (e.g., partnerships with businesses in Bangladesh in improving access to telecommunications in rural areas), and of community organizations linking up with the government (e.g., in India with joint forest management between the forest department of the government and local communities, or

SEWA, the well-known self-employed women's organization, covering health-related risks of its members through government-owned insurance companies, utilizing the larger risk-pooling advantages of the state or of the market in the insurance sector). Institutional economics will be much richer if we widen the discussion beyond institutions that secure private property against expropriation and admit a variety of institutional arrangements to cope with many different kinds of development problems.

The State

An unresolved issue in the institutional economics of underdevelopment is why dysfunctional institutions often persist for a long time. Why doesn't the social evolutionary process select fitter institutions? In general, there are certain regularities in the evolution of institutions as social agents repeatedly face the same type of social problems and adapt their behavior, but there are no necessary social welfare–maximizing mechanisms in the evolutionary process. In the recent literature on applications of evolutionary game theory to institutional change (see, for example, Bowles 2004) it is recognized that while efficiency generally contributes to a differential advantage in replication, it is highly unlikely that efficiency and success in replication will always go together, particularly because the positive and negative interactions of one institution with other institutions involve their complementarity and crowding-out, and the payoffs for adherence to particular institutions depend on adherence by others.

Before proceeding further, I should clarify what are considered efficient or inefficient institutions. We want to be up front about *not* necessarily referring to Pareto efficiency. We'll more often regard a movement toward a productivity-enhancing institution to be a change in the right direction. The Pareto criterion and insistence on unanimity are much too stringent (and politically a nonstarter) for most discussions of institutional change. In any case, when one is in search of Pareto efficiency, to make the compensating transfers from gainers to losers incentive-compatible in a situation where the valuation of gainers and losers is private information, it may be extremely difficult to change institutions even with no frictions at all in bargaining (beyond this information problem).[6]

In the recent institutional economics literature, what is considered to be a major stumbling block to realizing potential gains from institutional change is a political commitment problem, particularly in the sense of those in power finding it difficult to commit to not using that power. Looking over the last few hundred years of history, North, Weingast,[7] and others focused on a particular political mechanism of credible commitment that made much of the difference between the success story of Western Europe and North America and the stagnation in large parts of the rest of the world. This mechanism essentially involved self-binding by rulers (e.g., the king's giving up royal prerogatives and increasing the powers of the Parliament in 1688 in England) and rulers' credibly committing themselves to be nonpredatory, thus securing private property rights, and allowing private enterprise and capital markets to flourish. The standard prescription in this literature is for a *strong but limited* government, one that is strong enough to secure property rights, enforce contractual laws, and maintain stability but that commits not to transgress and make confiscatory demands.

While not denying that such self-binding mechanisms may have played an important role in Western history, I think it is possible to argue that they are neither necessary nor sufficient for economic development. They are not sufficient because there are other (technological, demographic, ecological, cultural) constraints on the development process, not all of which will be relaxed by rulers disabling themselves. They are not necessary, as a few non-Western success stories suggest (Japan since the Meiji Restoration, Korea and Taiwan since 1960, coastal China since 1980). In most of these cases, while rulers often adopted prudent policies (and sometimes even acquired a reputation[8] to this effect), they were far from disabling their own discretionary powers.

What is meant by a strong state? One must be careful to avoid circularity or endogeneity in definitions that include aspects of state performance in development. We may instead define the strength of a ruler (or a ruling group) as the ability to credibly precommit (measurable, however crudely, in terms of some aspects of the prior political-bureaucratic structure and preannounced decision rules) and think of him (her) as a Stackelberg leader, in a model where the ruler maximizes his objective function subject to the reaction function of the ruled. In the process, the ruler internalizes the economic costs and benefits of his actions in accordance with that reaction function. In contrast, one can say that the weak state is a Stackelberg follower: it cannot commit to a particular policy and merely reacts to the independent actions of private actors such as special-interest groups. Then, compared to the strong state, the weak state will have *too many* undesirable interventions (creating distortions in the process of generating rents for lobbying groups), and *too few* desirable interventions (as in the case of coordination failures) since the state does not take into account or internalize the effects of its own policies. So the distinction between a strong state (as in much of East Asia) and a weak state (as in much of Africa and South Asia) lies not in the *extent* of intervention but in its *quality*.[9] This also means that the beneficial effects of a strong state go beyond the North-Weingast ideal of a *strong but limited* government.

The East Asian state has often played a much more active role, for example, acting as a catalyst and coordinator for long-term finance in industrial development. It intervened in the capital market sometimes in subtle but decisive ways, using regulated entry of firms and credit allocation (sometimes threatening withdrawal of credit in not so subtle ways) in promoting and channeling industrial investment, underwriting risks and guaranteeing loans, establishing public development banks and other financial institutions, encouraging the development of the nascent parts of financial markets, and nudging existing firms to upgrade their technology and to move into sectors that fall in line with an overall vision of strategic developmental goals.[10] In this process, as Aoki, Murdock, and Okuno-Fujiwara (1997) emphasized, the state enhanced the market instead of supplanting it; it induced private coordination by providing various kinds of cooperation-contingent rents. In the early stages of industrialization, when private financial and other related institutions were underdeveloped and coordination was not self-enforcing, the East Asian state created opportunities for rents conditional on performance or outcome (in mobilization of savings, commercialization of inventions, export contests, and so on) and facilitated institutional development by influencing the strategic incentives facing private agents through an alteration of the relative returns to cooperation in comparison with the adversarial equilibrium. (Such contingent transfers are akin to the patent system, where the monopoly rent is contingent on successful innovation.) Of course, the state sometimes made mistakes and did not always succeed in picking winners, but the opportunities created allowed firms to experiment in exploring new directions. The prestipulated performance criteria used in East Asia often included export success, which in a world of international competition kept the subsidized firms on their toes and encouraged cost and quality consciousness.

One should not, of course, underestimate the administrative difficulties of such aggregate coordination, and the issues of micromanagement of capital may be too intricate for the institutional capacity and information-processing abilities of many a state in Africa, Latin America, or South Asia. There is also the problem of how credible the commitment of the state is in implementing the contingent transfer and actually carrying out the threat of withdrawing the transfer when performance does not measure up. The states in Africa, Latin America, or South Asia have often been rather lax in this compared to East Asia, and the contingent transfers soon degenerated into unconditional subsidies or entitlements for favorite interest groups. One should also be wary, as the East Asian experience of financial crisis (or the weakness of the Chinese financial sector) warned, about the moral hazard problems of too cozy a relationship[11] between public banks and private business (state-owned enterprises in the Chinese case) and the political pressures for bailout that a state-supported financial system inevitably faces.

Inequality and the Persistence of Dysfunctional Institutions

In the previous section I criticized the widely held view that the sole clue to persistence of dysfunctional institutions lies in the inability of the state to commit to nonintervention. The history of underdevelopment suggests that a major (but by no means the only) stumbling block to beneficial institutional change in many poor countries lies in the distributive conflicts and asymmetries in bargaining and mobilizing power among social groups. Institutional economists (including Marxists) used to point out how a given institutional arrangement serving the interests of some powerful group or class acts as a long-lasting barrier (or *fetter*, to quote a favorite word of Marx) to economic progress. As suggested by Bardhan (1989a) and Knight (1992), institutional economists now sometimes[12] understate the tenacity of vested interests, the enormousness of the collective action problem in bringing about institutional change, and the differential capacity of different social groups in mobilization and coordination. The collective action problem can be serious even when the change would be ultimately Pareto-superior for all groups. There are two kinds of collective action problems involved: one is the well-known free-rider problem about sharing the costs of bringing about change; the other is a bargaining problem where disputes about sharing the potential benefits from the change may lead to a breakdown of the necessary coordination. There are cases where an institution that nobody individually likes persists as a result of a mutually sustaining network of social sanctions when each individual conforms out of fear of loss of reputation from disobedience.[13] Potential members of a breakaway coalition in such situations may have grounds to fear that it is doomed to failure, and failure to challenge the system can become a self-fulfilling prophecy.

The problem may be more acute when, as is often the case, there are winners and losers from a productivity-enhancing institutional change. The costs of collective action of such a change may be too high. This is particularly true, as we know from Olson (1965), when the losses of the potential losers are concentrated and transparent while the gains of the potential gainers are diffuse[14] (or uncertain for a given individual, even though not for the group, as suggested by Fernandez and Rodrik 1991). There is also the inherent difficulty, emphasized by Dixit and Londregan (1995), that the potential gainers cannot credibly commit to compensate the losers ex post.[15] Ideally, the state could issue long-term bonds to buy off the losers and tax the gainers to repay. But in many developing countries there are serious limitations to the government's ability to tax and to keep inflation under control, and the bond market is thin. Losers may fear that once they give up an existing institution, they may lose the *locus standi* in lobbying with a future government when the promises are not kept (exit from a current institutional arrangement damaging their voice in the new regime in future), and so they resist a change today.

One can also formalize the obstruction by vested interests in terms of a simple Nash bargaining model, where the institutional innovation may shift the bargaining frontier outward (thus creating the potential for all parties to gain), but in the process the disagreement payoff of the weaker party may also go up (often because of better options for both exit and voice that institutional changes may bring in their wake), and it is possible for the erstwhile stronger party to end up losing in the new bargaining equilibrium (how likely this is will of course depend on the nature of the shift in the bargaining frontier and the extent of change in the disagreement payoffs).[16] As Acemoglu and Robinson (2006) emphasized, it may not be rational, for example, for a dictator to carry out institutional changes that safeguard property rights, law enforcement, and other economically beneficial structures even though these may fatten the cow that the dictator has the power to milk, if in the process his preexisting rent extraction machinery has a chance of being damaged or weakened. He may not risk upsetting the current arrangement for the uncertain prospect of a share in a larger pie.

Acemoglu and Robinson developed a theory where incumbent elites may want to block the introduction of new and efficient technologies because this will reduce their future political power. They gave the example from nineteenth-century history when in Russia and Austria-Hungary the monarchy and aristocracy controlled the political system but feared replacement and thus blocked the establishment of institutions that would have facilitated industrialization. These replacement threats are, of course, often driven by extreme inequality in society.

In explaining the divergent development paths in North America and South America since early colonial times, Engerman and Sokoloff (2002) provided evidence of how, in societies with high inequality at the outset of colonization, institutions evolved in ways that restricted to a narrow elite access to political power and opportunities for economic advancement. Initial unequal conditions had long-lingering effects, and through their influence on public policies (in distribution of public land and other natural resources, public investment in primary education and other infrastructure, the right to vote and in secret, patent law, corporate and banking law) tended to perpetuate those institutions and policies that atrophied development. Even in countries where initially some oligarchic entrepreneurs are successful in creating conditions (including securing their own property rights) for their own economic performance, as long as that oligarchy remains powerful it usually gets away with raising entry barriers for new or future entrepreneurs, and this blocks challenges to their incumbency and new technological breakthroughs. See Acemoglu (2008) for a theoretical analysis of this kind of dynamic distortion in oligarchic societies even when property rights are protected for the initial producers.

The classic example of inefficient institutions persisting as the lopsided outcome of distributive struggles relates to the historical evolution of land rights in developing countries. In most of these countries the empirical evidence suggests that economies of scale in farm production are insignificant (except in some plantation crops) and that the small family farm is often the most efficient unit of production. Yet the violent and tortuous history of land reform in many countries suggests there are numerous road blocks on the way to a more efficient reallocation of land rights put up by vested interests for generations. Why don't the large landlords voluntarily lease out or sell their land to small family farmers and grab much of the surplus arising from this efficient reallocation? There clearly has been some leasing out of land, but problems of monitoring, insecurity of tenure, and the landlord's fear that the tenant will acquire occupancy rights on the land have curtailed efficiency gains and the extent of tenancy. The land sales market has been particularly thin (and in many poor countries the sales go the opposite way, from distressed small farmers to landlords and moneylenders). With low household savings and severely imperfect credit markets, the potentially more efficient small farmer is often incapable of affording the going market price of land. Binswanger, Deininger, and Feder (1995) explained it in terms of land as preferred collateral (also carrying tax advantages and speculation opportunities for the wealthy) often having a price above the capitalized value of the agricultural income stream for even the productive small farmer, rendering mortgaged sales uncommon (since mortgaged land cannot be used as collateral to raise working capital for the buyer). Under these circumstances and if the public finances (and the state of the bond market) are such that landlords cannot be fully or credibly compensated, land redistribution will not be voluntary.

Landlords resist land reforms also because the leveling effects reduce their social and political power and their ability to control and dominate even nonland transactions.[17] Large land holdings may give their owner special social status or political power in a lumpy way (so that the status or political effect from owning 100 hectares is larger than the combined status or political effect accruing to fifty new buyers owning 2 hectares each). Thus the social or political rent of land ownership for the large landowner will not be compensated by the offer price of the numerous small buyers. Under the circumstances, the former will not sell, and inefficient land concentration persists.

An important aspect of political rent that is overlooked in the usual calculations of the surplus generated by a given institutional change is that all sides are often really interested in *relative* rather than absolute gain or loss. In a power game, as in a winner-take-all contest or tournament, it is not enough for an institutional change to increase the surplus for all parties to be acceptable. One side may gain absolutely and yet may lose relative to the other side, and thus it may resist change. If, in a repeated framework, both sides have to continue to spend resources in seeking (or preserving) power or improving their future bargaining positions, and if the marginal return from spending such resources for one party is an increasing function of such spending by the other party (power-seeking efforts by the two parties are strategic complements), it is easy to see why the relative gain from an institutional change may be the determining factor in its acceptability.[18]

That collective action problems in orchestrating institutional change from a low-level to a higher-level equilibrium are rendered particularly difficult by distributive conflicts is now slowly being recognized in both the macroeconomic and microeconomic literature. In macroeconomic comparisons of East Asia and Latin America in the last quarter of the twentieth century the point has been made that when wealth distribution is relatively egalitarian, as in large parts of East Asia (particularly through land reforms and widespread expansion of education and basic health services), it has been somewhat easier to enlist the support of most social groups (and isolate the extreme political wings of the labor movement) in making short-run sacrifices at times of macroeconomic crises and coordinating on stabilization and growth-promoting institutions and policies.[19] Rodrik (1998) cited cross-country evidence for his hypothesis that the economic costs of external shocks are magnified by distributional conflicts, and this diminishes the productivity with which a society's resources are utilized.

Below the aggregative or macroeconomic level there are many local self-governing institutions (elected local government bodies in charge of delivering local public goods like roads, extension service, public health, and sanitation; rural community organizations in charge of managing local environmental resources; urban neighborhood associations in charge of crime watch or activities promoting cultural-cum-social solidarity) where distributive conflicts lead to institutional failures. In areas of high social and economic inequality the problem of capture of even elected local government bodies by the local elite can be severe, and the poor and weaker sections of the population may be left grievously exposed to malfeasance.[20] Thus one beneficial by-product of land reform, underemphasized in the usual economic analysis, is that such reform, by changing the local political structure in the village, gives more voice to the poor and induces them to get involved in local self-governing institutions. In other cases, the problem of elite capture may be less but that of elite exit is quite serious in causing the erosion of political support from the provision of local public goods. When, for example, the rich do not send their children to local public schools and do not use the local health services, the public provision structure often crumbles, as is familiar in both rich and poor countries.

Similar problems arising from inequality may afflict local nongovernmental, often informal, community organizations in developing countries. The relationship between inequality and collective action (in the sense of participation in a regulatory group organization and of contributing to the provision or conservation of some common resource) is an underresearched area in economics. For a brief survey of the theoretical and empirical literature on this question, see Baland and Platteau (2006). Here I note that while the effect of inequality is in general ambiguous, there are many cases where the net benefits of coordination for each individual may be structured in such a way that in situations of marked inequality some individuals may not participate or contribute to the cost of collective action, and the resulting outcome may be more inefficient than in the case with greater equality.[21] Inequality may also lead to bargaining disputes arising from the distribution of benefits of collective action, and it may cause the negotiation and enforcement costs for cooperative arrangements to go up. In such situations, collective institutional structures and opportunities for cooperative problem solving may be forgone by societies that are sharply divided along social and economic lines.

In this section I have enumerated the various processes through which initial inequality may result in the persistence of dysfunctional institutions in poor countries. The hypothesis that high inequality predicts a high probability of bad institutions, and the latter in turn predict low income, could in principle be tested, but in practice it is quite problematic. Inequality, after all, is highly endogenous at the macroeconomic level, and any such exercise will be afflicted by the same kinds of problems as the ones Banerjee and Duflo (2003) pointed out about cross-country regressions on inequality and growth. With cross-sectional data one possibility is to use density of population in some historically early period as an instrument for predicting high inequality. As reported for cross-country regressions by Bardhan (2005), weak political rights today are associated with high density of population in 1500, possibly indicating that in areas of labor abundance relative to land and other resources workers and peasants have weak political power, and equality of political power may have been difficult to establish. But political inequality and economic inequality may not be closely associated. It is, of course, likely to be the case that, other things remaining the same, in areas where labor is scarce, labor may be valued more highly and thus there may be less inequality, as argued by Engerman and Sokoloff (2002) in their comparison of North America with the tropical parts of Latin America. But other things are often quite different. Land abundance and labor scarcity have not helped Africans in the same away as North Americans for various historical reasons. Also, by this logic, Asia (where density of population has been higher) should have more economic inequality than Latin America and Africa, but this is not the case. This may have something to do with inheritance practices. China and India, unlike Western Europe, North America, and Latin America, historically did not have primogeniture but rather equal partition (among sons) and subdivision of land, so there is a built-in tendency in Asia toward equality. There are also other factors involved. A historical density-of-population variable is therefore likely to be a weak instrument for economic inequality.

Commitment and Accountability

One other factor is the nature of political competition and the context-specific and path-dependent formations of political coalitions. An interesting example of this in terms of comparative institutional-historical analysis was provided by Nugent and Robinson (2005). Holding constant both colonial background and crop technology, they compared the divergent trajectories in institutions (particularly in terms of protection of smallholder property rights) and growth in two pairs of former Spanish colonies in the same region (Costa Rica–Colombia and El Salvador–Guatemala) producing the same principal crop (coffee). The political fragmentation of elites often helps in overcoming obstacles to institutional development. In Costa Rica, for example, the elites of different towns were induced to compete with each other for popular support, which they did by offering private property rights to smallholders. In El Salvador and Guatemala, on the other hand, the national elite remained unified in opposition to such an institutional change and instead went in the direction of mass land expropriation and militarized plantation societies. Institutional economics will be richer with more such comparative historical studies. In a statistical analysis of data from eighty-nine villages in contemporary West Bengal, Bardhan and Mookherjee (2007) found that political competition is more effective in bringing about land reforms and pro-poor targeting of programs than the redistributive ideology of the ruling party in the local governments.

Political competition, however, can sometimes lead to competitive populism. An inherent dilemma of governance institutions is involved here. On the one hand, one needs institutions of credible commitment to insulate the system from the populist pressures of special-interest groups and partisan or faction politics.[22] In particular, long-term investment projects or economic policy decisions that have consequences over a prolonged period will not get off the ground without such commitment. Even outside the economic sphere rule of law requires the system to display some degree of commitment that civil servants, judges, and the police are not beholden to the ruling politicians. (Examples are appointments of civil servants as political patronage in Latin America, or in India, where meritocratically appointed civil servants are dependent on politicians for promotion and transfers.) In the macroeconomics literature this is usually emphasized in the context of central bank independence, but the problem is much wider. (It should be added that there are reputational substitutes for mandatory independence of central banks, as the examples of not-so-independent central banks in postwar Japan, China, and India in the matter of inflation control suggest.)

On the other hand, too much insulation often means too little accountability. This leads to high-handed arbitrary governance, abuses, and waste. Even when the administration is benevolent, large-scale development projects directed from above by an insulated modernizing elite are often inappropriate technologically or environmentally, far removed from or insensitive to local community needs and concerns, and failing to tap the large reservoir of local information, initiative, and ingenuity. These projects often treat poor people as objects of the development process and end up primarily serving as conduits of largesse for middlemen and contractors and their political patrons; they also encourage parasitism on the state among the beneficiaries. In developing countries where much of the economy is in the vast informal sector and dispersed in far-flung villages and small towns, the accountability mechanisms are particularly important at the local community level.

In some sense the dilemma of commitment versus accountability is best resolved at the local level. If commitment is necessary for long-term projects, it may be easier to persuade the local people to make short-run sacrifices for local projects (like village roads, schools, health and sanitation, drinking water) that are to benefit them in the long run. There is more transparency of benefits, possibly more trust and peer monitoring among a small group of face-to-face people, and collective action may be easier in resisting populist pressures. In contrast, individuals and groups may perceive more uncertainty in the trickle-down from future growth arising out of large scale centrally administered projects, and they may instead opt for the bird-in-hand of current subsidies and short-term benefits. Accountability is also more direct at the local level, if the local democratic processes work. Electoral sanctions are more effective at the local level than at the central level, where multidimensionality of electoral issues dilutes responsibility. There is also more local vigilance on issues where there is more local stake ("it's our money you are wasting or stealing").[23]

Decentralization of governance in the sense of devolution of power to local governments is now in vogue in many countries, and there is a substantial literature on the pros and cons of decentralization, some of which has been surveyed by Bardhan (2002). In particular, the problem of local capture by collusive local elite groups or sectarian interests has often been mentioned. How acute this problem is depends, again, on the initial levels of inequality (both social and economic), how lopsided the nature of political competition is at the local level, and the context-specific and path-dependent formations of political coalitions.

Conclusion

In this chapter I started by showing how the recent institutional economics of development literature has ignored the substantive microeconomic institutional literature of the 1970s and 1980s and has been preoccupied with the macroeconomic impact of the security of property rights, to the neglect of other important institutions in the development process, particularly the participatory and coordinating institutions. I then showed that the persistence of dysfunctional institutions may have more to do with underlying distributive conflicts than with the political commitment problem of rulers not being able to bind themselves against making confiscatory demands.

I end with a comment on an implication of this central question of institutional persistence for future work on institutional economics. The persistence of something in history clearly makes the application of an empirical identification strategy easier, and it has been used as such, but it leaves open two issues in the study of institutional economics. One is that the procedure, widely adopted, of instrumenting recent institutions by referring to some historical fact is flawed because institutions change over time. An instrument for the initial institutions need not be a valid instrument for the current ones. As Przeworski (2004) commented on the use of "colonial settler mortality" by Acemoglu, Johnson, and Robinson (2001) as an instrument for current property rights institutions, if good institutions are more likely to survive in more affluent countries, then institutional quality today is still endogenous with respect to income.

Second, we need more theoretical models that can simultaneously handle the realistic case of some institutional durability with the possibility of institutional change, under different conditions with respect to perceptions of the costs and benefits of resisting change on the part of incumbent elites (in response to changes in the technological, political-organizational, and international environment).[24] The spread of the Green Revolution, say, in eastern India is a case in point. Initially, when the new technology became available, economists pointed to the oligarchic landlord-moneylender nexus of the region as a long-standing substantial institutional block. But over time in some parts of the region this nexus got weaker as the rate of return from investment in new technology improved with a package program of public and private irrigation infrastructure, credit, information, land reform, and social learning. The same question of institutional persistence and change is now relevant in pondering why the Green Revolution has been so slow in Africa so far. In general, continuity and change are complex dialectic processes in institutional life that need to be analyzed better.

Notes

1. Another collection of essays on institutions and development was edited by I. Adelman and E. Thorbecke for a symposium in the September 1989 issue of *World Development*.

2. For a discussion of this, see Bardhan (2005, ch. 1).

3. This otherwise good survey misses out on much of the large microeconomic literature on institutions in the 1970s and 1980s.

4. Security of property rights also facilitates access to credit, and thus production and trade.

5. See Seabright (1993) for an elaboration of this argument.

6. See Mailath and Postlewaite (1990) for a demonstration of this in the case of collective action on a public project.

7. See North and Weingast (1989). For some empirical criticisms of the argument for English history, see Carruthers (1990) and Clark (1995).

8. As Acemoglu (2003) pointed out in a model of repeated games, where reputation may act as a substitute for commitment contract, its efficacy depends on the patience and time horizon of the rulers. This is related to the point made by Evans (1995) on the importance of meritocratic career bureaucrats ("Weberian") with a longer time horizon in South Korea compared to the bureaucrats in Latin America, who are more dependent on short-term political patronage.

9. This idea was informally expressed in Bardhan (1990) and given a somewhat more formal exposition in Rodrik (1992) and Bardhan and Udry (1999). In a recent paper Acemoglu (2005) used a different definition of strong and weak states, which I have not found very useful. In this model the ruler is politically strong if he is not easily replaceable. I think authoritarian Korea was a strong state and democratic India was a weak state not so much because the leaders were more easily replaceable in the latter, but because in India extreme heterogeneity of interest groups often buffeted the state to go back on its long-term commitments and goals. Japan and Scandinavian countries have often demonstrated aspects of strong states in my sense, but leaders being easily replaceable makes them weak states in the Acemoglu sense.

10. For a recent account of the role of the state in facilitating and engendering coordination, networking, and technology upgrading in the electronics and information technology industry in Taiwan, see Lin (2003).

11. As the recent financial crisis in the United States illustrates, cozy relationships between regulators and the regulated in the financial sector are not unfamiliar in that country.

12. North (1990) is an exception in this tradition. He points to the contrasting and path-dependent processes of change in bargaining power of the ruler versus the ruled in different countries, particularly in the context of the fiscal crisis of the state. In an earlier historical literature on the transition from feudalism in Europe, Brenner (1976) provided a major departure from the usual analysis of transition in terms of demography or market conditions. He provided a detailed analysis of the contrasting experiences of transition in different parts of Europe (those between western and eastern Europe and those between the English and the French cases even within western Europe) in terms of changes in bargaining power of different social groups or in the outcomes of social conflicts. Brenner showed that much depends, for example, on the cohesiveness of the landlords and peasants as contending groups and their ability to resist encroachments on each other's rights and to form coalitions with other groups in society.

13. For a well-known static analysis of such a case, see Akerlof (1984). For a more complex model in terms of stochastic dynamic games explaining evolution of local customs or conventions, see Young (1998). Bowles (2004) provided an interesting extension of the Young model where institutional tipping is not generally induced by mutation-like accidents of behavior but rather results from intentional collective action of people. In this context he showed how highly unequal conventions may be difficult to dislodge.

14. As Machiavelli reminds us in *The Prince* (1513, ch. VI), "the reformer has enemies in all those who profit by the old order, and only lukewarm defenders in all those who would profit by the new."

15. Of course, some societies may be able to develop in repeated situations appropriate norms of compensation to losers, but preservation of such a norm itself may require collective action.

16. This is the case even if we abstract from the usual case of deadlocks arising in bargaining with incomplete information, with possible misrepresentation of the type of the bargaining players.

17. Busch and Muthoo (2002) developed a model where land redistribution may adversely affect a landlord's bargaining power in *other* markets (labor or credit). The inability to make binding commitments prevents the poor from committing not to exploit their increased bargaining power following land redistribution; and, of course, being wealth-

constrained, they cannot compensate the landlords up front either. The greater the degree of inequality in the players' bargaining powers, the more likely it is that inefficient institutions will persist.

18. For a model of power seeking on these lines to explain why two parties may not agree to obviously mutually advantageous transactions, even when there are simple enforceable contracts and side transfers of fungible resources to implement them, see Rajan and Zingales (1999).

19. See, for example, Campos and Root (1996).

20. For a theoretical analysis of the elite capture problem in the context of decentralization, see Bardhan and Mookherjee (2006a).

21. See Bardhan and Singh (2004) for a model where cooperation is beneficial in providing a public infrastructural facility, but subject to defection, and is supported by trigger strategy punishments in a repeated game. The paper explores the relationship between the nature of cooperation (size and composition of coalitions) and underlying inequality in the distribution of private productive assets.

22. For a theoretical model of competitive populism (as one of the costs of political competition), see Bardhan and Yang (2004).

23. Olken (2005) found from a field experiment in over 600 Indonesian villages on village road projects funded from above that increased grassroots monitoring tends to reduce theft of money that was supposed to be paid as wages to the villagers (but not so much the theft of the money supposed to be spent in procurement of materials from elsewhere). Such evidence for better performance of decentralization in the pro-poor targeting of *private* goods, in contrast to targeting of more public services, may also be found in Bardhan and Mookherjee (2006b) for rural West Bengal.

24. For the beginnings of a coherent theoretical explanation of the coexistence of frequent changes in political institutions with the persistence in certain aspects of economic institutions, in terms of a model with a Markov regime-switching process with state dependence, see Acemoglu and Robinson (2008).

References

Acemoglu, D. 2003. Why Not a Political Coase Theorem? Social Conflict, Commitment, and Politics. *Journal of Comparative Economics* 31 (4): 620–625.

———. 2005. Politics and Economics in Weak and Strong States. *Journal of Monetary Economics* 52 (7): 1199–1226.

———. 2008. Oligarchic vs. Democratic Societies. *Journal of the European Economic Association* 6: 1–44.

Acemoglu, D., S. Johnson, and J. A. Robinson. 2001. The Colonial Origins of Comparative Development: An Empirical Investigation. *American Economic Review* 91 (5): 1369–1401.

Acemoglu, D., and J. A. Robinson. 2006. Economic Backwardness in Political Perspective. *American Political Science Review* 100 (1): 115–131.

———. 2008. Persistence of Power, Elites, and Institutions. *American Economic Review* 98 (1): 267–293.

Akerlof, G. A. 1984. *An Economic Theorist's Book of Tales.* Cambridge: Cambridge University Press.

Aoki, M., K. Murdock, and M. Okuno-Fujiwara. 1997. Beyond the East Asian Miracle: Introducing the Market Enhancing View. In *The Role of Government in East Asian Economic Development: Comparative Institutional Analysis*, ed. M. Aoki, H. Kim, and M. Okuno-Fujiwara. Oxford: Oxford University Press.

Baland, J.-M., and J.-P. Platteau. 2006. Collective Action on the Commons: The Role of Inequality. In *Inequality, Collective Action and Environmental Sustainability*, ed. J.-M. Baland, P. Bardhan, and S. Bowles. Princeton, N.J.: Princeton University Press.

Banerjee, A., and E. Duflo. 2003. Inequality and Growth: What Can the Data Say? *Journal of Economic Growth* 8 (3): 267–299.

Bardhan, P. 1983. Labor-Tying in a Poor Agrarian Economy: A Theoretical and Empirical Analysis. *Quarterly Journal of Economics* 98 (3): 501–514.

———. 1984. *Land, Labor and Rural Poverty.* New York: Columbia University Press.

———. 1989a. The New Institutional Economics and Development Theory: A Brief Critical Assessment. *World Development* 17 (9): 1389–1395.

———, ed. 1989b. *The Economic Theory of Agrarian Institutions.* Oxford: Clarendon Press.

———. 1990. State and Economic Development. *Journal of Economic Perspectives* 4 (3): 3–7.

———. 2002. Decentralization of Governance and Development. *Journal of Economic Perspectives* 16 (4): 185–205.

———. 2005. *Scarcity, Conflicts, and Cooperation.* Cambridge, Mass.: MIT Press.

Bardhan, P., and D. Mookherjee. 2006a. Decentralization and Accountability in Infrastructure Delivery in Developing Countries. *Economic Journal* 116 (1): 101–127.

———. 2006b. Pro-Poor Targeting and Accountability of Local Governments in West Bengal. *Journal of Development Economics* 79 (2): 303–327.

———. 2007. Land Reform, Decentralized Governance and Rural Development in West Bengal. Working paper 314. Stanford Center for International Development.

Bardhan, P., and N. Singh. 2004. Inequality, Coalitions, and Collective Action. Working paper 71. Bureau for Research and Economic Analysis of Development (BREAD).

Bardhan, P., and C. Udry. 1999. *Development Microeconomics.* Oxford: Oxford University Press.

Bardhan, P., and T.-T. Yang. 2004. Political Competition in Economic Perspective. Working paper 78. Bureau for Research and Economic Analysis of Development (BREAD).

Bell, C. 1977. Alternative Theories of Sharecropping: Some Tests Using Evidence from Northeast India. *Journal of Development Studies* 13 (4): 317–346.

Berlin, I. 1969. *Four Essays on Liberty.* Oxford: Oxford University Press.

Binswanger, H. P., K. Deininger, and G. Feder. 1995. Power, Distortions, Revolt and Reform in Agricultural Land Relations. In *Handbook of Development Economics*, vol. 3, ed. J. R. Behrman and T. N. Srinivasan. Amsterdam: Elsevier.

Bowles, S. 2004. *Microeconomics: Behavior, Institutions and Evolution.* Princeton, N.J.: Princeton University Press.

Brenner, R. 1976. Agrarian Class Structure and Economic Development in Pre-industrial Europe. *Past and Present* 70 (1): 30–70.

Busch, L. A., and A. Muthoo. 2002. Power and Inefficient Institutions. Economics discussion paper 561. Department of Economics, University of Essex, UK.

Campos, E., and H. L. Root. 1996. *The Key to the East Asian Miracle: Making Shared Growth Credible.* Washington D.C.: Brookings Institution.

Carruthers, B. G. 1990. Politics, Popery, and Property: A Comment on North and Weingast. *Journal of Economic History* 50 (3): 693–698.

Carter, M. R. 1984. Resource Allocation and Use under Collective Rights and Labor Management in Peruvian Coastal Agriculture. *Economic Journal* 94 (4): 826–846.

———. 1989. The Impact of Credit on Peasant Productivity and Differentiation in Nicaragua. *Journal of Development Economics* 31 (1): 13–36.

Clark, G. 1995. The Political Foundations of Modern Economic Growth: England, 1540–1800. *Journal of Interdisciplinary History* 26 (2): 563–588.

Dixit, A. K., and J. Londregan. 1995. Redistributive Politics and Economic Efficiency. *American Political Science Review* 89 (4): 856–866.

Engerman, S. L., and K. L. Sokoloff. 2002. Factor Endowments, Inequality and Paths of Development among New World Economies. *Economia* 3 (1): 41–88.

Evans, P. 1995. *Embedded Autonomy.* Princeton, N.J.: Princeton University Press.

Feder, G., and T. Onchan. 1987. Land Ownership Security and Farm Investment in Thailand. *American Journal of Agricultural Economics* 69 (2): 311–320.

Fernandez, R., and D. Rodrik. 1991. Resistance to Reform: Status Quo Bias in the Presence of Individual-Specific Uncertainty. *American Economic Review* 81 (5): 1146–1155.

Greif, A. 1997. Microtheory and Recent Developments in the Study of Economic Institutions through Economic History. In *Advances in Economic Theory*, vol. 2, ed. D. M. Kreps and K. F. Wallis. Cambridge: Cambridge University Press.

Hoff, K., A. Braverman, and J. E. Stiglitz, eds. 1993. *The Economics of Rural Organization.* Washington, D.C.: World Bank.

Knight, J. 1992. *Institutions and Social Conflict*, New York: Cambridge University Press.

Kranton, R. E., and A. Swamy. 1999. The Hazards of Piecemeal Reform: British Civil Courts and the Credit Market in Colonial India. *Journal of Development Economics* 58 (1): 1–24.

Lin, J. Y. 1987. The Household Responsibility System Reform in China. *American Journal of Agricultural Economics* 69 (2): 410–415.

———. 2003. Industrial Structure, Technical Change, and the Role of Government in Development of the Electronics and Information Industry in Taipei, China. Working paper 41. Economics and Research Department, Asian Development Bank, Manila.

Mailath, G. J., and A. Postlewaite. 1990. Asymmetric Information Bargaining Problems with Many Agents. *Review of Economic Studies* 57 (3): 351–368.

Matoussi, M. S., and J. B. Nugent. 1989. The Switch to Sharecropping in Medjez-el-Bab. In *The New Institutional Economics and Development*, ed. M. Nabli and J. B. Nugent. Amsterdam: North-Holland.

Migot-Adholla, S., P. Hazell, and F. Place. 1991. Indigenous Land Rights Systems in sub-Saharan Africa: A Constraint on Productivity? *World Bank Economic Review* 5 (1): 155–175.

Morooka, Y., and Y. Hayami. 1989. Contract Choice and Enforcement in an Agrarian Community: Agricultural Tenancy in Upland Java. *Journal of Development Studies* 26 (1): 28–42.

Nabli, M., and J. B. Nugent, eds. 1989. *The New Institutional Economics and Development*. Amsterdam: North-Holland.

North, D. C. 1990. *Institutions, Institutional Change and Economic Performance*. New York: Cambridge University Press.

North, D. C., and B. Weingast. 1989. Constitutions and Commitment: Evolution of Institutions Governing Public Choice. *Journal of Economic History* 49 (4): 803–832.

Nugent, J. B., and J. A. Robinson. 2005. Are Endowments Fate? On the Political Economy of Comparative Institutional Development. Unpublished paper. Harvard University.

Olken, B. 2005. Monitoring Corruption: Evidence from a Field Experiment in Indonesia. NBER working paper 11753.

Olson, M. 1965. *The Logic of Collective Action: Public Goods and the Theory of Groups*. Cambridge, Mass.: Harvard University Press.

Otsuka, K. 1991. Determinants and Consequences of Land Reform Implementation in the Philippines. *Journal of Development Economics* 35 (2): 339–355.

Pande, R., and C. Udry. 2005. Institutions and Development: A View from Below. In *Proceedings of the 9th World Congress of the Econometric Society*.

Przeworski, A. 2004. Geography vs. Institutions Revisited: Were Fortunes Reversed? Unpublished paper. Department of Politics, New York University.

Rajan, R. R., and L. Zingales. 1999. The Tyranny of the Inefficient: An Enquiry into the Adverse Consequences of Power Struggles. Unpublished paper. Graduate School of Business, University of Chicago.

Rodrik, D. 1992. Political Economy and Development Policy. *European Economic Review* 36 (2–3): 529–536.

———. 1998. Where Did All the Growth Go? External Shocks, Social Conflicts, and Growth Collapses. NBER working paper 6350.

Roumasset, J. A. 1984. Explaining Patterns in Landowner Shares: Rice, Corn, and Abaca in the Philippines. In *Contractual Arrangements, Employment, and Wages in Rural Labor Markets in Asia*, ed. H. P. Binswanger and M. R. Rosenzweig, 82–95. New Haven, Conn.: Yale University Press.

Seabright, P. 1993. Managing Local Commons: Theoretical Issues in Incentive Design. *Journal of Economic Perspectives* 7 (4): 113–134.

Shaban, R. 1987. Testing between Competing Models of Sharecropping. *Journal of Political Economy* 95 (5): 893–920.

Skinner, Q. 2002. A Third Concept of Liberty. *Proceedings of the British Academy* 117: 237–268.

Udry, C. 1990. Credit Markets in Northern Nigeria: Credit as Insurance in a Rural Economy. *World Bank Economic Review* 4 (3): 251–269.

Williamson, O. 1985. *The Economic Institutions of Capitalism.* New York: Free Press.

Young, H. P. 1998. *Individual Strategy and Social Structure: An Evolutionary Theory of Institutions.* Princeton, N.J.: Princeton University Press.

2 Spontaneous Markets, Networks, and Social Capital: Lessons from Africa

Marcel Fafchamps

Recent years have witnessed a renewed interest in institutions as an essential ingredient for growth (World Bank 2002). There is now an abundant literature documenting the role that institutions play in the development process (Keefer and Knack 1997; Acemoglu, Johnson, and Robinson 2002). Market institutions in particular appear central to this process (North 1973; Acemoglu, Johnson, and Robinson 2005), so much so that they are now commonly seen as a critical component of a good business environment. However, beyond generalities about courts and the respective merits of common law versus Roman law, little practical advice is available on how to improve market institutions.

Detailed analysis of how markets operate in practice has been provided by John McMillan, Chris Woodruff, and co-authors for Vietnam and Eastern Europe (McMillan and Naughton 1996; Johnson, McMillan, and Woodruff 2002; 2000; McMillan and Woodruff 1999a; 1999b; 2000) and by myself, with various co-authors, for sub-Saharan Africa (Bigsten et al. 2000; Fafchamps 2002b; 2003; 2004; Fafchamps and Minten 1999; 2001; 2002). What this analysis reveals is that courts play a less important role than is often assumed. This may be the case even in developed economies, as has been shown, for instance, by Lisa Bernstein's insightful analysis of the New York diamond trade and of U.S. grain markets (Bernstein 1992; 1996). But, for reasons made clear in this chapter, it is certainly true in developing countries.

Policymakers need to understand the forces that shape market interactions in order to intervene effectively. The purpose of this chapter is to provide a conceptual framework with which to make sense of market institutions. The principles presented here are applicable to any country and to any market, for instance, for credit, insurance, or labor. But most of the discussion focuses on developing countries, and it is couched in terms of markets for goods, such as manufacturing inputs or agricultural produce. Markets for such goods are usually thought to be less problematic than markets for credit, insurance, and labor. Consequently they have received much less attention. The empirical evidence has nevertheless shown that the difficulties normally associated with credit, insurance, and labor markets are equally present in markets for goods. It is therefore useful to take markets for goods as a starting point. Other markets can be seen as special cases of the principles outlined here.

Although I use equations in this chapter, it should not be thought of as a theoretical contribution. Math is used as a didactic device to illustrate a process or principle. Although the chapter draws heavily from the theoretical literature, the choice of model is primarily determined by many years of experience studying markets in Africa and, more recently, in Asia. What is presented here is what I believe should be the backbone of any economic theory of markets in developing countries. The principles outlined in this chapter will help the practitioner see through many empirical puzzles, and they set a firm foundation on which to base policy.

I begin by describing the central role that contract enforcement plays in any form of exchange, but particularly in market exchange. Trust and breach deterrence are the focus. The next section examines the value of commercial relationships, shows how markets can spontaneously emerge without external enforcement, and discusses information sharing and how it facilitates or potentially hinders exchange. I examine different forms of information sharing and investigate under what conditions collective punishment can be self-enforcing. Discrimination and networks are examined next. Many policy interventions in markets can be understood as attempts to correct inequitable market outcomes. I show that ethnic or gender bias arises naturally in all markets but can have multiple origins. Which origin dominates determines whether an affirmative action policy, for instance, targeted credit, is likely to succeed. The chapter concludes with an extensive application of the conceptual framework to policy issues. I cover not only issues surrounding courts and other formal market-supporting institutions, but also how to upgrade informal markets and how to aim for efficiency and equity.

Markets and Contract Enforcement

The starting point for understanding market institutions is to realize that any market transaction is a contract. As a contract the transaction has a set of mutual obligations. There are many opportunities for cheating in trade, from misrepresenting quality to absconding with payment. For market exchange to take place, buyer and seller must trust each other. This is indeed what survey respondents say over and over again. But where does trust come from? When is it rational to trust someone?

Trust and Breach Deterrence

It is possible to think about trust not as an emotion but as a rational thought process. To rationally trust someone, one must believe that the person has adequate incentives to behave in a trustworthy manner. Several such incentives have been suggested in the literature. They include items such as guilt and shame, the fear of court action or of strong-armed enforcement, the unwillingness to spoil a valuable relationship, and the fear of losing one's reputation.

Guilt is internal to each individual. The ability to feel guilty for breaking a promise varies among individuals (Levitt 2006). Honesty is largely a by-product of upbringing, what psychologists call secondary socialization (Platteau 1994b). It is also influenced by cultural values and religious beliefs. Shame is a related concept. It is the capacity to feel bad if exposed as a cheater. Unlike shame, guilt does not require public knowledge and does not rely on information sharing.[1]

Enforcement mechanisms that rely on coercion are of two types: legitimate and illegitimate. The legal enforcement of contracts through courts ultimately relies on the state's monopoly over legitimate force. It is the state's backing that allows buyers to seize a debtor's assets, thus granting collateral value to unmovable property. Illegitimate force can also be used to enforce contractual obligations. Parties may resort to insults and violence directly, or hire thugs and bribe policemen to intervene. In the great majority of cases, the actual use of force is not required; implicit or explicit threats are sufficient.

Threats, however, are not always credible. The use of coercion is costly. For small transactions, legal costs are typically too high to justify court action. Even when legal costs are low relative to the size of the transaction, the person being sued may have nothing to foreclose on. This is particularly true in developing countries where many people are poor. In these cases, the threat of court action is not credible, and it fails to induce compliance.[2]

A third type of enforcement mechanism is based on quid pro quo: "I will continue to behave if you continue to behave." It is the threat of retaliation that induces compliance with contractual obligations. For such a mechanism to work, parties must interact repeatedly over time. The simplest form of retaliation is the refusal to further transact. For this punishment to deter breach, the relationship must be something worth preserving. Retaliation may also be inflicted by a group of people who were not party to the contract. Group punishment requires a coordination mechanism and the circulation of information about contractual breach. Reputation is this coordination and information-sharing device.

The Passage of Time

I now illustrate these concepts formally. Consider a contract by which a buyer promises something in exchange for something else, for instance, to pay p in exchange for quantity q. If payment is immediate, there is little room for cheating.[3] Such cash-and-carry transactions are the norm in a "flea market economy" such as the occasional roadside markets found in developed economies (Fafchamps and Minten 2001). Flea markets require little trust but only allow very limited forms of exchange. They are the least developed form of market institution.

Trust becomes more essential when the contract implies the passage of time. In many markets—credit, labor, insurance—time is inherent to the nature of the transaction itself because by definition one party fulfills its obligations before the other. Time also enters sales transactions in many ways, for instance, ordering, warranty, invoicing, payment by check or credit card. With the possible exception of microenterprises, businesses would find it extremely costly to conduct all their transactions with suppliers on a pure cash-and-carry basis. The capacity to enter into contracts with delayed obligations is an essential condition for a good business environment.

The analysis that follows focuses on sales transactions with delayed payment. Nearly all commercial supply purchases fall into this category.[4] Similar principles apply to other types of transactions like credit, labor, insurance, and most services. In sales contracts they also apply to other delayed contractual obligations, such as warranty or time of delivery.[5] So the focus on sales transactions is without loss of generality.

Imagine that a buyer receives q today (t_0) and promises to pay p tomorrow (t_1). For the purpose of this example, breach of contract is defined as nonpayment, whether it is excusable or not.[6] We want to know what makes the promise credible. To find out, we proceed by backward induction. Focus first on t_1, the time at which the buyer decides whether or not to comply with the contract. In case of payment, the buyer pays p. To reflect the fact that the marginal utility of p may vary across buyers, let $u(q)$ be the buyer's utility from q, and let $u(p)$ denote the utility loss associated with paying p. The cost of compliance may depend on external shocks. In case of nonpayment, the buyer keeps p but incurs punishment.

As mentioned, there are many different types of punishment to consider: guilt and shame, whose utility cost to the buyer is denoted G; various forms of coercive action including harassment, threats, and court action, whose cost to the buyer is denoted $P(C)$; the suspension of future trade with the seller resulting in the loss of relationship R; and damage to the buyer's reputation leading to a loss W of trade with other suppliers. I have allowed the strength of $P(C)$ to depend on the form of contract C. R and W are discussed in great detail in the rest of this chapter; for now they are taken as given. A rational buyer fulfills the contract if the cost of complying is smaller than all penalties combined[7]—that is, if

$$u(p) \leq G + P(C) + R + W. \tag{2.1}$$

Willingness to Trade

Let us now turn to the seller's incentives. The seller is asked to part with q at t_0 in exchange for a promise p at t_1. Let $v(p)$ and $v(q)$ be the values of p and q to the seller. Assume that there are gains from trade so that $v(p) > v(q)$. But this is not sufficient for trade to take place. When deciding whether to trust the buyer, a rational seller must evaluate the chance of being paid. This is given by the probability that equation (2.1) is satisfied. The expected gain to the seller is

$$v(p)\,\Pr(payment) - v(q) = v(p)\,\Pr(u(p) < G + P(C) + R + W) - v(q). \tag{2.2}$$

The seller may affect the probability of repayment by adjusting the form of the contract C, for instance, written contract, formal guarantees, posting a bond. Say there are N possible contract forms C_n, each with cost B_n. The seller must choose C_n to maximize the value of the transaction net of transaction cost $v(p)\,\Pr(payment|C_n) - v(q) - B_n$. If mechanisms other than $P(C)$ ensure the respect of the contract, the form of the contract does not matter, in which case formal guarantees or even a written contract will not be required. If no contractual form C_n exists so that $v(p)\,\Pr(payment|C_n) - B_n \geq v(q)$, it is optimal for the seller not to trade.

The buyer, too, must agree with the contract ex ante. A rational buyer does so if and only if the expected benefit from the contract is positive, that is, if

$$u(q) \geq u(p)\ \Pr(payment) + (G + P(C) + R + W)(1 - \Pr(payment)). \tag{2.3}$$

Equation (2.3) states that the buyer's gain from the contract (first term) must be greater than the expected cost of complying when compliance occurs (second term) plus the expected cost of punishment when compliance does not occur (third term).

Equations (2.2) and (2.3) illustrate the tension inherent in any contract. If enforcement is too lenient, buyers agree to any price p because they are not penalized for failing to pay, and hence will not pay. In this case, $\Pr(payment) = 0$, and it is not rational for the seller to trade. In contrast, if enforcement is very harsh, the expected cost of punishment is larger than any gain from trade for the buyer. If the buyer is not absolutely sure of being able to pay at t_1, a small chance of facing a very severe penalty may deter the buyer from trading. In both cases, no contract is concluded even though there are significant gains from trade. For trade to occur, enforcement must be sufficiently strong to deter opportunistic breach but not so strong that it scares away potential buyers.

Excusable Default

The previous conclusion hinges on the assumption that the contract is not contingent: a good is delivered, and payment is expected, irrespective of the circumstances. In this situation, any failure to pay is by definition a breach of contract. Buyers are punished even if nonpayment results from an exogenous shock beyond their control. The fear of such punishment is what drives honest buyers away.

To avoid this outcome, parties may opt for a contingent contract instead, stipulating explicit circumstances in which default is excusable. Examples of such contingent contracts can be found in practice, for instance, in large public works contracts. But for most contracts the time and effort required to stipulate all possible contingencies is prohibitively costly. Moreover, doing so may reveal information that parties would rather conceal to preserve their bargaining power when negotiating contract terms. For this reason, contracts normally remain incomplete in the sense that they do not specify all the conditions under which breach is excusable (Hart 1995; Hart and Moore 1988).

Most legal systems recognize that excusable default is essential to market exchange and include provisions on "force majeure" and "acts of God." These provisions apply to all contracts by default. Bankruptcy law can also be seen as a way of codifying excusable default while at the same time guaranteeing equality of treatment among creditors. The law also criminalizes fraudulent default, which is an extreme form of opportunistic breach of contract.[8] In all these cases, an outside party—the court—is empowered to investigate the circumstances of the debtor to ascertain ex post whether default was excusable and whether bankruptcy was fraudulent.

These mechanisms eliminate the need for detailed contingent contracts in most circumstances. But they only work for contracts enforced via $P(C)$. When enforcement relies on guilt, reputation, or relationships alone, there is no outside party to whom buyer and seller can delegate an ex post assessment of the excusable character of contractual nonperformance. For these contracts, contingencies themselves become subject to breach: even if the supplier ex ante accepts to relinquish payment in a certain state of the world, ex post he can default and insist on payment anyway. This means that negotiating excusable default clauses is not only costly but also futile. Contracts that are enforced via reputation and relationships may de facto be contingent but in a way that must be self-enforceable. This important point is revisited later in connection with the flexible enforcement of relational contracts.

Buyers' Types

So far I have implicitly assumed that all buyers are of the same type. This need not be true in practice. Buyers are likely to differ in their payoffs $v(p)$ and $v(q)$. They may also vary in their vulnerability to exogenous shocks, for instance, because of differences in experience, spare capacity, and financial wherewithal. Finally, clients may differ in their susceptibility to various types of punishments, for example, honesty, time horizon, or capacity to elude legal sanctions. These complications can be added to the model without affecting the earlier conclusion that punishment for breach of contract cannot be either too weak or too strong (Fafchamps 1996). It is also possible to allow for nonobservable effort on the part of the buyer and hence for moral hazard, not in payment itself, but in the actions the buyer takes to make himself able to pay.

Contractual incentives have been studied extensively, and there is a vast literature devoted to contractual issues with multiple types and unobservable effort. The interested reader is referred to Hart and Holmstrom (1987) and Salanié (1997) for summaries of the theoretical literature on contracts. Much of the literature has focused on the optimal design of contracts to minimize moral hazard and adverse selection. For instance, it has been noted that high penalties can be used to attract low-risk types while discouraging high-risk types, thereby providing incentives for buyers to reveal their type. As Stiglitz and Weiss (1981) showed, this mechanism breaks down if agents can avoid the high penalties by declaring bankruptcy or, more generally, by avoiding punishment for breach of contract. The same observation holds for moral hazard: if parties can breach the contract without incurring penalties, it is futile to seek a resolution of moral hazard problems through contractual incentives. The issue of contract enforcement is, in this sense, more fundamental than that of optimal contract terms.

This is why, in the remainder of this chapter, I look at market institutions from the vantage point of contract enforcement. The focus is on a topic that has received relatively little attention, namely, on incentive issues in contracts that are enforced by extracontractual punishment mechanisms, such as reputation and relationships. After clarifying the determinants of R and W, I progressively allow for multiple types and shocks, building bridges with the rest of the literature whenever possible.

What Has Been Learned

From this overview of the contract enforcement problem, it has been learned that penalties for breach of contract play a crucial role in making exchange possible whenever delivery and payment are not instantaneous. In spite of its simplicity, the conceptual framework developed so far delivers a number of important lessons:

- The ideal of an anonymous market is a fallacy. To trust someone, one must know who he or she is. This does not mean that all trade is personalized. But being able to identify the other party is nearly always essential, particularly if there is a problem with payment, delivery, or warranty. One important function of business registration is precisely to facilitate unambiguous identification. Those who complain that banks do not lend to unregistered firms have never tried to collect from them. An immediate corollary is that if precise identification is problematic, agents may use alternative methods for identifying people, such as personal introduction or the creation of a business community in which individual agents are identified in person.

- It is erroneous to think that perfect contract enforcement can ever be achieved or is even desirable. Existing legal codes understand this well; both Roman law and common law traditions allow for excusable default ("force majeure" and "acts of God"). Debt is no longer inherited as it was during the Roman empire. Indenture contracts have long been abolished, and prison for debt belongs in Dickens novels. Bankruptcy is allowed everywhere for limited liability firms. But countries differ with respect to personal bankruptcy, which is allowed in the United States but not in much of Europe. They also differ in their attitude toward punitive damages, which are allowed in U.S. law but frowned upon in continental Europe.

- Some likelihood of breach of contract is unavoidable, and it must be anticipated by economic agents. Fafchamps, Gunning and Oostendorp (2000) showed that in Zimbabwe manufacturing firms hold large inventories to shelter themselves from late delivery resulting from transport problems. How much breach is acceptable probably depends on the context. In much of Africa late payment is common and widely tolerated (Bigsten et al. 2000; Fafchamps and Minten 2001; Fafchamps and Gabre-Madhin 2006). Economic agents nevertheless go to great trouble to avoid it, most often by refusing any payment method other than cash in hand.

- Legal institutions are most relevant for large anonymous transactions, such as the sale of a house. They can provide a lot of security but typically at a high cost B_n. Small transactions, in contrast, are difficult to enforce through courts and, if they are anonymous, cannot rely on expected future trade. Small anonymous transactions must therefore be self-liquidating, with immediate cash payment and no delayed obligations. This form of trade, the "flea market economy," characterizes most trade in poor countries, especially in the so-called informal sector. Nearly all of Africa, for instance, is fed by such a marketing system. Needless to say, it is not very efficient; it raises the risk of theft and requires that transactions be conducted in person, not over the phone. This in turn raises transport costs and limits the size of firms because traders are too busy running from market to market. It is difficult to envisage how agricultural markets could be improved without finding sources of increasing returns to foster concentration.

- Commercial transactions can be enforced through repeated interaction alone, that is, through R and W. Courts are not necessary for market exchange. Perhaps the most obvious example of this is the drug trade, which spans over many countries and churns billions of dollars in trade every year without any court enforcement. When agents do not rely on courts to enforce contracts, formal guarantees are irrelevant and contracts do not even need to be written. Markets are decoupled from formal institutions. In Africa most trade among medium- to large-scale firms takes this form. The question then becomes how one can understand markets without legal institutions. Do they follow the same rules? How can we improve them? Do we have to throw away informal institutions before putting in place formal ones? Doing so is likely to be fraught with problems.[9] Is there a way to upgrade informal markets? If so, how? Answering these questions is the focus of the remainder of this chapter. The key is to understand R and W.

Relational Contracting and Reputation

It is clear from the previous section that the fear of losing R or W can serve as a deterrent to opportunistic breach of contract. But where do the values of R and W come from? Why should economic agents fear losing a commercial relationship? There are so many other agents around, so why care? I begin with R. In the following sections, I draw liberally from Ghosh and Ray (1996) and from my own work on these issues.

A Two-Agent Example

To illustrate how a commercial relationship can be valuable, I begin with a simple example. Consider two agents, a client A and a supplier B. Assume they are in a long-term relationship with no end in sight. Each month A receives merchandises from B and must pay upon receipt of a monthly invoice. We wish to know under what circumstances the fear of losing a relationship can deter opportunistic breach. To focus on this, assume that the client is always able to pay. Hence, without loss of generality, let $u(p) = p$. If A pays, her gain from trade is her profit margin α. If A does not pay, she does not pay p, which for simplicity is normalized to 1; her total gain is thus $1 + \alpha$. The client has a discount factor:

$$\beta = \frac{1}{1+\delta} < 1,$$

where δ is the (monthly) rate at which A discounts the future. If A pays, the relationship continues and more supplies arrive the following month. If A cheats, B stops supplying forever.

What is the value for A of the relationship with supplier B? If A does not pay, she gains 1 this month but B refuses to trade from then on. Hence A loses α in all future periods, that is,

$$\sum_{t=1}^{\infty} \beta^t \alpha = \frac{\beta\alpha}{1-\beta}.$$

It is not optimal for the client to cheat if

$$1 + \alpha + \beta 0 \leq \alpha + \frac{\beta\alpha}{1-\beta} \tag{2.4}$$

$$1 \leq \frac{\beta\alpha}{1-\beta} \quad \text{or} \quad \delta \leq \alpha. \tag{2.5}$$

Inequality (2.4) is called the voluntary participation constraint or non-cheating constraint. Provided β is close enough to 1 (that is, provided the discount rate δ is small enough) and α is strictly positive, $\frac{\beta\alpha}{1-\beta}$ can be arbitrarily large. To facilitate comparison with the first section, note that inequality (2.4) can also be derived in terms of the instantaneous gain from cheating $1 + \alpha - \alpha = 1$ and the long-term loss from losing the relationship:

$$u(p) = 1 \leq \frac{\beta\alpha}{1-\beta} = R. \tag{2.6}$$

We see that the future value of the relationship is simply $\frac{\beta\alpha}{1-\beta}$. For β close enough to 1, the fear of losing the relationship can by itself deter opportunistic breach.

An N-Agent Example

The two-agent example illustrates the value of a relationship if no outside option exists at all. What happens if outside options exist? Imagine a situation with two groups of agents, clients and suppliers, trading repeatedly over time. As before, each transaction is such that payment takes place after delivery. There are two types of suppliers: good and bad. Good suppliers deliver quality inputs; bad suppliers do not. When the client buys from a bad supplier, she makes zero profit. When she buys from a good supplier, she makes α profit as before. The type of an individual supplier is not immediately observable. To discover the supplier's type, the client has to experiment, that is, purchase a sample and try it out. Experimentation costs $c > 0$ and takes one period. The proportion of good suppliers in the total population is θ.

A client without a supplier has to sample a supplier at random and incur cost c to find out whether the supplier is good or bad. If the supplier turns out to be good, they enter into a long-term relationship in the following period. If the supplier is bad, the client has to sample another supplier in the following month. The payoff of a client matched with a good supplier is as before:

$$V^M = \frac{\alpha}{1-\beta}.$$

The expected payoff of a client when searching is

$$V^S = -c + (1-\theta)\beta V^S + \theta\beta V^M.$$

Solving for V^S, we obtain

$$V^S = \frac{\theta\beta\alpha - c(1-\beta)}{(1-\beta)(1-\beta+\theta\beta)}. \tag{2.7}$$

Now we can ask, would A cheat a good supplier? If A cheats, she gets an instantaneous payoff of 1 as before, but the continuation payoff is different from the first example: she now gets V^S. The noncheating constraint now is

$$1 + \alpha + \beta V^S \leq \alpha + \beta V^M = V^M \tag{2.8}$$

or written as in (2.6),

$$u(p) = 1 \leq \beta(V^M - V^S) = R. \tag{2.9}$$

In this case, the value of the relationship R is the difference $\beta V^M - \beta V^S$. This is because a cheater still has a chance of forming a new relationship but must incur a cost of search to do so.

Plugging equation (2.7) into the noncheating constraint (2.8) enables rewriting the noncheating constraint as

$$1 \leq \beta\frac{c+\alpha}{1-\beta+\beta\theta} = R \quad \text{or} \quad \delta + \theta - c \leq \alpha. \tag{2.10}$$

Thus, if $\theta = 0$ (no replacement supplier) and $c = 0$, condition (2.9) boils down to (2.6). Consider what happens if $c = 0$. R is a decreasing function of θ; the higher θ is, the lower R is. At the limit, if $\theta = 1$, condition (2.9) becomes

$$1 + \delta \leq \alpha. \tag{2.11}$$

If the profit margin is less than 100 percent, the value of the relationship is too small and condition (2.11) is violated. There is still a penalty, however, because matching is not immediate, that is, the cheater loses α for one period. This is what condition (2.11) says.

Now imagine that the cheating client can immediately find a new supplier and does not have to wait. This case can be represented by letting $\theta = 1$ as before and by setting $c = -\alpha$, meaning that the client makes a profit α in period 1 instead of incurring a cost of c. The non-cheating constraint becomes

$$1 \leq \beta \frac{-\alpha + \alpha}{1 - \beta + \beta} = 0.$$

In this case, the relationship has no value. This is not surprising; since the supplier can be replaced immediately at no cost, the fear of losing the supplier has no value. It follows that the fear of losing a business relationship can only deter opportunistic breach when replacing this relationship takes time or is costly. This arises, for instance, if there is only one supplier or if it is difficult to identify reliable suppliers.

Spontaneous Market Emergence

The contract enforcement mechanism just described rests on relational contracting. It is rudimentary yet extremely powerful. It implies that if search is time-consuming or costly, markets with delayed contractual obligations (credit, insurance, warranty) can arise spontaneously in a completely decentralized manner, without any external enforcement or information sharing. This idea was first applied to labor markets by Shapiro and Stiglitz (1984). Kranton (1996) contrasted relation-based markets with more impersonal exchange and showed that the former can be an equilibrium although the latter is in general more efficient.

It is beyond the scope of this chapter to explain in detail how markets can spontaneously emerge (see Fafchamps 2002b for details), but the basic intuition is straightforward. Consider a drug addict who wishes to purchase his daily fix. He knows there is plenty of adulterated supply on offer. He cannot tell without trying it, and consuming bad stuff is potentially lethal. In this environment, an addict who has found a reliable source of supply wants to continue buying from the same source. The difficulty of finding another reliable supplier is what gives value to the relationship and allows the supplier to extend a little bit of credit to regular customers.[10] This is called relational contracting, that is, repeated exchange between two parties over an extended period of time based on the relationship between them.

This market emergence process appears to be natural to most people and arises spontaneously in many environments. Staal, Delgado, and Nicholson (1997) described the milk market in Addis Ababa in exactly the same terms, for instance. But this process has a surprising twist: What makes contract enforcement possible is the existence of search costs. Asymmetric information is what allows the emergence of markets for credit, insurance, and the like. Eliminate search costs and information asymmetry, and spontaneous contract enforcement collapses. This is worth emphasizing because information asymmetries and search costs are usually viewed as evils that take us away from first best. But in a second-best world, they are what make sophisticated markets possible.

Second, gains from trade cannot be eliminated by competition; if α falls to 0, clients have nothing to lose from cheating suppliers. Contract enforcement requires that buyers get rents. Too much competition can thus undo contract enforcement by eliminating these rents. This forces exchange to take a flea market form. This means no orders, no checks, no invoicing, no warranty, no credit, no insurance, just cash-and-carry. Flea markets—produce markets, roadside shops and services—litter the streets of all towns and cities of the developing world. This is perhaps a testimony to the strength of competition in undermining market development, or at least one form of it. To be fair, relational contracting can survive the pressure of competition but only provided that trust reduces transaction costs relative to cash-and-carry, for example, by allowing delivery to be organized over the phone.

Some markets inherently involve the passage of time and cannot operate on a cash-and-carry basis. This is true of credit, for instance. In a credit market based on relational contracting, competition for funds cannot bring borrowers' gains from trade below the level required to guarantee repayment. This limits the interest rate the lender is able to charge. With a limited supply of funds, this naturally leads to rationing; some borrowers get a loan, others do not. Patronage relationships can be seen in this light as a way of solving the rationing problem. By forming a long-term relationship with a landlord, potential borrowers ensure future access to credit in a rationed world. The bottom line is that markets based on relational contracting do not behave in a conventional way.

The Different Kinds of Reputation

Having clarified R, the value of business relationships, I now turn to W, the value of reputation. The word *reputation* has been used with different meanings in the literature, so it is imperative to first distinguish among them. *Reputation* is sometimes used as synonymous with *relationship*: "If I cheat Jack, I will lose my reputation with him." That meaning has already been discussed. A second meaning refers to the type of the agent or to the good produced, as in: "Toyota is a car manufacturer with a good reputation." What we mean is that Toyota produces reliable cars. We rely on the manufacturer's reputation to assess a hidden characteristic of the product we buy—how long it will operate before breaking down. A third meaning of the word refers to the past behavior of an agent, as in: "Andersen lost its reputation when it helped Enron circumvent regulation on public securities." In this case, we are not talking about the quality of Andersen's service but about the fact that the firm cheated. I focus on the last two meanings.

Reputation so defined implies the sharing of information. The reputation of Toyota cars for reliability is based on the experience of past buyers. By sharing their driving experiences with us, they help us draw an inference about a hidden attribute of Toyota cars. Similarly, Andersen's cheating behavior is known to us because it was described in the newspapers. It is because this information has been circulated that Andersen has lost customers. If the information had been kept secret, it would only have affected Andersen's relationship with Enron and the Securities Commission. But the two types of reputation have different effects on markets.

Sharing Information about Supplier Types To illustrate the role of reputation about type, let us expand our earlier model to allow information sharing. Assume that clients share information about suppliers' types. Does this affect incentives to cheat? The answer is yes because when clients share information on good and bad suppliers, they no longer have to incur the screening cost c.[11] The noncheating constraint becomes

$$1 \leq \beta \frac{\alpha}{1-\beta+\beta\theta}$$

$$< \beta \frac{c+\alpha}{1-\beta+\beta\theta} \quad \text{if } c > 0. \tag{2.12}$$

Sharing information about types reduces incentives to respect contractual obligations because it reduces screening costs and thus reduces the penalty for cheating. This kind of reputation effect makes contract enforcement more difficult.

Sharing Information about Client Behavior If we assume instead that suppliers share information about the past behavior of clients, we get the opposite result: Reputation can make contract enforcement easier.

To see why, suppose that (good) suppliers agree never to sell again to clients who have not paid in the past. In the literature, the situation in which economic agents collude to exclude cheaters from future trade goes by various names. Kandori (1992) called it a reputational mechanism or equilibrium. Greif (1993) called it a multilateral punishment strategy. Sometimes it is also called collective punishment or exclusion. This kind of enforcement mechanism has many problems. For now let us assume that collective exclusion is an equilibrium.

With this assumption, a cheating client can never buy from a good supplier ever again. We are back to our first model, even though there are many agents. The short-term gain from cheating is, as before, 1. The long-term loss from cheating is all future trade, i.e.,

$$\sum_{t=1}^{\infty} \beta^t \alpha = \frac{\beta\alpha}{1-\beta}.$$

Consequently, in this case, we have

$$R + W = \frac{\beta\alpha}{1-\beta} > \beta\frac{\alpha}{1-\beta+\beta\theta}, \tag{2.13}$$

from which we see that sharing information about behavior raises the penalty for cheating and thus provides better contract enforcement incentives.[12]

The Information-Sharing Process

Collective punishment assumes that agents share information about all past behavior of all agents. This seems like an impossible requirement to satisfy, given the enormous amount of information processing that this would require. Kandori (1992) showed that information processing can be dramatically simplified by resorting to individual specific labels.

Kandori's idea was to summarize information about past behavior into a single variable or label $z_i(t)$ for each client i. This variable takes integer values between 0 and T. If a client has not cheated in the past, $z_i(t) = 0$. If a client cheats, he is punished for T periods. In the first punishment period, $z_i(t) = T$, in the second punishment period, $z_i(t+1) = T - 1$, and so on, until the punishment phase is over, at which time $z_i(t + T + s) = 0$ for all s. If a player cheats during the punishment phase, the punishment is restarted. Kandori showed that this simple strategy can enforce cooperation in a large class of repeated interaction games that include the buyer-seller game.

This equilibrium resembles the way credit reference agencies operate. They simplify the information about each agent i with a credit report showing when the agent last cheated (paid late or not at all). This information is kept on the agent's record for a set number of years T, after which time it is erased.

Reputation and Meta-Punishment Reputational punishment has received an inordinate amount of attention in the literature, so much so that it is customarily believed that collective punishments are easy to sustain and are pervasive in practice. Any evidence that economic agents share information is usually taken to imply that they collude to exclude cheaters, often without acknowledging the possibility that they may exchange information about types, not about cheaters. In my own empirical work, I have found only limited evidence of reputational punishment. My interpretation for these findings is that a coordinated punishment strategy is difficult to sustain.

To illustrate this difficulty, consider suppliers' incentives to share information. Suppose client A has not paid one of his suppliers. This supplier tells the others. Suppliers have agreed not to deal with cheaters. Clients know this. Now A approaches supplier B, promising he will not cheat anymore. The question is, is it in B's interest to refuse to deal with A?

To answer this, imagine that B agrees to trade with A, and consider A's incentive to cheat B. Since A is already blacklisted by all other suppliers, if he were to cheat on B he would not find any other supplier to trade with afterwards. Consequently, A's incentive to pay is the value of the relationship

$$1 \leq \frac{\beta\alpha}{1-\beta}.$$

This is the same noncheating constraint as (2.13): A has as much incentive to pay B as any other client. From B's perspective, if (2.13) is satisfied for all clients, then it also ensures that A will pay. In other words, A's future behavior is as reliable as any other client's, irrespective of his past cheating. Now consider B's incentive to trade with A. The alternative is to refuse to trade and wait for another client. To the extent that it is costly for B to refuse to trade and wait, it is in his interest to trade with A. Hence it is not in the interest of suppliers to participate in collective punishment.

This problem is known as the meta-punishment problem. To incite suppliers to jointly punish cheaters, those who refuse to punish must themselves be punished. If other suppliers could impose some social sanction on B, they might be able to force B to refuse A and wait. The problem with meta-punishment is that trade between A and B need not be observable to other suppliers. Since it is not in the interest of either A or B to advertise the fact that they are circumventing the sanction, meta-punishment is only implementable if suppliers observe each others' dealings. This requirement to some extent runs contrary to the requirements of competition, which assumes some secrecy. Meta-punishment is thus difficult to satisfy for commercial contracts.

If meta-punishment is impossible, collective punishment unravels. Even though there is information sharing about past cheating, suppliers cannot coordinate their actions to permanently exclude cheaters. We fall back on the N-agent case with noncheating constraint:

$$1 \leq \beta \frac{c+\alpha}{1-\beta+\beta\theta}.$$

Self-Enforcing Collective Punishment The difficulty of enforcing collective punishment originates in the assumption that clients are identical. The fact that a client has cheated in the past does not reveal anything about the client. Since his payoff is unchanged, his incentive to cheat again is also unchanged. If the threat of exclusion deters cheating from all clients, it also deters future cheating by past cheaters. This is what creates an incentive problem for suppliers.

Things are different if clients come in several types τ. Say there are two types of clients, good and bad. Good clients are as before. Bad clients are very impatient—low β—and cannot resist the temptation to cheat.[13]

Suppose A does not pay B. The behavior of A now serves as a signal regarding A's type. A is a bad client, a cheater, because in equilibrium only bad clients cheat. Cheating thus reveals one's type. Now suppose that B tells other suppliers. Will other suppliers refuse to sell to A? The answer is yes; past behavior predicts future behavior through inference about types. When cheating is interpreted as a signal of a bad type, sharing information about past behavior results in collective punishment without meta-punishment. Collective punishment is self-enforcing.

In the framework of the earlier model, this is equivalent to saying that the probability of payment depends on the client's type. Let the proportion of bad types in the economy be μ. If the type is unknown, the supplier must take a chance, and her payoff is

$$v(p)\ \Pr(payment) - v(q) = v(p)(1-\mu) - v(q). \tag{2.14}$$

However, if the type of the client is known, the probability of payment is either 1 (if the client is good) or 0 (if the client is bad).

This model can be extended to the case in which clients' types change over time, for instance, they do not pay because they are going bankrupt. The same mechanism applies. If information about their behavior circulates, they will be excluded from future trade in a decentralized, self-enforcing manner.[14]

The appeal of this approach is that it accords with field observations. Based on microsurveys of manufacturing firms and agricultural traders in many countries, Fafchamps (2004) found no evidence of coordinated exclusion of cheaters in sub-Saharan Africa. No respondent ever described a refusal to trade as punishment for past breach, and no evidence was found of meta-punishment or of coordination to punish. Survey respondents displayed little fear that failing to pay a supplier would affect their credit among other suppliers. But discussions with numerous respondents indicated that they interpret information about nonpayment to other suppliers as a possible indication of liquidity problems. If they fear a client is on the verge of bankruptcy, they withdraw their credit. Respondents nevertheless understand that withdrawing credit for fear of bankruptcy can be self-fulfilling. For this reason, they act with caution and dislike spreading rumors. The evidence shows that although there is much sharing of information about trade opportunities and agent type, little information is exchanged about breach of contract. Could it be that there are incentive problems associated with the sharing of information?

Incentives to Share Information about Cheaters There are many incentive problems associated with the circulation of information about cheaters. First, it must be possible to identify agents unambiguously. Second, cheated suppliers do not have an incentive to share the information with others. One reason is that by telling other suppliers who the cheater is, they actually help competitors. Even if this is not a consideration, sharing information requires an effort without immediate counterpart. As a result it is difficult to incite suppliers to circulate accurate and current information about breach of contract. Finally, agents may seek to capture clients by telling other suppliers that they are cheaters.

In my empirical work, I have encountered examples of all of these phenomena, so that I am convinced they explain why information sharing is not more prevalent. Milgrom, North, and Weingast (1991) proposed an elegant solution to the incentive problems surrounding the information-sharing process. This solution is meant to mimic an old institution, called the Law Merchant, who is the repository of information about past breach of contract. This is similar to Kandori's credit reference bureau argument, but Milgrom and colleagues focused on the incentives for buyers and sellers to refer to the Law Merchant. The problem is to incite agents to report accurate information about breach of contract. In the model, this is achieved by making the Law Merchant adjudicator of disputes. In this manner, he is provided with accurate information about past cheating. The punishment for breach of contract is a fine. Cheaters are asked to pay a judgment that exceeds the gain they made from cheating. Part of this payment goes to the cheated, who thus have an incentive to report cheating. In equilibrium nobody cheats, but if they do, they pay their fines in order to clear their names and be allowed to trade again. The Law Merchant keeps track of unpaid judgments.

According to Milgrom and co-authors, the Law Merchant proposes a combined contract to buyers and sellers whereby agents pay a query fee to learn whether their client has any outstanding judgments. This fee then enables them to seek the adjudication of the Law Merchant in case of contractual dispute. Suppliers who fail to consult the Law Merchant before contracting are refused help. This part is essential because in equilibrium there is no cheating. Consequently, if the Law Merchant could not collect a query fee, he would generate no income and thus would disappear. Milgrom, North, and Weingast (1991) show that this system is incentive-compatible and can enforce impersonal spot contracts.

In my empirical work, I have not encountered any Law Merchant. But I have observed that credit reference agencies rely critically on publicly available information about contractual cases brought to court. This alone may explain why, of nine African countries that I studied, the only one with a large credit reference agency, Zimbabwe, was the only country in the group where unpaid debts were customarily brought to court.[15] Private arbitration has been said to mimic the Law Merchant. I have hardly observed any use of private arbitration in Africa, although it may be relevant elsewhere. What I have observed is that credit reference agencies often offer credit recovery or debt mediation services. Just as in the case of the Law Merchant, these activities provide them with valuable (and accurate) information about cheating. In a rural African context, village chiefs play an arbitration role, especially in land disputes and family law (Udry 1991). It is unclear whether their authority is called upon to enforce commercial transactions that transcend village boundaries.

Flexibility and Breach

So far, breach of contract has been regarded as a simple affair: the client either pays or does not pay. If he does not pay, this signals he has a bad type or is on the verge of bankruptcy. In practice, things are not so clear-cut because all economic agents are faced by shocks. As a result, even good clients sometimes cannot comply with the contract.

A more accurate representation of reality is to assume that bad clients never pay but that, with some probability, good clients find themselves temporarily unable to pay. Observing nonpayment raises the probability that the client is a bad type but not with absolute certainty. To make this clear, consider the following situation.

In each period, a good client—someone who has paid in the past—has a probability γ of becoming permanently bad. This is meant to represent massive shocks that force a firm out of business. Good clients can also face temporary difficulties that make them unable to pay during one period. The probability of such occurrences is denoted $\sigma < 1$.

Imagine a supplier B who has been selling to A for some time and has always been paid. But now B is not paid. What should B do? This depends on whether A has become bad or not. If A has become bad, B should stop supplying; otherwise, B should continue selling to A. What are the odds that A has become bad?

$$\Pr(A \text{ is bad}|A \text{ cheated}) = \frac{\Pr(A \text{ is bad})}{\Pr(A \text{ cheated})} = \frac{\gamma}{\gamma + (1-\gamma)\sigma}.$$

Suppose further that suppliers make a positive profit margin on each sale, and let V^T denote the supplier's expected utility from selling to a good client.[16] For simplicity, assume that it takes exactly one period for the supplier to find a good new client. The supplier must choose between keeping the client and risk losing 1 a second time, or reject the client and lose potential sales for one period. If A has failed to pay once, it is in the interest of the supplier to continue selling to this client if

$$\frac{\gamma}{\gamma+(1-\gamma)\sigma}(-1)+\frac{(1-\gamma)\sigma}{\gamma+(1-\gamma)\sigma}V^T \geq 0,$$

$$(1-\gamma)\sigma V^T \geq \gamma,$$

which, for a large enough V^T and a small enough γ, is satisfied. In this case, it is in supplier B's interest to be flexible, that is, to allow A to skip payment once. Breach of contract does not automatically destroy the relationship.

Flexibility does not last forever, however. Suppose that A cheats a second time immediately afterwards. What is now the probability that A is bad? Bayes' law says that

$$\Pr(T_1|E) = \frac{\Pr(E|T_1)\Pr(T_1)}{\sum_{j=1}^{2}\Pr(E|T_j)\Pr(T_j)}.$$

Let E be "cheat twice in a row," and let T_1 be "A is bad" and T_2 be "A is good." We have[17]

$$\Pr(A \text{ is bad}|\text{cheat twice}) = \frac{1\gamma}{1\gamma+\sigma\sigma(1-\gamma)} = \frac{\gamma}{\gamma+(1-\gamma)\sigma^2}.$$

Since $\sigma < 1$ by assumption,

$$\Pr(A \text{ is bad}|\text{cheat once}) = \frac{\gamma}{\gamma+(1-\gamma)\sigma} < \frac{\gamma}{\gamma+(1-\gamma)\sigma^2} = \Pr(A \text{ is bad}|\text{cheat twice}).$$

This is because a good client is unlikely to cheat twice in a row. The supplier's incentive to continue selling to A now becomes

$$\frac{\gamma}{\gamma + (1-\gamma)\sigma^2}(-1) + \frac{(1-\gamma)\sigma^2}{\gamma + (1-\gamma)\sigma^2}V^T \geq 0$$

$$(1-\gamma)\sigma^2 V^T \geq \gamma.$$

Since the left-hand side is smaller, the supplier is less likely to sell again to A.

This argument can be extended to N cheating periods simply by raising σ to the Nth power. We have

$$\lim_{N\to\infty} \Pr(A \text{ is bad}|\text{cheat } N \text{ times in a row}) = 1$$

with very rapid convergence to 1 if σ is small.

This demonstrates that suppliers may be flexible for a while but after some time will gradually begin to suspect that A has become a bad client. How long the seller is willing to give the buyer the benefit of the doubt depends on σ. If the business environment is very risky, and σ is large relative to γ, many businesses face difficulties meeting their short-term financial obligations, but they are accommodated by their creditors. This in turn generates financial uncertainty in the creditors' business, generating a multiplier effect. Another source of multiplier effect arises because it is easier for firms to claim having been hit by a shock than to admit that they were just sloppy or disorganized. The risk-sharing benefit that flexibility confers generates the standard moral hazard problem associated with any insurance: The insured has less incentive to apply proper care. Bigsten et al. (2000) documented that African manufacturing firms first adopted a conciliatory attitude toward nonpaying clients. Only if negotiation failed did they sever the business relationship or seek reparation in court. Similar results for agricultural traders were reported by Fafchamps and Minten (2001).

What Has Been Learned?

The excursion into the world of relational contracting and reputation has taught a few useful lessons:

- Commercial relationships are valuable only if they are not easily replaceable, for instance, because of screening costs or because of search time. The more bad agents there are, the more valuable relationships are, and the easier it is to sustain contracts on the strength of relationships alone. Relational contracting is the dominant form of contract enforcement in sub-Saharan Africa.

- Contrary to what is often believed, information sharing does not necessarily improve contract enforcement. To illustrate this, the chapter described a model in which sharing information about supplier types weakens contract enforcement. The reason is that doing so reduces search costs and thus lowers the value of relationships. It was also shown that sharing information about past behavior is necessary but not sufficient for collective punishment of cheaters. Exclusion of cheaters is not decentralizable unless economic agents can observe other agents' trading partners, or unless agents interpret breach of contract as a sign of impending bankruptcy. Empirical work in Africa uncovered no evidence of coordination devices to punish cheaters but found some indications that breach raises concerns about the financial viability of the debtor.
- In a risky business environment, such as the one characterizing much of the developing world, economic agents face many shocks that make it difficult for them to comply with contractual obligations. This observation applies to payment but also to on-time delivery, quality control, worker absenteeism, and so on. Firms operating in this environment show more flexibility with respect to contractual obligations, preferring to renegotiate contracts when difficulties arise rather than impose a rigid interpretation of the contractual terms. Foreign firms entering such an environment may be surprised by the difference in business culture. Biggs, Moody, von Leewen, and White (1994), for instance, documented the indignation of large U.S. firms trying to source garment products from sub-Saharan Africa and experiencing failed deadlines and inconsistent quality standards. What is normal in Africa clearly is not in the United States.

Discrimination and Networks

Information sharing and its effect on contract enforcement has been discussed. The presence of good and bad types was found essential to grant value to commercial relationships and to support decentralized exclusion of cheaters. The coexistence of multiple types raises other issues, discussed in this section. First, I examine how trust can be built over time when there are many types of clients. The problem is con artists. Next I allow for observable characteristics that are correlated with hidden types and introduce the concept of statistical discrimination. Finally, I discuss the network effects that arise as a result of multiplicity of types and information sharing within networks.

Building Trust

So far it has been assumed that economic agents can ascertain each other's type by incurring a screening cost c. But where does this cost come from?

Two Types Let us start with a simple example. Suppose that suppliers share information perfectly and that collective punishment is enforced via meta-punishment.[18] There are two types of clients, good and bad. Clients can be bad for many reasons, for instance, because they are genuinely dishonest or short-sighted, or because they do not value the merchandise offered by the supplier.

Here I define good and bad clients in terms of discount factor.[19] Good clients have discount factor β_h, and bad clients have discount factor β_l, with $\beta_h > \beta_l$. Being more patient, good clients value long-term gains more and thus have less incentive to cheat. To make this clear, assume that

$$\frac{\beta_l \alpha}{1-\beta_l} < 1 < \frac{\beta_h \alpha}{1-\beta_h}. \tag{2.15}$$

It follows that bad clients cannot be deterred from cheating. How can suppliers force bad types to reveal themselves?

One possibility is for suppliers to propose a small transaction, for instance, by granting a small amount of supplier credit. By reducing the size of the transaction, the supplier reduces her exposure in case of nonpayment. Let κ be the size of the transaction. What is the smallest transaction required to induce the bad agent to reveal his type by not paying?

If κ is chosen too small, bad clients may choose to pay the small transaction only to cheat on a larger transaction later. To see this, suppose that the supplier first sells κ and, if paid, sells 1. What is the bad client's incentive to mimic good behavior in the first period to cheat more later? By cheating right away, the bad client gets κ. By cheating later, the bad client gets $\alpha\kappa$ now and $\beta_l 1$ next period. To induce the bad client to reveal his type in the first period, κ must be large enough that cheating now is better for the bad client:

$$\kappa \geq \alpha\kappa + \beta_l.$$

$$\kappa^* \geq \frac{\beta_l}{1-\alpha}. \tag{2.16}$$

$\kappa^* < 1$ since, by inequality (2.15), a size 1 transaction induces immediate cheating by bad clients.[20] Good clients repay any size transaction because

$$1 < \frac{\beta_h \alpha}{1 - \beta_h} \Rightarrow \kappa < \frac{\beta_h \alpha \kappa}{1 - \beta_h} \quad \text{for any } \kappa.$$

Having found κ^*, we now easily derive c as the expected loss associated with the test transaction κ^*. Suppliers have a unit profit margin of λ on repaid transactions. Let φ be the probability of being matched with a bad client. We have

$$-c = -\varphi\kappa^* + (1 - \varphi)\lambda\kappa^*.$$

$$c = \kappa^*(\varphi - (1 - \varphi)\lambda).$$

A longer trial period may be better than a one-period trial period. Intuitively, insisting on a longer trial period enables the supplier to reduce κ^* because the impatient bad client has to wait longer before being able to fully cheat the supplier. For instance, if the trial period lasted two periods, the optimal level of κ would be given by

$$\kappa \geq \alpha\kappa + \beta_l \alpha\kappa + \beta_l^2.$$

$$\kappa^{**} \geq \frac{\beta_l}{1 - \alpha - \beta_l \alpha}.$$

This is clearly smaller than (2.16). When choosing how long the trial period should be, the supplier must trade lower exposure for reduction in trade volume in case the client turns out to be a good one. I leave this as an exercise. In practice, trial periods in commercial relationships last from three to six months in sub-Saharan Africa. Trial periods of a similar length are often found in labor contracts, where they serve a similar role.[21]

N Types Now suppose that there are N types ranked $\beta_1 < \beta_2 < \cdots < \beta_N$. Partition these types into all the good types G for whom

$$1 \leq \frac{\beta_h \alpha}{1 - \beta_h} \quad \text{for all } h > t,$$

and all the bad types for whom

$$\frac{\beta_l \alpha}{1-\beta_l} < 1 \quad \text{for all } h \leq t.$$

The index t denotes the most patient bad type. We know from (2.16) that type t is the hardest to force to reveal his type because it requires the highest κ^* to induce cheating.

One possibility would be for the supplier to set

$$\kappa^* = \frac{\beta_t}{1-\alpha},$$

in which case all bad types would reveal themselves in period 1, and the supplier would be fully informed. But this is an expensive strategy for the supplier because it requires a high exposure κ^*. If there are lots of cheaters in the economy, this is probably too expensive. Another approach is to start small, first forcing the really bad types to reveal themselves. Then, in the second period, the supplier would raise κ^* slightly to induce another batch of bad types to reveal themselves. And so on until all bad types have been revealed. It is also conceivable to lengthen the trial period for each group in order to further reduce exposure, albeit at the cost of delaying full trade.[22]

The exact shape of the screening strategy depends on the precise distribution of types—their level of impatience and the proportion of clients of various types—as well as on the supplier's margin λ. This gradual screening process closely resembles what survey respondents in Africa usually call the building of trust (Fafchamps 2004). In practice, human beings are much better at inferring type than the crude model used here would suggest. They may rely on facial expression, verbalization, and various interpersonal interactions to improve screening (Cornell and Welch 1996).

Statistical Discrimination

Building trust can be a lengthy and complicated process. It is reasonable to expect economic agents to use any information that reduces screening costs by facilitating inference.

One such possibility arises whenever agents observe external characteristics that are correlated with unobserved type (Akerlof 1985; Coate and Loury 1993). The most likely candidates are characteristics that are easily observable, such as gender, race, ethnicity, religion, appearance, age, and firm size. Any characteristics that are correlated with hidden type, even slightly, can be used to improve inference. As a result, populations with different observable characteristics end up being treated differently by the market. This is called statistical discrimination.[23] We expect statistical discrimination to be pervasive in all economic transactions where hidden type or hidden quality are at issue: labor, credit, insurance, rentals, goods and services, pretty much all markets.

Statistical discrimination is not equitable. People are treated differently purely on the basis of external characteristics that are by themselves irrelevant for contractual performance. The equity loss due to statistical discrimination is particularly large in markets driven by relational contracting because failure to be selected has long-term consequences. Yet statistical discrimination is individually rational for the person doing the screening. Furthermore, in many cases it is (second-best) Pareto-efficient. It is therefore pervasive. Short of eliminating the information asymmetry that is the cause of discrimination, it is difficult to uproot.

There is abundant empirical evidence that business communities in Africa are not representative of the population at large (Fafchamps 2002a). Minorities—some of them native, some of them not—tend to be overrepresented among middle- and large-scale entrepreneurs, those that operate outside the flea market economy. While there often are historical reasons why a particular minority has become overrepresented in a particular business, evidence suggests that overepresentation is long-lasting and even survives efforts to dismantle it (Fafchamps 2002a; Himbara 1994). It is therefore no surprise that many development projects seek to correct welfare imbalances resulting from such discrimination, for instance, by targeting assistance toward minorities, women, microenterprises, scheduled castes, and so on. Understanding statistical discrimination is essential to a proper grasp of market institutions.

Statistical discrimination can manifest itself in various ways. I focus here on the simplest form, which is simply to exclude B clients from trade.[24] To illustrate this possibility in the modeling framework, assume there two types of clients, good and bad, and two ethnic groups, B and W. The share of B clients in the population is b. Without loss of generality, assume that the proportion of bad types in the B population is higher than in the W population:

$$\sigma_B > \sigma_W.$$

Consider the decision of a supplier approached by an unknown B client. The supplier can choose either to screen the client or to reject the client and wait until the next period in the hope of being faced with a W client. For simplicity, assume that the screening exposure κ is the same for both populations of clients and that screening is done in one period.[25] If the supplier screens the B client, his payoff is

$$V^B = \sigma_B(-\kappa + b\beta V^B + (1-b)\beta V^W) + (1-\sigma_B)\left(\lambda\kappa + \beta\frac{\lambda}{1-\beta}\right), \qquad (2.17)$$

where λ is the supplier's profit margin and β his discount factor. If the client is bad, the supplier loses κ and is matched with a new client in the following period, who could either be B or W. This is captured by the first term. The second term captures what happens if the client is good, in which case the supplier earns margin λ on a transaction of size κ today and gets λ thereafter.

A similar equation can be written for V^W:

$$V^W = \sigma_W(-\kappa + b\beta V^B + (1-b)\beta V^W) + (1-\sigma_W)\left(\lambda\kappa + \beta\frac{\lambda}{1-\beta}\right). \qquad (2.18)$$

It is immediately obvious that $V^B < V^W$ since $\sigma_B > \sigma_W$.

If the supplier refuses to screen B prospective clients, the payoffs are

$$\bar{V}^B = b\beta\bar{V}^B + (1-b)\beta\bar{V}^W. \qquad (2.19)$$

$$\bar{V}^W = \sigma_W(-\kappa + b\beta\bar{V}^B + (1-b)\beta\bar{V}^W) + (1-\sigma_W)\left(\lambda\kappa + \beta\frac{\lambda}{1-\beta}\right). \qquad (2.20)$$

The question is, does the supplier refuse to screen B clients? This is an important question because such discrimination is bound to be deeply resented by good B types.

To answer this question, we first solve the system made of (2.17) and (2.18). This yields the value of V^B. We then solve the system made of (2.19) and (2.20). This yields $\bar{V}^B$. We then compare V^B to $\bar{V}^B$ and check whether it is ever the case that the second is larger than the first. Let us first consider the case where $\kappa = 1$. Skipping the algebra, we obtain

$$V^B - V^B = [\lambda(1-\sigma_B) + \sigma_W(1-b)\beta - \sigma_B(1-b\beta)]M,$$

where M is a long expression guaranteed to be positive. The sign of $V^B - \bar{V}^B$ depends upon the sign of the expression in brackets. This expression increases with λ: the higher the supplier's margin, the more he has to lose by delaying the chance of finding a good client. The expression is also decreasing in $\sigma_B - \sigma_W$. The higher the proportion of bad clients in the B population, the less likely the supplier is to screen prospective B clients.[26] Finally, σ_B does not have to be much larger than σ_W for discrimination to arise. If the supplier is very patient but the margin λ is small, even a small difference between σ_B and σ_W results in discrimination.

To see the effect of screening cost κ, consider the formula for $\kappa \neq 1$:

$$V^B - \bar{V}^B = \{\kappa[\lambda(1 - \sigma_B) + \sigma_W(1 - b)\beta - \sigma_B(1 - b\beta)] + (1 - \kappa)\beta\lambda(1 - \sigma_B)\}M.$$

The expression now has two terms, the second of which is always positive. It follows that when the cost of screening κ is small, the supplier always prefers to screen. This is because not screening delays finding a good client.

An immediate policy implication is that reducing the cost of identifying good B agents should reduce if not eliminate discrimination. There are many examples of such institutions, such as a credit reference agency, a certification or vetting program, personal recommendation, and so on. Of course, by helping good B agents to distinguish themselves from bad B agents, bad B agents find it harder to be screened.

Vetting can have negative externalities on unvetted good agents. To see this, suppose that the cost of screening κ varies across suppliers so that, for any σ_B, some suppliers agree to screen B agents. The likelihood L that a new B client is turned down is equal to the proportion of suppliers who find it optimal not to screen. From these results, this proportion is a decreasing function of σ_B: the more bad clients, the fewer suppliers agree to screen. Now imagine that only half of the good B agents benefit from vetting. The proportion σ'_B of bad agents among unvetted B agents is now

$$\sigma'_B = \frac{\sigma_B}{\sigma_B + 0.5(1 - \sigma_B)} > \sigma_B.$$

It follows that with partial vetting, unvetted good B agents are even more likely to be discriminated against.

Insiders and Outsiders

Processes other than statistical discrimination can generate differential treatment. One of them is network effects. To understand how this is possible, assume that potential clients are observationally equivalent but that some suppliers share (accurate) information about clients' types. Call these suppliers insiders. Other suppliers—the outsiders—do not share information with anyone. For instance, by socializing with each other—visiting the mosque or temple or golf club together—insiders may have opportunities to exchange information that outsiders do not have.[27]

Consider an insider supplier approached by a prospective client. The client can be an insider or an outsider. If the client is an insider, the supplier learns the client's type from other insiders. Either the client is good or bad. If the client is good, no need to screen. The supplier offers to trade immediately. If the client is bad, the client is rejected right from the start. If the client is an outsider, the supplier can either screen at cost κ or reject the client and wait until the next period. If the screening cost κ is high and there is high chance of meeting a good insider client next period, waiting is better than screening.

To show this formally, consider the supplier's decision to screen or wait. We keep much of the same notation as previously: B stands for outsider; W stands for insider. Assume that the proportions of good clients are the same in both, i.e., $\sigma_B = \sigma_W = \sigma$, so that there is no room for statistical discrimination. The proportion of insider clients in the economy is b. If the supplier screens outsiders,

$$V^B = \sigma(-\kappa + b\beta V^B + (1-b)\beta V^W) + (1-\sigma)\left(\lambda\kappa + \beta\frac{\lambda}{1-\beta}\right), \tag{2.21}$$

where as before λ is the supplier's profit margin and β his discount factor. The first term is what happens if the client is bad, in which case the supplier loses κ and is matched with a new client in the following period, who could either be B or W. The second term is what happens if the client is good, in which case the supplier earns his margin on the κ transaction today and gets λ thereafter. A similar equation[28] can be written for V^W:

$$V^W = \sigma(b\beta V^B + (1-b)\beta V^W) + (1-\sigma)\frac{\lambda}{1-\beta}. \tag{2.22}$$

If the supplier refuses to screen outsiders, the payoffs are

$$\bar{V}^B = b\beta\bar{V}^B + (1-b)\beta\bar{V}^W. \tag{2.23}$$

$$\bar{V}^W = \sigma(b\beta\bar{V}^B + (1-b)\beta\bar{V}^W) + (1-\sigma)\frac{\lambda}{1-\beta}. \tag{2.24}$$

Solve each system of equation separately, and compute the difference $V^B - \bar{V}^B$, which, for $\kappa = 1$, simplifies to

$$V^B - \bar{V}^B = [\lambda(1-\sigma) - \sigma(1-\beta(b+(1-b)\sigma))]Q,$$

where Q is a positive expression. The larger σ is, the less likely the supplier is to screen outsiders. Furthermore, if $\kappa = 0$ it is always optimal to screen. The bottom line is that information sharing among insiders can generate discriminatory exclusion toward outsiders.[29] Information sharing by insiders hurts outsiders, an outcome that is similar to partial vetting.

My empirical work on manufacturing firms and agricultural traders in sub-Saharan Africa shows that a significant proportion of the ethnic bias pervasive in business can be explained by network effects. In Fafchamps (2000), for instance, I showed that access to supplier credit among Kenyan and Zimbabwean manufacturing firms is ethnically biased, even after controlling for firm size. If I also control for social network capital, however, the ethnic bias disappears. In Fafchamps (2003), I looked for evidence of ethnic bias in agricultural trade using survey data from Benin, Madagacar, and Malawi. I failed to find systematic evidence of ethnic bias, but I found strong evidence of social network effects.

What Has Been Learned?

The presence of multiple types singularly complicates the operation of markets and has a number of unpleasant features.

- The building of (rational) trust is like peeling an onion. It is a gradual discovery process in which temptation forces various layers of bad clients to reveal themselves. In the end, only the good clients are left. Crooks are patient bad agents who manage to gain other people's trust in order to cheat them on a large scale. Examples include pyramid schemes (such as the ones that wreaked havoc in Albania some years ago)[30] and fraudulent banking schemes (such as the ones that plague the Nigerian banking sector today). As these examples demonstrate, regulation is often necessary to protect markets from the deleterious effects of crooks.

- When unobservable type is correlated, even mildly, with observable characteristics, statistical discrimination naturally arises. Discriminatory exclusion is particularly rife if screening costs are high and suppliers earn low margins. This process tends to amplify the natural disadvantages that may handicap certain groups, such as native entrepreneurs, women, and microenterprises.
- Insider networks can have effects similar to those of discrimination, leading to the exclusion of outsiders and, more generally, of less well connected firms and individuals. This shows that while information sharing serves useful purposes, it can also lead to inequitable outcomes. This is, in a sense, normal. If information sharing generates a positive externality (e.g., by economizing on screening costs and reducing the likelihood of breach) *and* if not everyone shares that information, then those who share the information have an advantage over those who do not. Social capital only helps those who have it.
- Markets characterized by relational contracting are unfriendly to newcomers. Because trading relationships last a long time, people prefer to deal with people they already know. Consequently, newcomers are less frequently offered the chance of proving themselves. This is particularly true in stagnant economies where new economic opportunities do not arise that could upset the status quo and allow significant entry. These detrimental effects are compounded by statistical discrimination and insider information sharing. The end result is a market environment that is inimical to newcomers and outsiders alike. Such an environment restricts entry and reduces competition. Add a corrupt government and an incestuous banking sector, and one gets a business mentality that does not favor growth.

Policy Implications

We have taken a rapid tour of the market institution landscape, building a conceptual framework that can account for field observations from Africa and elsewhere. We have learned that markets do not work quite as expected, that there is a lot of inefficiency and rigidity, that entering a flea market may be easy for a newcomer, but it is difficult to graduate to the upper echelons of the market economy where contracting takes place.

Are there any policy implications that come out of this new understanding? Should we simply aim to eliminate the informal institutions that exist and start with a clean slate, based on formal legal institutions? Or should we try to upgrade the information institutions that exist? The literature has agonized over this question, hesitating between an incremental approach—scaling up informal institutions (Dixit 2004)—and a big bang approach—replacing informal institutions by imported modern institutions (Bauer 1954). An intermediate path has also been discussed, whereby foreign direct investment induces a gradual adoption of modern market institutions under the impetus of the market. China, for instance, seems to fit this model up to a point.

To answer these questions, we have to ask whether market institutions in developed economies are fundamentally different from those described here. The economic textbooks say so. But what about actual markets? Certainly there is less market inefficiency and rigidity in the large vibrant economies of developed countries than in the poor backwater economies of Africa. There are more opportunities to switch suppliers and less flexibility—and thus more predictability—in contracts. But can we say that the features I have described are nonexistent in developed economies?

Let us look at our main findings in turn. Can we reasonably claim that relational contracting is absent from developed economies? Certainly not from labor markets. The employment contract is the most common form of relational contracting anywhere. Daily labor contracts only arise when worker characteristics are irrelevant or easily observable, such as in agriculture. Consumers repeatedly eat in the same restaurant, shop in the same supermarket, and buy the same brand of baked beans. Relational contracting is also present in sectors such as banking and insurance—whenever screening is costly or time-consuming. Relationships may be easier to break in developed economies, but the evidence suggests that they are not valueless.

What about information sharing? It is true that valuable screening information is provided in an impersonal manner by a variety of experts from the Michelin guide to movie critics. Credit reference agencies canvas the economy and provide credit reports on anyone with a credit card. Yet we go to conferences, talk to colleagues over lunch, and write reference letters for our students and former employees. This suggests that some of the same informal information-sharing processes persist in developed economies, even though many of their functions have been superseded by formal institutions and paid experts.

What about crooks? Are developed economies able to completely eliminate opportunistic breach of contract and white-collar crime? Well, they may do a better job than in Africa, but it would be a wild exaggeration to claim that crooks are totally absent from, say, the U.S. corporate and economic landscape. Think of insider trading, of the savings and loans debacle, of Enron and Andersen, of Bernie Madoff, or of the U.S. rise in personal bankruptcies in the midst of an economic boom. Clearly some people, anywhere, are happy to gamble with other people's money. What protects the economy from them is a complex mix of regulation and social norms.

What about discrimination? There is plenty of evidence of it in developed countries, manifesting itself in many different ways. The social tensions that it generates in rich countries are no different from those that arise in poor ones. They can be inflamed for political gain, or they can be attenuated by a combination of affirmative action and community development.

What about networks? Are developed economies so impersonal that who you know does not matter? Some years ago Granovetter (1995) brought to our attention the role that referral plays in getting a job (see also Montgomery 1991). More recently Munshi (2003) illustrated the role of networks among Mexican migrants in the United States. It is not a secret that in the corporate world, business contacts are key to success, and that people pay a fortune for an M.B.A. degree in part for the networking opportunity it confers.

What this superficial overview suggests is that market institutions in developed economies are not so different from what they are in Africa. Many of the same features are present. Business ethics and informal networks matter everywhere. But many informal features have been superseded by regulation and formal institutions, such as external audits, prudential regulation for banks and insurance corporations, affirmative action laws, consumer protection laws, a free press with defamation laws, experts who can be exposed for circulating false information, and so on.

Market institutions in developed economies can thus be described as a combination of informal and formal features that structure the environment in which firms and individuals operate. It would be futile and counterproductive to even attempt to eliminate informal institutions. What is needed is a way to improve and upgrade what exists.

This is not a once-and-for-all process. Market institutions are not a fixed, never-changing set. At the time of Adam Smith, markets in Scotland probably operated in a way very similar to those in Africa today.

Based on these observations, an incremental or intermediate approach seems more likely to succeed. If informal institutions remain at work even in the most developed economies, it would be futile to seek their elimination. But a variety of institutional innovations can be introduced to facilitate a transition toward a market environment that is more conducive to growth. How these innovations can percolate through Africa is unclear. My personal view is a pragmatic one. If foreign direct investment (FDI) can serve as a Trojan horse for modern market institutions, then the impetus for institutional innovation can be left to the private sector. But past experience suggests that simply waiting for FDI to do the job may fail to deliver results. A more proactive approach may be required, whereby government and donors intervene to jump-start the innovation transfer process. The political environment must also be such that the business community, whether foreign or local, is encouraged to participate in the definition of incremental institutional changes that favor growth and innovation.

In the remainder of this chapter, I outline some ideas about the kind of reforms that are worth considering for Africa today. They are costly, so not all countries can implement them all—the environment has to be ripe for change. But hopefully they point in the right direction.

Judges and Courts

At the beginning of the chapter I pointed out that if the transaction is too small to justify court action or if agents have no assets to seize, the threat of court action is not credible.[31] This simple observation implies that small transactions and transactions among poor people remain largely outside the purview of the law. Since developing countries have many poor people, this means it is futile to think that the enforcement of contracts through judges and courts can ever suffice to provide suitable market institutions for the poor. This issue is typically discussed in the literature under the guise of the "credit constraint" poor households face. But the issue is much broader than just loans; it also affects their access to insurance, education, equity, supplier credit, and many other markets.

Several avenues for providing market institutions for the poor have been suggested, such as building on reputation and long-term relationships. In this context, microcredit initiatives can be seen as efforts to harness contract enforcement mechanisms, including guilt and shame, to serve the contracting needs of the poor. Much more work is needed to expand these initiatives to include some of the most glaringly absent markets for the poor, such as insurance and supplier credit for agricultural inputs.

Saying that legal institutions are insufficient does not imply that judges and courts have no role to play in the development of markets. Empirical work has shown that court sanctions are important for large firms and for large transactions (Fafchamps 2004). This is particularly true of foreign investors, who need the protection of the law to guarantee that they will be not be expropriated unlawfully. Legal institutions can also serve an important role by criminalizing extreme forms of opportunistic breach such as fraud and fraudulent bankruptcy. Last but not least, legal institutions play a crucial supportive role for informal institutions.

So what is the situation regarding judges and courts in sub-Saharan Africa today? Most African countries inherited laws and judicial systems from a colonial power. Commercial law may not have kept up with all the legal developments that took place in developed economies over the last few decades. But the basic legal principles are the same as those that allowed Europe to develop. The problem lies not so much with the laws themselves but with the way they are enforced.

One important issue in this respect is that courts are underfunded in much of sub-Saharan Africa. As documented by Widner (2000), African courts often lack basic supplies and even access to the laws themselves. The author contends that it would not cost much to provide African courts with the minimum required for them to do their job. In addition to delays due to underequipment and underfunding, African judges also seem to have a conciliatory attitude toward debtors, granting them frequent reprieves and de facto helping them evade contractual obligations. This is, in a sense, the translation of contractual flexibility to legal precedent. It is also easy for individuals to avoid contractual obligations by moving where they cannot be traced.

Corruption in the legal system is rampant. Perhaps the most outrageous case I have seen documented is jails in Madagascar, where criminals customarily pay prison officials to be set free (Ministère de la Justice 1999). Political interference with court activity is common in certain countries. Corruption and underfunding combine to form a weak legal environment. But the legal and institutional foundations are there, and it is possible to invest in strengthening the court system by providing better funding and training for judges and legal support staff.

Formal Support Institutions

Perhaps more than functioning courts, what distinguishes developed market economies from undeveloped ones is the plethora of formal market support institutions. Most of them are private, such as credit reference agencies, standards and grades, quality certification (ISO), franchising, trademarks, and brand names. But nearly all of them are protected or promoted in some way by legal institutions, for instance, laws on quality certification, on weights and measures, on intellectual property rights, on defamation, or on the protection of privacy. It would be difficult for private market institutions to exist without protection from the law. For instance, franchising, branding, and trademarks are not possible if other firms can usurp the same name. Standards and grades offer little protection if no one enforces them. Expert systems find it difficult to establish their credibility if defamation laws are not implemented and consumers are not protected against fraudulent claims.

More sophisticated market institutions, like commodity exchanges and stock markets, cannot exist without external certification. For the stock market, this role is fulfilled by external auditors; for commodity markets, by bonded warehouses and grading and quality certification agencies. The credibility of these outside experts depends not only on a free press but also on the implementation of antidefamation laws, so that readers can believe what they read in newspapers.[32] Regulation is essential to the credibility of many high-powered financial instruments, such as futures and derivatives. This is needed in developed economies and more so in developing ones.

When market support institutions are locally weak or absent, it is still possible for expert agencies (e.g., credit reference agencies, agencies that rate credit risk, external auditors) to use their internationally recognized brand names to guarantee the credibility of their operations in developing countries. Provided brand-named products are hard to imitate, it is also possible for transnational corporations to sell internationally recognized brands of goods and services through franchising and direct investment. The presence of major hotel chains and soft drink manufacturers in virtually all countries is an illustration of this principle. ISO certification and credit ratings can be provided by internationally recognized certification agencies to firms located in countries where the legal system is weak.

By the same reasoning, firms in poor countries can apply to be publicly traded in another country's stock market. Some South African corporations, for instance, opted to be listed on the London stock exchange instead of the South African one. Firms and governments in poor countries can use established commodity markets elsewhere to trade in futures and derivatives. The Ethiopian government, for instance, is said to trade actively in coffee futures. From these examples, we see these developments already happening.

One could argue that what makes multinational corporations successful is not just their knowledge base and know-how but their ability to use the good market institutions in one country to support their activities in countries with less adequate institutions. For these firms, inadequate market institutions in Africa are not necessarily a major obstacle to investment. But such inadequacies hinder the activities of small and medium-sized firms, a fact that is partly responsible for the existence of relatively few mid-sized firms in sub-Saharan Africa (Fafchamps 1994). Yet small and mid-sized firms are essential to long-term economic success. Without them, the knowledge and know-how brought by foreign investors remain within the confines of a small number of large firms. There is no relay to ensure that this knowledge will make its way through the local economy. Poor market institutions penalize small and mid-sized firms, one reason that technology transfer and its corollary, productivity growth, remain elusive in sub-Saharan Africa.

Equal Opportunity and Entrepreneurship

If foreign investors have access to market support institutions elsewhere while local firms do not, this gives the foreign investors an advantage. When they invest in a country, they bring with them business norms and practices developed elsewhere. Using superior norms of commercial behavior among themselves gives them an edge over local entrepreneurs. As a result, foreign business enclaves can develop and prosper even in the absence—or perhaps because of the absence—of formal market support institutions locally.

In such an environment, assistance to native entrepreneurs becomes a hot political issue. Organizational know-how and norms of behavior must spread to domestic firms for their full productivity to be felt. This can only be accomplished if native entrepreneurs are given a chance to join the group of firms using the best institutional practices. This may require some form of affirmative action or targeting to correct for statistical discrimination and network effects penalizing young entrepreneurs.

One possible approach is to initiate a vetting program that screens local entrepreneurs' ability to repay credit and helps the successful ones graduate to credit from suppliers and formal financial institutions. The vetting of entrepreneurs can be used at all levels of enterprise development, e.g., for women, minorities, and the like. The sustainability of many development programs, such as microcredit for women and microenterprises or training for small entrepreneurs, should be judged on their capacity to eliminate the underlying causes of discrimination. As the analysis of Coate and Loury (1993) suggests, programs that are not designed to assist aid recipients to wean themselves from external aid are unlikely to succeed in the long run; once they are removed, preexisting discrimination will reassert itself.

Policy Choice and Civil Society

Setting up appropriate market institutions is a complex process. For instance, judging from what is in place in developed economies, the number of market support institutions is potentially quite large. Not all of them can be put in place overnight, and probably not all of them are needed in all countries. How can one prioritize?

To paraphrase Easterly (2006), this is something that each country has to sort out for itself. There is no one-size-fits-all market institutions solution. A government is unlikely to identify priorities without talking to civil society in general and to local businessmen and businesswomen, preferably through business associations. The formation of civil society organizations and business associations should thus be promoted. For reasons discussed earlier, they should be required to be inclusive, that is, to foster socialization across ethnic, religious, and gender lines. Failure to achieve business integration across ethnic and racial lines is, in my view, one of the most serious problems facing Africa today.

Because local entrepreneurs may not know of institutional innovations developed elsewhere, it is important to foster the insertion of local business interests in international networks and to consult foreign investors on their needs. International development agencies too can assist the upgrading of local institutions by bringing talent from elsewhere. Market institutions are an area where the transfer of knowledge is essential and can be nurtured.

Finally, as was pointed out in chapter 1, one should not ignore domestic political forces. In my experience, political elites in most poor countries wish to develop their country, but not at the cost of losing their economic independence. This is plainly true everywhere, but is particular true in Africa because of its specific history. We have seen that foreign investors often are at a strong advantage relative to domestic entrepreneurs, not only because of their technological know-how but also because of their access to market support institutions elsewhere. The solution, in my view, is not to shut foreign investors out either directly, or indirectly by condoning rampant corruption, but to provide domestic entrepreneurs with market support institutions locally or facilitate their access to these institutions elsewhere.[33] What is needed is the political will.

Notes

I am grateful for the excellent comments received from Debraj Ray, Tim Besley, an anonymous referee, and participants at the CESifo conference held in Venice in July 2006. This work is part of the program of the ESRC Global Poverty Research Group.

1. Note that for people to incur the cost of sharing information to shame people, they must derive some kind of satisfaction from shaming others, e.g., retribution or self-righteousness.

2. Unless the offending party is persuaded that the aggrieved party will go to court or will resort to violence even at a cost, e.g., because she wishes to preserve a reputation of toughness or because her moral sense compels her to do so. I ignore these complications here, the main point being that the threat of court action need not be credible.

3. It is still possible to misrepresent the quality or quantity of the good, or to pay with false money; hence the need for close inspection.

4. Common business practice is for the supplier to send a monthly invoice and expect payment within a stipulated number of days, typically thirty.

5. The possibility of breach of contract also arises in simple purchases whenever the quality of the good cannot be inspected on the spot. For instance, when I purchase a can of peas or a bottle of milk, I cannot assess the quality of the good inside the package. Consequently, I either must trust the supplier or the brand name on a sealed package. This usually implies some kind of long-term relationship either with the brand or with the supplier.

6. I revisit the issue of excusable default when discussing contingent contracts.

7. Inability to pay can be represented by $u(p) = \infty$: in this case, the contract cannot be fulfilled. These are also the situations in which $u(p) < \infty$ and the buyer can pay, but equation (2.1) is not satisfied, making the buyer unwilling to pay. The distinction

between inability and unwillingness to repay is blurred in practice. For equity reasons, debtors often are regarded as unable to repay when compliance would be unduly costly, that is, when $u(p)$ rises above a socially acceptable level $B < \infty$. The reason is that insisting on payment in all circumstances would encourage unlucky debtors to engage in criminal activity in order to repay their bills. Here I consider that a buyer who is unable to pay is also unwilling to pay.

8. Contractual guarantees can often be seen as a way of modifying the attribution of a debtor's assets upon bankruptcy. Without specific guarantees, all the debtor's assets serve all his debts, and thus all assets constitute collateral. Registering a mortgage does not increase the collateral of the debtor. All it does is earmarks an asset to serve a specific debt, to the detriment of other creditors.

9. In a sense we can see Idi Amin's expulsions of Asians from Uganda in the 1970s as an attempt to replace one market institution—Asian business networks—with native traders. As history tells us, the transition was far from smooth.

10. Obviously, drug addicts also have a short time horizon and discount the futue heavily. As a result, their β is small. But their α is probably quite large.

11. Strictly speaking, screening costs have to be incurred once—the first time a supplier is approached by a client. But in the long run, this cost is a vanishingly small proportion of expected average payoffs and can be ignored.

12. The split of $\frac{\beta\alpha}{1-\beta}$ into its two components, $EV(\tau,\varepsilon)$ and $EW(\tau,\varepsilon)$, is a bit arbitrary in this case. But it is useful to think of it as having two distinct parts. What the client would economize by not having to look for another supplier, which is given by $\beta\frac{c+\alpha}{1-\beta+\beta\theta}$, and lost future trade opportunities because other suppliers refuse to sell. We also have to take into account the fact that since no supplier would agree to sell, it is not in the client's interest to incur screening cost c. We obtain

$$EV(\tau,\varepsilon) = \beta\frac{\alpha}{1-\beta+\beta\theta}.$$

$$EW(\tau,\varepsilon) = \frac{\beta\alpha}{1-\beta} - \beta\frac{\alpha}{1-\beta+\beta\theta}$$

$$= \frac{\beta^2\theta\alpha}{(1-\beta)(1-\beta+\beta\theta)}.$$

13. Alternatively, we can see that they are incompetent, so their profit margin is low or negative—low α. Consequently, bad clients have less incentive to pay.

14. The model would be generalized to a situation in which the enforcement mechanism is guilt, not relationships or reputation. Certain agents are honest in the sense that they would feel very bad if they cheated, whereas others are dishonest in the sense that they would not care. Past behavior can then be used to infer someone's honesty, that is, innate or acquired capacity to self-inflict punishment by feeling guilty. These issues are discussed in detail by, for instance, Platteau (1994a; 1994b). This interpretation seems to be the most natural one, the one we would probably volunteer if asked to explain how we interpret cheating.

15. This was before 2000.

16. This is itself a combination of the probability of being paid, etc. But these details are not essential to the point I am trying to make, so they can be ignored for now.

17. I have simplified this a bit. To be completely correct, we would have to allow for the fact that A cheated the first time because of a shock and the second time because he switched type. This would only complicate the math without changing the qualitative conclusion.

18. Alternatively, assume a single monopolistic supplier.

19. Similar results are obtained if bad clients are defined in terms of the size of their profit margin α.

20. To see this, note that (2.15) can be rewritten:

$\beta_l \alpha < 1 - \beta_l$.

If $\kappa = 1$, (2.16) becomes

$\alpha < 1 - \beta_l$,

which is clearly always satisfied if (2.15) is satisfied.

21. In labor contracts, the worker may not know whether she is able to complete the task assigned to her without first trying to learn it. A similar situation often arises when a client approaches a new supplier. For instance, the client may be unsure whether the new input can successfully be processed or whether there is a demand for goods produced with the new input. If the client discovers the input is not usable, he loses interest in the relationship and, from the point of view of the model, becomes a bad client. In this case, we expect to observe a trial period, although its purpose is slightly different, that is, to enable the client to learn his type.

22. See also Watson (1999) for in-depth coverage of this issue.

23. Statistical discrimination can also arise between two observationally distinct populations that are on average identical but have a different variance. To see this, consider an employer. If the employer is looking for exceptional talent—the upper tail—he is better off sampling from the more variable population. If the employer is trying to avoid exceptionally bad workers—the lower tail—he is better off sampling from the less variable population.

24. It is possible to show that for certain parameter values, price discrimination obtains instead. In this setup, B agents have to accept a lower profit margin α (and thus must guarantee suppliers a higher profit margin λ) in order to convince suppliers to screen them. There also exist equilibria in which suppliers screen only a proportion of B agents, not all. See Fafchamps (2003) for details.

25. Because $\sigma_B > \sigma_W$, the supplier may opt for a different screening strategy for each group, e.g., by choosing a longer screening period and lower κ for B clients. See Fafchamps (2003) for details.

26. To see this, note that since β is close to 1, $(1 - b)\beta \simeq 1 - b\beta$.

27. Here I abstract from strategic network formation issues and regard information exchange as exogenously given.

28. In contrast to (2.18), the supplier does not lose κ if the client is bad and earns the full λ immediately.

29. In Fafchamps (2003), I show that insider information sharing can also generate equilibria with discriminatory pricing.

30. Enron could also fit into this category.

31. Unless the aggrieved party seeks revenge through court action or wishes to establish a reputation of toughness for the future.

32. Many African countries now have a free press—or at least much freer than before. There are many tabloids making outrageous claims without fear of being held accountable. Sometimes it seems as if disinformation has replaced lack of information.

33. For instance, it is probably not necessary for all African countries to have a stock market. Under certain conditions, firms incorporated in one country can list themselves on the London or New York exchange. A number of South African corporations have done so, for instance. The same is true for commodity exchanges. Countries with a currency agreement, such as the CFA zone, could fairly easily institute shared market support institutions.

References

Acemoglu, D., S. Johnson, and J. A. Robinson. 2002. Reversal of Fortune: Geography and Institutions in the Making of the Modern World Income Distribution. *Quarterly Journal of Economics* 117 (4): 1231–1294.

———. 2005. The Rise of Europe: Atlantic Trade, Institutional Change, and Economic Growth. *American Economic Review* 95 (3): 546–579.

Akerlof, G. A. 1985. Discriminatory, Status-Based Wages among Tradition-Oriented, Stochastically Trading Coconut Producers. *Journal of Political Economy* 93 (2): 265–276.

Bauer, P. T. 1954. *West African Trade: A Study of Competition, Oligopoly and Monopoly in a Changing Economy*. Cambridge: Cambridge University Press.

Bernstein, L. 1992. Opting out of the Legal System: Extralegal Contractual Relations in the Diamond Industry. *Journal of Legal Studies* 21: 115–157.

———. 1996. Merchant Law in a Merchant Court: Rethinking the Code's Search for Immanent Business Norms. *University of Pennsylvania Law Review* 144 (5): 1765–1821.

Biggs, T., G. Moody, J. von Leewen, and E. White. 1994. Africa Can Compete! Export Opportunities and Challenges in Garments and Home Products in the U.S. Market. Technical report. Washington, D.C.: World Bank.

Bigsten, A., P. Collier, S. Dercon, M. Fafchamps, B. Gauthier, J. W. Gunning, A. Isaksson, A. Oduro, R. Oostendorp, C. Patillo, M. Soderbom, F. Teal, and A. Zeufack. 2000. Contract Flexibility and Dispute Resolution in African Manufacturing. *Journal of Development Studies* 36 (4): 1–37.

Coate, S., and G. C. Loury. 1993. Will Affirmative Action Policies Eliminate Negative Stereotypes? *American Economic Review* 83 (5): 1220–1240.

Cornell, B., and I. Welch. 1996. Culture, Information and Screening Discrimination. *Journal of Political Economy* 104 (3): 542–571.

Dixit, A. K. 2004. *Lawlessness and Economics: Alternative Modes of Governance*. Princeton, N.J.: Princeton University Press.

Easterly, W. 2006. *The White Man's Burden: Why the West's Efforts to Aid the Rest Have Done So Much Ill and So Little Good*. New York: Penguin.

Fafchamps, M. 1994. Industrial Structure and Microenterprises in Africa. *Journal of Developing Areas* 29 (1): 1–30.

———. 1996. The Enforcement of Commercial Contracts in Ghana. *World Development* 24 (3): 427–448.

———. 2000. Ethnicity and Credit in African Manufacturing. *Journal of Development Economics* 61 (1): 205–235.

———. 2002a. The Role of Business Networks in Market Development in sub-Saharan Africa. In *Communities and Markets in Economic Development*, ed. M. Aoki and Y. Hayami. Oxford: Oxford University Press.

———. 2002b. Spontaneous Market Emergence. *Berkeley Electronic Press* 2 (1): article 2. ⟨http://www.bepress.com/bejte/topics/vol2/iss1/art2⟩.

———. 2003. Ethnicity and Networks in African Trade. *Berkeley Electronic Press* 2 (1): article 14. ⟨http://www.bepress.com/bejeap/contributions/vol2/iss1/art14⟩.

———. 2004. *Market Institutions in sub-Saharan Africa.* Cambridge, Mass.: MIT Press.

Fafchamps, M., and E. Gabre-Madhin. 2006. Agricultural Markets in Benin and Malawi. WPS 2734. World Bank.

Fafchamps, M., J. W. Gunning, and R. Oostendorp. 2000. Inventory and Risk in African Manufacturing. *Economic Journal* 110 (466): 861–893.

Fafchamps, M., and B. Minten. 1999. Relationships and Traders in Madagascar. *Journal of Development Studies* 35 (6): 1–35.

———. 2001. Property Rights in a Flea Market Economy. *Economic Development and Cultural Change* 49 (2): 229–268.

———. 2002. Returns to Social Network Capital among Traders. *Oxford Economic Papers* 54: 173–206.

Ghosh, P., and D. Ray. 1996. Cooperation in Community Interaction without Information Flows. *Review of Economic Studies* 63: 491–519.

Granovetter, M. S. 1995. *Getting a Job: A Study of Contacts and Careers.* 2d ed. Chicago. University of Chicago Press.

Greif, A. 1993. Contract Enforceability and Economic Institutions in Early Trade: The Maghribi Traders' Coalition. *American Economic Review* 83 (3): 525–548.

Hart, O. 1995. *Firms, Contracts, and Financial Structure.* Oxford: Clarendon Press.

Hart, O., and B. Holmstrom. 1987. The Theory of Contracts. In *Advances in Economic Theory*, ed. T. F. Bewley. Cambridge: Cambridge University Press.

Hart, O., and J. Moore. 1988. Incomplete Contracts and Renegotiation. *Econometrica* 56 (4): 755–785.

Himbara, D. 1994. The Failed Africanization of Commerce and Industry in Kenya. *World Development* 22 (3): 469–482.

Johnson, S., J. McMillan, and C. Woodruff. 2000. Entrepreneurs and the Ordering of Institutional Reform: Poland, Slovakia, Romania, Russia and Ukraine Compared. *Economics of Transition* 8 (1): 1–36.

———. 2002. Courts and Relational Contracts. *Journal of Law, Economics, and Organization* 18 (1): 221–277.

Kandori, M. 1992. Social Norms and Community Enforcement. *Review of Economic Studies* 59: 63–80.

Keefer, P., and S. Knack. 1997. Why Don't Poor Countries Catch Up? A Cross-National Test of Institutional Explanation. *Economic Enquiry* 35 (3): 590–602.

Kranton, R. E. 1996. Reciprocal Exchange: A Self-Sustaining System. *American Economic Review* 86 (4): 830–851.

Levitt, S. D. 2006. An Economist Sells Bagels: A Case Study in Profit Maximization. NBER working paper 12152.

McMillan, J., and B. Naughton. 1996. *Reforming Asian Socialism: The Growth of Market Institutions.* Ann Arbor: University of Michigan Press.

McMillan, J. and C. Woodruff. 1999a. Dispute Prevention without Courts in Vietnam. *Journal of Law, Economics, and Organization* 15 (3): 637–658.

———. 1999b. Interfirm Relationships and Informal Credit in Vietnam. *Quarterly Journal of Economics* 114 (4): 1285–1320.

———. 2000. Private Order under Dysfunctional Public Order. *Michigan Law Review* 98 (8): 2421–2458.

Milgrom, P. R., D. C. North, and B. Weingast. 1991. The Role of Institutions in the Revival of Trade: The Law Merchant, Private Judges, and the Champagne Fairs. *Economics and Politics* 2 (19): 1–23.

Ministère de la Justice. 1999. Justice selon les justiciables: Une enquête auprès des usagers du système judiciaire [Justice according to citizens: A survey among users of the judicial system]. Gouvernement de Madagascar.

Montgomery, J. D. 1991. Social Networks and Labor Market Outcomes: Toward an Economic Analysis. *American Economic Review* 81 (5): 1408–1418.

Munshi, K. 2003. Networks in the Modern Economy: Mexican Migrants in the U.S. Labor Market. *Quarterly Journal of Economics* 118 (2): 549–599.

North, D. C. 1973. *The Rise of the Western World.* Cambridge: Cambridge University Press.

Platteau, J.-P. 1994a. Behind the Market Stage Where Real Societies Exist. Part I: The Role of Public and Private Order Institutions. *Journal of Development Studies* 30 (3): 533–577.

———. 1994b. Behind the Market Stage Where Real Societies Exist. Part II: The Role of Moral Norms. Journal of Development Studies 30 (4): 753–815.

Salanié, B. 1997. *The Economics of Contracts: A Primer.* Cambridge, Mass.: MIT Press.

Shapiro, C., and J. E. Stiglitz. 1984. Equilibrium Unemployment as a Worker Discipline Device. *American Economic Review* 74 (3): 433–444.

Staal, S., C. Delgado, and C. Nicholson. 1997. Smallholder Dairying under Transactions Costs in East Africa. *World Development* 25 (5): 779–794.

Stiglitz, J. E., and A. Weiss. 1981. Credit Rationing in Markets with Imperfect Information. *American Economic Review* 71 (3): 393–410.

Udry, C. 1991. Rural Credit in Northern Nigeria. Ph.D. diss., Department of Economics, Yale University.

Watson, J. 1999. Starting Small and Renegotiation. *Journal of Economic Theory* 85 (1): 52–90.

Widner, J. 2000. *Building the Rule of Law.* New York: W.W. Norton.

World Bank. 2002. *Building Institutions for Markets. World Development Report 2002.* Washington, D.C.

3 Financial Markets and Conflict in the Developing World

Eliana La Ferrara

A significant part of the developing world, especially in sub-Saharan Africa, has been plagued by a massive wave of civil conflicts in the past thirty years. It is estimated that in the last sixty years "about 40 percent of countries with a 1990 population of at least half a million have had at least one internal conflict that killed at least 1,000 people" (Fearon 2005, 1). This has captured the attention of policymakers, who have singled out violent conflict as one of the major causes of underdevelopment (e.g., World Bank 2003), and it has spurred a growing number of studies in the economics literature aimed at understanding the causes and consequences of violent conflict.

One thesis put forward in the academic debate is that these conflicts are both the cause and the result of a weak institutional environment that many of these countries inherited at independence or developed shortly thereafter. On the other hand, many commentators have emphasized the role that economic interests play in today's civil wars. In this chapter I explore the link between civil conflict, economic interests, and weak institutions in the developing world.

I argue that we can learn a lot about the economic effects of conflict by looking at investors' perceptions as measured by asset market reactions. I do this by relying on a methodology that is widely applied in finance but seldom employed in the conflict literature: the event study approach. This approach consists of identifying a set of companies that are economically active in a country and a set of exogenous political events (in this case, related to conflict onset, deterioration, or termination), and examining how the returns on these companies' stock respond to these events. This approach is a useful complement to recent contributions that have analyzed the role of markets and institutions in conflict environments from a macroeconomic perspective. In fact, while empirical studies on this topic at the macroeconomic level face serious endogeneity problems, in the event study framework identification is possible by construction, given the exogeneity of political events. The approach also relies on a rich set of microeconomic information both at the company level and at the political level; daily indicators are typically used on both sides.

I first review the extensive macroeconomic literature on conflict and economic performance, highlighting what we can learn from it. The arguments revolve around the economic causes and effects of conflict as well as the relationship between conflict and institutions. The next section reviews the (less extensive) microeconomic literature on the economics of conflict and underlines some important questions (which in my view are still unanswered) about the relationship between firms' behavior and conflict in the developing world. After briefly illustrating the event study methodology, I present two empirical illustrations from my own work and emphasize how these results highlight the weaknesses of the institutional context under study. Finally, I outline some policy implications of the proposed approach, including the role of corporate social responsibility.

What We Know about Conflict and Economic Performance

Since the seminal contribution of Collier and Hoeffler (1998), a great deal has been written on the economics of conflict in poor countries. This chapter highlights those contributions that have shaped subsequent research or that have the potential to spur further work in this field.

Economic Causes of Conflict

It may be useful to start by summarizing Collier and Hoeffler's (1998) main findings. Their goal was to investigate the *economic causes* of civil war. They set up a simple theoretical framework in which rebels are utility maximizers and initiate a civil war if their expected benefits outweigh the costs, along the lines of previous models by Azam (1995) and Grossman (1995). Using cross-country data, Collier and Hoeffler estimated the probability of conflict onset as well as conflict duration as a function of the following variables: per capita income, the share of primary commodity exports to GDP, population size, and ethnolinguistic fractionalization. They found that increases in per capita income are associated with lower incidence and duration of wars, whereas larger population size is associated with greater risk of war (possibly due to secessionist forces). The relationship between war occurrence or duration and natural resource endowment, as proxied by the share of primary commodity exports, is nonlinear. Generally speaking, resource-abundant countries are more likely to experience a civil war and have wars that last longer, except at very high levels of endowments, where the relationship becomes negative. Ethnolinguistic fractionalization also has a hump-shaped relationship with conflict onset and duration, indicating that intermediate levels of ethnic diversity are most associated with conflict.

While Collier and Hoeffler's 1998 paper provided the first attempt to list the main factors related to civil wars, in subsequent contributions Collier and Hoeffler (2004) and Fearon and Laitin (2003) showed the relative importance of each of these factors as well as some additional variables. In particular, Collier and Hoeffler (2004) explored whether the leading motive underlying rebellions is greed or grievance. The former relates to the opportunities that rebel groups may see in initiating a war, such as the prospect of appropriating natural resources but also their ability to organize and grow, as typically affected by the geography of the country (e.g., the presence of mountains and forests). Grievance factors, on the other hand, are the lack of civil liberties and political rights and the extent to which society is divided in terms of ethnicity, religion, and income distribution. Drawing on an empirical strategy similar to that of their previous paper, Collier and Hoeffler (2004) found that opportunistic motives seem to prevail over grievance in terms of explanatory power. In particular, natural resource endowments but also the presence of diasporas that can offer financial capital to rebel groups were found to be significantly associated with the probability of war.

In a related study, Fearon and Laitin (2003) found that after controlling for income levels and growth, ethnic and religious heterogeneity did not significantly affect the likelihood of civil conflict after the Cold War. But they emphasized the role played by country characteristics that favor rebel recruitment (e.g., poverty, unemployment, weak states, rough terrain).

The studies of Collier and Hoeffler (2004) and Fearon and Laitin (2003) spurred a large body of research. One of the factors highlighted in the former paper is the role of *natural resources*. The main contention in the substantial literature on natural resource wars (e.g., Klare 2001; Ross 2004) is that wars are more likely to involve resource-abundant countries because of the competition over (geographically concentrated) resource rents. In other words, resources matter because of looting; they constitute an endowment for rebel groups. An interesting complement to this explanation is given by Weinstein (2005), who argued that resources matter not so much because they constitute endowments (after all, many rebel groups have mobilized in resource-poor countries) but because they shape the *type of individuals* who will join the group as well as their behavior. Weinstein proposed a "recruitment game" where rebel leaders face informational asymmetries and collective action problems. In his model, leaders from resource-poor countries obtain political support by making credible promises of future rewards to members who are willing to invest their time in the groups. Leaders in resource-abundant countries can recruit members who are interested in short-term rewards and are not committed to the goals of the group. In this sense, natural resources can be a curse for the rebel groups as much as for the country. Through some interesting case studies of rebel groups in Uganda, Mozambique, Eritrea, and Sierra Leone, Weinstein showed that some of the differences in the membership of these groups can be traced to differences in their resource base. Although further work is needed to validate and generalize these conclusions, this represents a new trend in the analysis of the causes of conflict that is moving from macroeconomic to microeconomic analysis, in this case the microeconomics of rebel groups' organization.

One important finding presented by Fearon and Laitin (2003) is the relative unimportance of ethnic heterogeneity. This has led to a growing interest in the way in which social divisions may fuel conflict, and particularly in the appropriate measure of social divisions to be employed. Early work by Horowitz (1985) suggested that the likelihood of conflict depends not so much on the existence of few or many ethnic groups, but on the balance of power between them. For example, a society with many small ethnic groups would be more diverse but less conflict-prone than a society with only two groups, a majority and a (large) minority. Similar arguments were put forward by Posner (2005), who focused on the relationship between ethnic politics and institutions in Africa. The argument that it is *ethnic polarization* that matters, not ethnic fragmentation per se, was tested empirically by Montalvo and Reynal-Querol (2005; 2007). In their 2005 article they constructed an index of ethnic polarization that measures how far the distribution of ethnic groups is from the bipolar distribution where two groups of equal size are opposed. They found that although ethnic fractionalization does not have significant explanatory power for the likelihood of civil wars, ethnic polarization does, both in itself and after accounting for the degree of fractionalization itself. In their 2007 paper they showed that ethnic polarization increases the *duration* of civil wars as well, possibly because of its effects on the bargaining process among rival groups (see Slantchev 2004).

Although this literature has played an important role in spurring the debate on the causes of violent conflict, its findings should be interpreted largely as correlations rather than causal statements. In fact, as acknowledged by many of the authors, several explanatory variables employed are endogenous. For example, GDP per capita is likely to be lower in a country where agricultural (and possibly industrial) production has been undermined by violence and instability. Variables like population size and ethnolinguistic fractionalization or polarization are also potentially endogenous if some groups are disproportionately killed during the war or leave the country seeking refuge elsewhere. Furthermore, some of the observed correlations may reflect a spurious relationship driven by omitted variables (such as institutional quality).[1]

Addressing the issue of causality is particularly difficult in the context of conflict analysis and is likely to be a challenge for future work in the field. Miguel, Satyanath, and Sergenti (2004) attempted to test the causal effect of (low) growth on conflict. They instrumented GDP growth with rainfall shocks (measured as percentage change in rainfall from the previous year) and found that a decrease in annual growth of 5 percentage points led to a 12 percent higher probability of conflict incidence.

Do Weak Institutions Cause Conflict?

One of the findings presented in Fearon and Laitin (2003) is that weak states, identified as states with a high degree of political instability in the three years before the period under study, have a significantly higher likelihood of conflict onset. According to the authors, political instability implies relatively disorganized political institutions at the center, which in turn facilitate the emergence of rebel movements. Although the empirical evidence on the relationship between institutional quality and conflict is very sparse, several channels could be identified which help to explain how weak local institutions may be at the root of conflict.

The first, intrinsically microeconomic, channel relates to the way in which a weak institutional setting is unable to enforce the security of property rights. As shown in the models of Hirshleifer (1991),

Skaperdas (1992), and Grossman and Kim (1995), when property rights are insecure, more resources are devoted to predation and to defense expenditure than to productive activities. Indeed, a significant part of the revenue of rebel groups in many conflict episodes came from looting in contexts characterized by weak property rights enforcement by the central state.

Another channel operates through the inability of weak states to commit to delivering certain policies that are viewed as a precondition for peace. For example, Azam (2006) presented a framework in which the government would like to prevent civil war by giving a transfer to its opponents but is unable to commit to do so; hence conflict breaks out. This in turn increases the costs of the required tranfers, making them unfeasible. The framework fits some recent experiences of civil war, such as that in the Ivory Coast. In a similar vein, Grossman (2004) studied the properties of a self-enforcing constitution that can serve as an alternative to civil conflict. One of the conditions under which such a constitution can be designed is that parties place a relatively high weight on the future, which is sometimes not the case in unstable political environments.

Another contribution linking institutional weakness and potential conflict is that of La Ferrara and Bates (2001). The authors analyzed a setting in which states lack a monopoly over violence and politicians compete to build a revenue-yielding constituency either by supplying local public goods or by mobilizing security services. Under certain conditions, an equilibrium can emerge in which both parties invest only in building up their military capabilities and not in public goods provision. Furthermore, despite being Pareto-inefficient, in the absence of external coordination and enforcement, militarization remains privately advantageous and the best response to the anticipated actions of the other.

An additional channel through which weak institutions may affect conflict operates through the "resource curse" hypothesis. Mehlum, Moene, and Torvik (2006) showed that the detrimental effects on growth of natural resource abundance only occur in countries with low institutional quality (as measured by the rule-of-law index), not in countries with "good" institutions. In their theory, this occurs because in the former set of countries, rent seeking and production are complements, whereas in the latter they are substitutes. In other words, in countries with "grabber-friendly" institutions—characterized by a weak rule of law, inefficient bureaucracy, high corruption, and risk of expropriation—individual talent is diverted into unproductive activities. These may include the organization of rebel movements, although this point is not explicitly made by the authors.

Empirical analyses of the effects of institutions on the likelihood and duration of conflict face the same difficulties as the previously surveyed studies on the economic causes of conflict, that is, the potential endogeneity of institutional variables.[2] Efforts to look at the historical determinants of institutions were made by Djankov and Reynal-Querol (2007), who examined the "colonial origins" of civil wars.

Economic Consequences of Conflict

The preceding studies addressed the relationship between conflict and economic performance in the direction that goes from economic conditions to the likelihood (duration) of war. In other words, they investigated the economic *causes* of conflict. Another strand of the literature has focused on the economic *effects* of war, in particular on the costs that violent conflict impose on the countries involved.

Early work in this area explored the relationship between political instability and investment (e.g., Alesina and Perotti 1996 and Svensson 1998). For example, Alesina and Perotti showed that there is a negative relationship between the occurrence of violent phenomena of political unrest and investment rates, hence on growth. A shortcoming of this and similar studies is that they rely on cross-country variation in political instability; hence it is difficult to identify a causal relationship between conflict and economic performance. Furthermore, the analyses in these papers deal with instability broadly defined; hence it is not easily comparable to the literature reviewed before, which focuses on violent conflict.

A different approach exploits variation *within* countries in the intensity of conflict to identify the effects of war on a set of financial indicators, under the assumption that changes in conflict intensity are not the result of economic conditions but rather of political and strategic considerations. Looking at financial market reactions has an advantage in that it mitigates problems of unobserved heterogeneity intrinsic in cross-sectional studies but only allows assessment of the relationship between conflict and *investors' perceptions*.[3] One can certainly say that changes in investors' perceptions will translate into different conditions of access to capital markets; it is more difficult to say whether they automatically translate into higher or lower investment and growth for the countries involved.

Among a set of recent studies focusing on financial market reactions to conflict, Rigobon and Sack (2005) computed an indicator of war risk for the Iraqi conflict between January and March 2003 and estimated how changes in this indicator reflect changes in asset prices. In particular, they found that higher perceived war risk during this period was associated with higher oil futures prices, lower Treasury yields, lower equity prices, and a fall in the dollar. War risk was also responsible for a high fraction of the volatility of these assets.

Wolfers and Zitzewitz (2009) proposed an innovative approach, the use of prediction markets to estimate the ex ante probability of war. In particular, they studied the Iraqi conflict and looked at changes in the price of a "Saddam Security" traded on Tradesports that would have paid $10 if Saddam Hussein had been removed from office by June 30, 2003. They studied the period September 2002–February 2003 and interpreted changes in the price of this Saddam Security as changes in the probability of war against Iraq. According to their estimates, a higher probability of war leads to increases in oil prices and to lower equity prices, consistent with Rigobon and Sack's paper. The magnitude of the effect estimated by Wolfers and Zitzewitz is such that increasing the probability of war by 10 percent would increase (spot) oil prices by $1 and decrease the S&P 500 index by 1.5 percent.

While these studies focused on the ex ante risk of war, other efforts have been made to use financial market reactions to assess the effects of the initiation of conflict or the effects of changing intensity of conflict ex post.

Guidolin and La Ferrara (2005a) used the PRIO-Uppsala Armed Conflict Database to construct a sample of 112 conflicts worldwide, that is, all the conflicts for which the initiation can be dated in a precise week during the period 1974–2004. They estimated the reactions of stock market indices and major commodity prices during the week in which such conflicts were initiated. They found that national stock markets are more likely to display positive reactions to conflict onset compared to the world market, suggesting the possibility of war-induced rallies in which investors tend to buy stocks and the initiation of conflict is seen as a sign of resolution. The U.S. stock market is the one that displays the strongest reactions. When the type of conflict is taken into account (international versus internal), the results indicate that *international* conflicts tend to have a more significant impact on stock markets and on the dollar exchange rate. The prices of commodities react to both types of conflict, whereas the price of gold typically only reacts to *internal* conflicts. Guidolin and La Ferrara classified events according to the *region* where they occurred; they found that Asia and the Middle East are the regions where conflicts tend to have the strongest effects on asset markets. Location in the Middle East is obviously important for commodity indices including oil prices: 60 percent of the conflict onsets occurring in this region have an impact on oil futures that is significantly different from zero.

What We Know about Conflict and Private Businesses

The preceding studies convey useful information on the aggregate effects of conflict in the sense that they quantify the impact of certain conflict events on broad financial indicators, such as national stock market indices, commodity prices, and the value of currencies. It is, however, equally interesting to investigate the economic effects of conflict from a microeconomic perspective, that is, to assess the implications of increasing conflict levels for firms and consumers located in the areas where conflict occurs. In what follows I focus only on firms because the tools and the data that can be used to address this part of the question are most similar to the ones described for macroeconomic financial studies.

One of the few studies that, to my knowledge, used econometric tools to quantify the economic costs of conflict for private businesses was by Abadie and Gardeazabal (2003). The authors used as a case study the terrorist conflict in the Basque region and conducted an event study on the announcement (and subsequent end) of a cease-fire by ETA between 1998 and 1999. I illustrate the event study methodology in the next section. For the moment, it suffices to say that it is a tool that allows measurement of the impact on stock prices of unexpected pieces of news. Abadie and Gardeazabal collected data on seventy-three companies traded on the Madrid Stock Exchange and divided them into Basque and non-Basque stocks depending on whether they had a significant part of their business in the Basque Country. They then constructed two buy-and-hold portfolios, a Basque one and a non-Basque one, and compared their performance in the period from the announcement of the truce in 1998 to the end of the truce in November 1999. They found that the Basque portfolio outperformed the other one during the intermediate months of this period, when the truce was considered credible by investors and by public opinion in general. The Basque portfolio did worse at the beginning of the truce (when it was not yet credible) and toward the end (when it became increasingly clear that the truce would no longer be respected). The magnitude of their estimate suggests that the compounded effect of the "good news" period was an extra return of about 10 percent for the Basque portfolio over the non-Basque one, whereas for the "bad news" period it was about −11.2 percent. To sum up, financial markets perceived the political uncertainty associated with ETA's terrorism as bad news, consistent with the macroeconomic literature.

The study of Abadie and Gardeazabal (2003) pertained to a conflict region that is not quite representative, in the sense that it is an industrialized country in which conflict takes the form of terrorism. The typical conflict in the past thirty years has occurred in a poor country with a nondemocratic government and little or no accountability embedded in its institutions. Can we assume that the effects of conflict will be similar in such a setting, or *is there something in the interplay of political uncertainty and weak institutional settings that may differently affect investors' perceptions of conflict?* Historical and qualitative arguments that this may indeed be the case have been proposed for a variety of African conflicts (see, e.g., Le Billon 2001). Econometric evidence on the subject is hard to find. One exception is the work by Guidolin and La Ferrara (2007), which is reviewed later.

In the next section I briefly illustrate a methodology that can help bridge this gap and then present two applications that actually suggest a nontrivial relationship between conflict, institutions, and firm value.

Using Financial Markets to Learn More: Methodology

All studies that look at investors' reactions to news about conflict share a common premise. The price of an asset characterized by an uncertain stream of future cash flows should reflect the present discounted value of the long-run stream of cash flows generated by the asset. If a political event affects the value of the asset, then the economic effects of such a political event can be quantified by looking at changes in the price of the asset that occur in a short interval of time around the event. This approach relies on the assumption that security markets are informationally efficient and that they form rational (unbiased) expectations. Most important, the political events considered must be exogenous with respect to the change in market value of the security.

Two approaches have been used in the literature based on this premise. The first can be referred to as "dummy regression tests" and the second as "event studies."[4]

Dummy Regression Tests

The dummy regression approach is the closest correspondent to large sample studies that regress economic indicators on a set of political variables. The difference is that the dependent variable in this case is the rate of return on a given asset, and the regressors of interest are a series of dummy variables corresponding to days (weeks, months) in which given political events occurred.

Formally, denote with r_t the rate of return on an asset at time t, defined as the percentage change in the price of the asset in the unit of time. Let r_t^M be the rate of return on the local index of the market where the security is traded, and let D_t be a dummy variable (or a set of dummy variables) that takes value 1 if an event occurred at time t and zero otherwise. One can estimate the following augmented market model:

$$r_t = \alpha + \beta r_t^M + \gamma D_t + \varepsilon_t, \qquad t = 1, \ldots, N, \tag{3.1}$$

where ε_t is a white noise error and N is the number of observations (periods) in the full sample. The parameter γ is the one we are interested in, as it captures the impact of the event(s) considered on asset returns. Testing the hypothesis that the event did not affect asset returns thus amounts to testing the null that $\gamma = 0$, once we account for the movements of the market through r_t^M.

Alternatively, the dummy regression approach is often implemented in two stages. The first is to estimate the simple market model

$$r_t = \alpha + \beta r_t^M + \varepsilon_t, \qquad t = 1, \ldots, N, \tag{3.2}$$

which is used to predict the abnormal return

$$e_t = r_t - \hat{\alpha} + \hat{\beta} r_t^M, \qquad t = 1, \ldots, N. \tag{3.3}$$

In the second stage, the abnormal return is regressed on one or more event dummies:

$$e_t = \lambda D_t + \eta_t, \qquad t = 1, \ldots, N. \tag{3.4}$$

Again, the null of no effect of the event(s) under study is a test on the coefficient λ. The idea underlying this method is to separate price reactions that are driven by normal factors, such as market conditions, from abnormal reactions that are due to the event of interest. That is why the residuals of the normal model are used to identify abnormal price fluctuations.

This method is very simple to implement in both versions, and it allows the full set of observations available to be exploited. However, it has one shortcoming: if more than one event occurs during the entire period, and if their occurrence affects the stochastic process followed by asset returns, this will be embedded in the estimates of the coefficients α and β in equations (3.1) or (3.2), which are estimated on the entire period. In particular, observations that *follow* certain political events will influence the value of beta that is used to predict reactions to *previous* events. This could lead to underestimating or overestimating the reactions to these events, depending on the direction of the distortion in the estimated coefficients of (3.2). To avoid this problem, one can resort to a slightly different implementation, which is known in the finance literature as event study.

Event Studies

The classical event study methodology is summarized very well in Campbell, Lo, and MacKinlay (1997). As in the dummy regression approach, the goal is to quantify the reaction of the price of an asset to the occurrence of events, the timing of which is known. The difference is that the null model is estimated on a *subset* of available observations for which the researcher can be confident that no significant event related to the one under study occurred. To illustrate the procedure, consider the time line in figure 3.1.

Let t_0 be the date of the event of interest. If there is uncertainty on the precise date on which investors learned about the event, one should define an *event window* $[t_0 - k, t_0 + k]$ around the event date. This window need not be symmetric, and it typically depends on the degree to which the event is anticipated. The key difference between this method and dummy regression is that here the normal model is estimated using T observations that immediately precede the event window. In other words, the market model

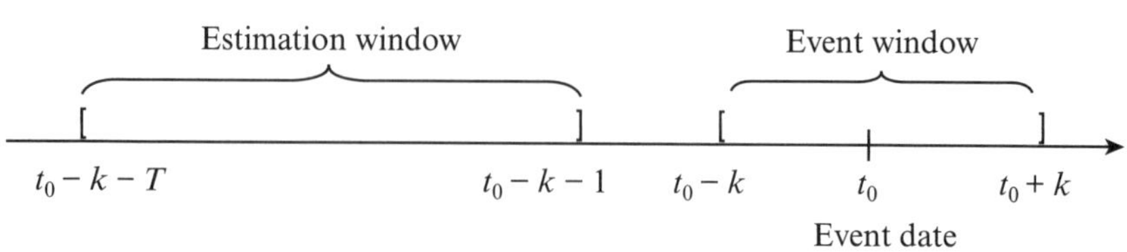

Figure 3.1
Time line for event study.

$$r_t = \alpha + \beta r_t^M + \varepsilon_t, \qquad t = t_0 - k - T, \dots, t_0 - k - 1, \tag{3.2'}$$

is estimated over an *estimation window* $[t_0 - k - T, t_0 - k - 1]$ that never overlaps with the event window. The parameter estimates from (3.2′) are then used to predict the abnormal returns in the event window, that is,

$$e_t = r_t - \hat{\alpha} + \hat{\beta} r_t^M, \qquad t = t_0 - k, \dots, t_0 + k. \tag{3.3'}$$

Note that the benchmark used to estimate abnormal returns need not be the market model as in (3.2′) but can also be any other model such as the CAPM.

In order to assess the impact of the event on asset prices one can examine the pattern of abnormal returns during the event window or build a (less noisy) synthetic measure of the *cumulative* effect of the event over the event window. The latter is typically known as the cumulative abnormal return (CAR) and is constructed as follows:

$$\text{CAR}_t \equiv \sum_{t=t_0-k}^{t} e_t, \qquad t = t_0 - k + 1, \dots, t_0 + k. \tag{3.5}$$

Visual inspection of the evolution of CAR_t over the event window thus allows a first assessment of whether the event had any cumulative impact on asset returns. An upward (downward)-sloping CAR indicates that the event positively (negatively) affected abnormal returns.

To assess the significance of the effect, the null hypothesis that the CAR had no impact on prices, $H_0 : \text{CAR} = 0$, can formally be tested either parametrically or nonparametrically. Parametric tests rely on the fact that the standardized CAR is distributed as a student's t with a number of degrees of freedom that depends on the length of the estimation window (see Campbell, Lo, and MacKinlay 1997 for details). Nonparametric rank and sign tests are sometimes preferred because they are less influenced by departures from normality that characterize high-frequency data and have better small sample properties (see Corrado 1989 and Corrado and Zivney 1992 for a specification of these tests).

Conflict, Firms, and Institutions: Illustrative Examples

In what follows I illustrate two applications of the event study methodology that attempt to use financial markets to shed light on firms' behavior in conflict environments. The first concerns diamond-mining companies in Angola and uses data from Guidolin and La Ferrara (2007). The second concerns arms-producing companies all over the world and uses data from DellaVigna and La Ferrara (2007). It is interesting to note that the issues of conflict diamonds and of illegal arms trade are among those that have attracted much attention on behalf of nongovernmental organizations and public advocacy groups in their campaigns. Action on these matters, however, is constrained by the difficulty of finding hard evidence of inappropriate behavior on the part of the economic agents involved. In both cases, the challenge for the proposed research agenda is to indirectly form hypotheses on firms' behavior based on systematic patterns of reactions by financial investors.

Diamond-Mining Firms in Angola

The diamond-mining sector in Angola is a very interesting case study because it allows us to explore certain characteristics that are representative of a fairly broad set of conflicts in sub-Saharan Africa. First, the Angolan civil war was a long conflict that plagued the country since its independence in 1974 and until the year 2002. Many African countries have experienced long wars, so long that economic agents have learned to operate in a conflict environment and have developed strategies that are specific to such a setting. Second, the Angolan conflict is typically interpreted as a resource war, one where command over lucrative natural resources—oil and diamonds—has been key in allowing the government and the rebels to sustain their military efforts for so many years. Resource-abundant countries often develop "grabber-friendly" institutions (Mehlum, Moene, and Torvik 2006), and when this type of institution is combined with a conflict setting, the consequences of political instability for firms' behavior can be counterintuitive. Finally, the type of resource from which rebel groups derived their revenue, alluvial diamonds, is one that does not require prohibitive levels of fixed investment and that is relatively easily lootable. This implies that the Angolan setting until the end of the war was one where the state did not have a monopoly over property rights enforcement, in the sense that there were areas of the country where mining operations could not be conducted without some form of noninterference by rebel forces.

To illustrate the implications of these features of the Angolan conflict for the behavior of diamond-mining companies in the country, it is useful to start by summarizing the findings of Guidolin and La Ferrara (2007). They conducted an event study on the death of Jonas Savimbi, leader of the rebel organization União Nacional para a Independência Total de Angola (UNITA), on February 22, 2002. Savimbi's death was unanimously considered to be a prerequisite (if not a sufficient condition) for peace in the country. On the other hand, no one could predict when Savimbi would be captured or killed, after years in which the national army had been hunting him. His unexpected death during an ambush at the border with Zambia can therefore be considered an ideal natural experiment for an event study on the end of the war. Starting from this premise, Guidolin and La Ferrara (2007) collected data on stock prices of publicly traded diamond-mining companies holding concessions in Angola during the period January 2, 1998 to June 30, 2002, and examined how the abnormal returns of these stocks evolved around the date of Savimbi's death. To ensure that their findings did not reflect some unobserved shock that interested the diamond industry over the same period, the authors constructed a control portfolio of otherwise similar diamond-mining companies that did not hold concessions in Angola over the same period, and compared the results for the Angolan portfolio with those of the control portfolio.[5]

The main result is that on the day of Savimbi's death the abnormal return of the Angolan portfolio was −4 percentage points; five days later, the cumulative abnormal return was −12 percentage points. These effects were statistically different from zero according to both parametric and nonparametric tests. On the other hand, the CAR of the control portfolio over the same period displayed an upward trend that was not statistically significant. What these results suggest is that financial investors perceived Savimbi's death not as good news but rather as *bad news* for diamond-mining companies that were operating in the country. This result is prima facie counterintuitive, if one thinks of the argument that political instability deters investment. Notice that the effect is not due to a potential *increase* in uncertainty about UNITA's leadership after Savimbi's death because the same result is obtained if one conducts an event study on the cease-fire signed by both parties on April 4, 2002.

Several explanations can be put forward for this pattern of investors' reactions. The first is that the end of the war would increase the competition faced by incumbent firms, for instance, because of new entry by companies that had previously been discouraged by the conflict environment, and this would shrink the profit margins of incumbents. A second explanation is that somehow investors feared increased rent extraction by the government after the end of the war. In fact, one could argue that during the war the existence of UNITA curbed the bargaining power of the government vis-à-vis foreign companies. On the one hand, the extremely insecure environment should have made the government willing to attract any company that was willing to enter the country and pay royalties. On the other hand, UNITA's direct control of some of the mining areas posed a limit to the monopoly power of the government over mining rights. Finally, the need of immediate funds to pay for the war could also translate into relatively more attractive deals for incumbent firms compared to a situation of peace. Note that this explanation does not require the rebel movement to be less rent-seeking than the official government, although in the case of Angola it can be argued that investors indeed perceived UNITA as more friendly toward foreign investors than the government party, the Movimento Popular de Libertação de Angola (MPLA), possibly because of the Marxist-Stalinist origin of the latter. In 2000 and 2001, Political Risk Services, a country-risk rating agency, reported that "business would have little to fear from a UNITA government. Most of UNITA's leaders are receptive to foreign private investment. Savimbi himself has acknowledged that Angola needs international input. . . . The party has promised that once in power, it would honor existing contracts that were fairly negotiated."[6] All that is needed is for civil war to create an environment in which neither party can fully monopolize the management of natural resources, which limits the scope for rent extraction from private businesses.

All this suggests that the increase in government rent extraction after the end of the war was a very concrete possibility in the mind of investors. To further illustrate this point, I present an event study of an episode that preceded Savimbi's death and that gives a sense of how common the perception of mismanagement was in the Angolan diamond sector.

On January 26, 1999, Jose Dias, the managing director of Endiama, was unexpectedly suspended from office due to allegations of corruption. Endiama (Empresa Nacional de Diamantes de Angola) had been created in 1986 to control the production and marketing of Angolan diamonds. By law every foreign company willing to mine Angolan diamonds had to enter a production-sharing arrangement with the state-owned Endiama. Partnerships with Endiama and with other local mining companies were well known to be very costly but at the same time essential to obtain mining licenses—a phenomenon that is fairly common to other lines of business in developing and transition countries and that has sometimes been referred to as "parasitic rent appropriation" (Mehlum, Moene, and Torvik 2003).

Figure 3.2 reports the cumulative abnormal returns of the Angolan and the control portfolios of diamond-mining companies, constructed as in Guidolin and La Ferrara (2007), corresponding to the event of January 26, 1999. Angolan stocks show a significant increase in their abnormal return of about 2 percentage points following the suspension of the corrupt director (figure 3.2A), whereas stocks in the control portfolio display no significant reaction to the news (figure 3.2B). The null of a zero CAR for the Angolan portfolio is rejected against the alternative of a positive CAR at the 1 percent level for the event window of three trading days around the date of the event. The corresponding p-value for the control portfolio is .29.

This result suggests that the management of Endiama by government-appointed Jose Dias was seen as damaging to diamond-mining companies holding concessions in Angola (at least the publicly traded ones in the sample of Guidolin and La Ferrara 2007), which is consistent with the negative reaction of the same stocks to the news of Savimbi's death.

Obviously investors should be wary that conflict not only brings about potential gains in terms of limits to competition and bargaining power but also risk of disruption of production activities and loss of assets. In related work, Guidolin and La Ferrara (2005b) constructed a continuous indicator of conflict intensity for Angola over the same period, based on the number of military attacks, civilians and military killed or wounded, and press coverage.[7] They performed nonparametric regressions of the abnormal returns of the Angolan and control portfolios over this continuous tension indicator during the full period January 2, 1998 to February 22, 2002. They found that the relationship between companies' abnormal returns and political tension is hump-shaped for the Angolan portfolio, whereas no clear pattern emerges for the control portfolio. In other words, while extremely low or extremely high levels of political tension are associated with lower abnormal returns, intermediate levels of conflict increase the abnormal returns of companies holding concessions in Angola.

Arms-Producing Firms and Embargoes

A second example of firms potentially benefiting from conflict comes from the arms trade. That the defense industry should profit from the occurrence of wars is no surprise at all. What should be a surprise,

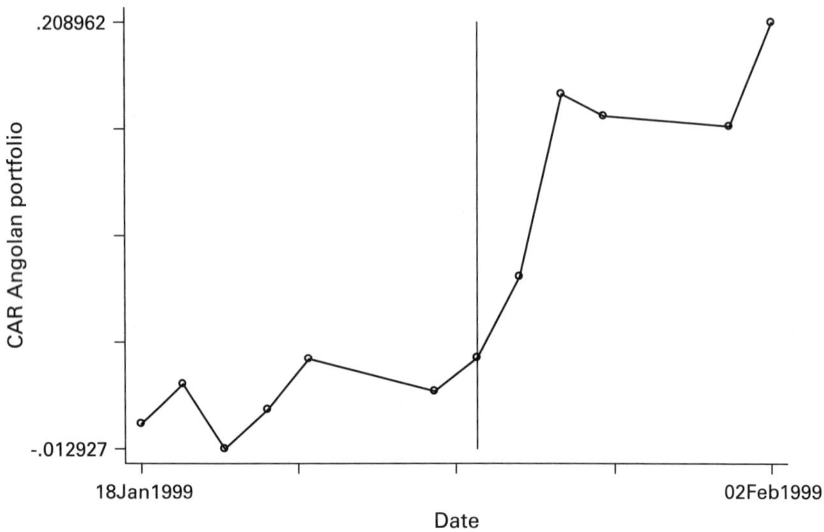

(A) Angolan Portfolio

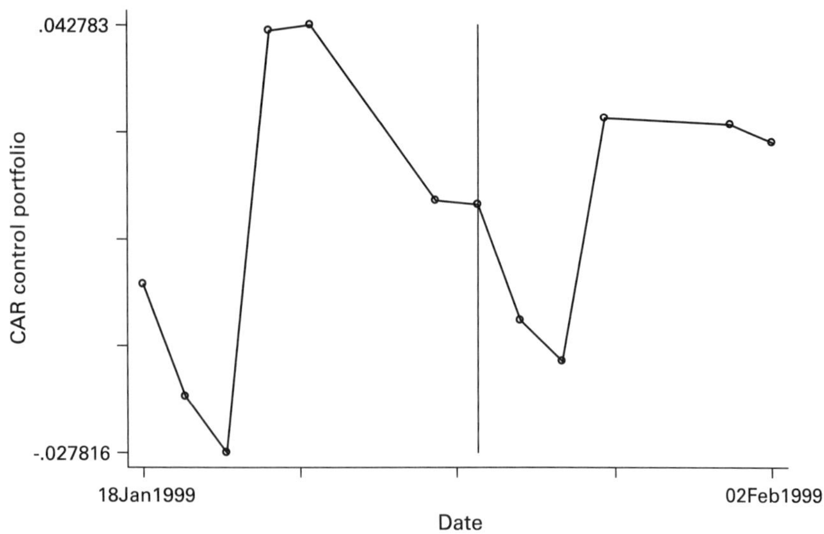

(B) Control Portfolio

Figure 3.2
Cumulative abnormal returns of diamond-mining companies corresponding to the event "Corrupt Endiama director suspended."

though, is that some companies benefit from the existence of wars in countries where by law they should *not* be selling arms. I briefly illustrate a research project aimed at detecting the violation of arms embargoes that builds on DellaVigna and La Ferrara (2007).

The authors collected the stock prices of over 160 arms-producing companies around the world that were publicly traded (though not necessarily for the entire period) from the mid-1980s to the current time. They then isolated eight arms embargoes imposed by the UN Security Council in the period 1990–2004 on the basis of availability of stock prices during the period of the embargo and of the existence of salient and unanticipated conflict events during the same period. The eight embargoed countries analyzed were Angola, Ethiopia, Liberia, Rwanda, Sierra Leone, Somalia, Sudan, and Yugoslavia.

For these countries, the authors collected information on the history and evolution of the conflicts to identify events that *unexpectedly* increased or decreased the intensity of the conflict during the embargo.[8] The political events selected for the analysis satisfied three criteria: (1) they were unanticipated; (2) they received broad media coverage; and (3) their impact on the perceived duration of the conflict was an unambiguous increase or decrease.[9]

The working hypothesis was as follows. If a company never sold to a country under embargo, political events affecting the duration of the conflict (and of the embargo) in that country should not affect the company's stock price, absent general equilibrium effects. If a company sold to the country in question but stopped after the embargo was imposed, then any event increasing the duration of the conflict would postpone the moment at which the embargo would be lifted and the company would be able to resume selling; hence it should have a *negative* effect on stock prices. Finally, if a company was (illegally) trading with the country during the embargo period, increases in conflict intensity that increase the demand for arms would *increase* the company's stock price. Note that the company involvement with the embargoed country may be direct (hence constituting a breach of the embargo) or indirect, through third countries or middlemen. As long as informed investors were aware of the final destination of the arms, and the surplus in the transaction was not entirely absorbed by the third party, one would still observe effects on the stock price.

Figures 3.3 and 3.4 provide an illustration of the type of test that is employed on a larger scale by DellaVigna and La Ferrara (2007). The figures plot the cumulative abnormal returns of a South African

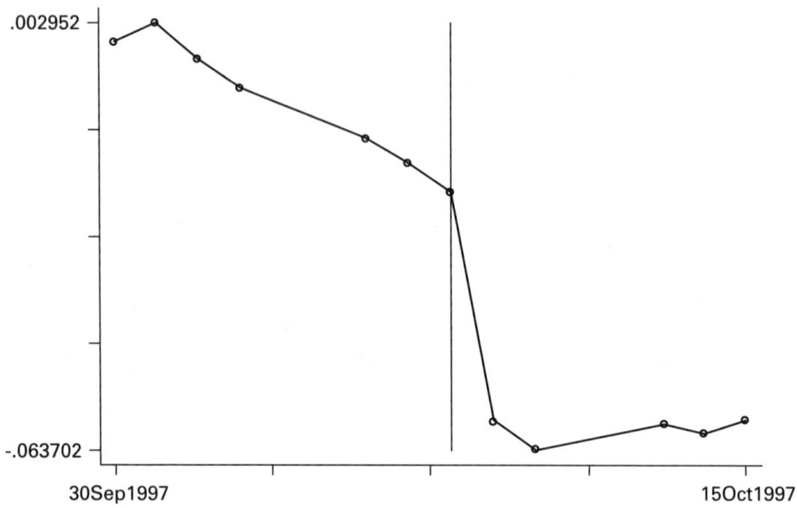

Figure 3.3
Cumulative abnormal return of an arms-producing company corresponding to the event "UN arms embargo imposed against Sierra Leone."

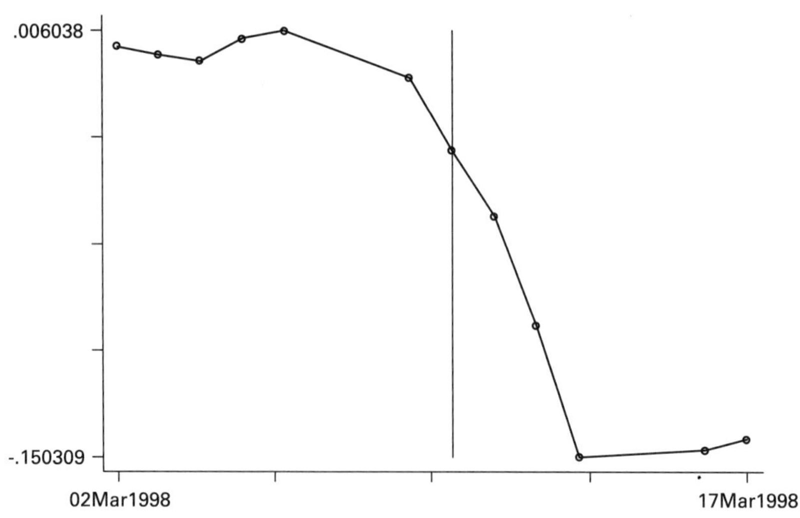

Figure 3.4
Cumulative abnormal return of an arms-producing company corresponding to the event "president returns from exile following truce."

arms-producing company corresponding to two events in the civil war in Sierra Leone. The first event (figure 3.3) is the imposition of the UN arms embargo against Sierra Leone on October 8, 1997. The figure shows a sharp drop in the company's CAR on the day of the event. Between that day and the following one, the CAR of this company dropped by over 3.5 percentage points. Over the entire window going from five trading days before the event to five trading days after, the loss was 6.4 percentage points. One possible interpretation for this finding is that investors believed the company was selling some of its production to Sierra Leone, either directly or through brokers, and they expected it would stop doing so after the imposition of the embargo.

The CAR of the same company corresponding to a subsequent event in the war in Sierra Leone is shown in figure 3.4. On March 10, 1998, the elected president Kabbah returned from exile following a truce between the government and the RUF (the rebel organization). At that time, the arms embargo was still in place. In principle, this event should have positively affected the stock price of this company because it was a sign of resolution of the conflict. At worst, it should have had no impact if investors did not trust the two parties to actually agree on negotiations. On the contrary, this event had a *negative* and significant effect on the company's abnormal returns, so large that between the week preceding March 10 and the following one the CAR declined by 15 percentage points. One interpretation for this result is that in the meantime investors came to learn (or to believe) that the company was still selling to Sierra Leone and that the existence of the embargo actually made it much costlier for Sierra Leone to acquire arms and much more profitable for the company to sell them.[10]

Deriving conclusions on illegal behavior based on one instance of anomalous investor reaction would clearly be irresponsible as well as methodologically wrong. However, thanks to the availability of multiple events for the same conflict and multiple observations for the same company in different conflicts, one could search for *systematic patterns* of reactions all in a consistent direction and for the same company. While it is possible that something else occurred on March 10, 1998, that induced a fall in the stock price of that particular company, it would be less plausible (and statistically very unlikely) that a reaction in the same direction to *several other* conflict events always occurred to that company during the embargo on Sierra Leone.

To draw a parallel with a different literature, this research agenda has a similar spirit as Duggan and Levitt (2002) and Jacob and Levitt

(2003), who detected cheating behavior using systematic patterns in the data. The difference is that whereas they have available data on the *outcomes* of interest (sports match results or grades given by the teachers), DellaVigna and La Ferrara had only information on investors' *beliefs*. How much one is willing to trust investors' knowledge is open to discussion. What is generally accepted is that financial investors should not systematically lose money holding erroneous beliefs.

Note, however, that since a large fraction of the illegal trade in weapons is in the secondhand market, an approach based on equity prices of manufacturers cannot convey a global estimate of the extent of embargo breeches.

Conclusions and Policy Lessons

This chapter has reviewed some well-known contributions on the economic causes and effects of civil conflict and has compared the widespread macroeconomic approach used in the literature with a microeconomic one that has been proposed for the study of conflict and that relies on event studies. Leading themes through the analysis have been (1) how the microeconomic analysis of financial market reactions can help detect anomalous behavior by companies, and (2) to what extent these reactions systematically differ when companies operate in weak institutional environments as opposed to well-regulated markets.

It may be useful at this point to go back to the macroeconomic literature on conflict and compare the policy lessons that can be drawn from that literature with some lessons that emerge from the microeconomic research agenda. One key recommendation stemming from the finding that income levels and growth rates are negatively correlated with the risk and duration of war has been that policies (including aid) designed for poverty reduction and growth should also help restore peace. A second well-known argument is that given the role played by natural resources in civil conflict, strategies of diversification that make these economies less heavily dependent on primary exports should also make them less prone to conflict.

On the other hand, the microeconomic approach targeted to understanding how private businesses operate in conflict environments has highlighted different, and sometimes conflicting, patterns. Given the weak institutional environment present in many conflict economies, it is possible for some firms to actually profit from the political uncertainty generated by conflict. This was suggested by the two illustrations in this chapter on diamond-mining and arms-producing companies, but it also fits well with the opinions of those who operate in these environments. For example, Berman (2000) reports the results of a survey in which the managers of large multinational companies overseeing their operations in conflict regions were interviewed about the factors affecting their willingness to operate in countries affected by conflict. Most respondents declared they would not be discouraged from operating in such regions provided the supply conditions were sufficiently attractive (e.g., because of natural resource endowments) and the conflict was contained in certain parts of the country. The availability of political-risk insurance was also a significant factor in their decisions.

It is commonly believed that multinational corporations and private businesses operating in conflict environments are sufficiently hurt by the uncertain political climate so as to be the first stakeholders in restoring peace. The main message of this chapter is that a deeper understanding of what investors perceive to be the costs (or benefits) of conflict is needed to provide a realistic assessment of how much effort these economic actors will spontantously exert in peace-building operations.

In addition, while most of the academic debate focuses on the inadequacy of *local* governments and institutions as means of preventing civil wars, the case study of arms embargoes presented in this chapter suggests that international regulations and institutions also play a crucial role. In other words, it can be misleading to focus only on two actors—government and rebels—without looking at the incentives of other players, such as private companies involved in conflict countries.

Institutional reforms, emphasis on corporate social responsibility, and initiatives aimed at improving transparency and accountability may be needed to align the interests of governments, corporations, and citizens. One such example is the Extractive Industry Transparency Initiative (EITI), which targets the governments of resource-abundant countries to solicit the publication and verifiability of government revenues from oil, gas, and mining. Similarly, companies operating in countries that implement the EITI commit to full disclosure of their payments to local governments. The goal of this initiative is to improve the accountability of governments to their citizens, thus increasing the share of revenues that gets spent for the social good. While this initiative is confined to the extractive industry, the emphasis on microeconomic policies to improve accountability is gaining momentum in other sectors as well and may indeed constitute a very effective means of addressing poverty reduction.[11]

Notes

Some of the results described in this chapter come from joint work with Massimo Guidolin and Stefano DellaVigna. I am grateful to both for their invaluable inputs into this research agenda. The chapter also benefited from the comments of Tim Besley, Raji Jayaraman, one anonymous referee, and seminar participants at the BREAD/CESifo conference in Venice. Maria Aleksinskaya provided excellent research assistance. This chapter is part of the Polarization and Conflict Project CIT-2-CT-2004-506084 funded by the European Commission-DG Research Sixth Framework Programme. The usual disclaimer applies. Correspondence: ⟨eliana.laferrara@unibocconi.it⟩.

1. Note that employing lagged values of these variables, as is sometimes done in this literature, does not necessarily alleviate endogeneity problems if conflict can be anticipated or there is persistence.

2. For a thorough analysis of how conflict leads to disruption of local institutions, see Reno (1998).

3. The reasons why problems of unobserved heterogeneity are mitigated by approaches that look at financial market reactions will become clear later, when the event study methodology is described. For the moment, it suffices to mention that this approach exploits variation in abnormal reactions of company stock prices (reactions that are not predicted by market movements or by company fixed effects), thus allowing to control for time-varying unobserved differences among markets (countries) or time-invariant unobserved differences among companies.

4. While the term *event study* is often used to indicate the first approach as well, I prefer to use it in conformity with its original use in the finance literature.

5. The Angolan portfolio was equally weighted and was composed of seven companies traded on one of three stock exchanges: Toronto, Johannesburg, and Sydney. The control portfolio was a weighted average of forty-two companies traded on the same three markets, but the weights were optimally derived to minimize the distance between the Angolan and the control portfolio on several dimensions before February 2002. For details about the construction of the two portfolios, see Guidolin and La Ferrara (2007).

6. Source: Angola Update, August 1, 2000, through January 1, 2002.

7. Daily data on the occurrence of these casualties was collected through a search on the Lexis-Nexis database. For details on the search parameters, see Guidolin and La Ferrara (2005b).

8. Unexpectedness was gauged from the time profile of the number of hits in Lexis-Nexis searches during the days preceding and following the event.

9. See DellaVigna and La Ferrara (2007) for a quantitative assessment of these criteria.

10. Advocacy groups have been quite adamant in denouncing that most if not all of the UN arms embargoes have been systematically violated, and that one of the effects has been to make it simply more costly, but not impossible, for the embargoed countries to acquire arms (see, e.g., Wood 2006).

11. For some examples of accountability reforms implemented by the government of Uganda, see Reinikka and Svensson (2004) and Björkman and Svensson (2009).

References

Abadie, A., and G. J. Gardeazabal. 2003. The Economic Costs of Conflict: A Case Study of the Basque Country. *American Economic Review* 93 (1): 113–132.

Alesina, A., and R. Perotti. 1996. Income Distribution, Political Instability, and Investment. *European Economic Review* 40: 1203–1228.

Azam, J.-P. 1995. How to Pay for the Peace? A Theoretical Framework with References to African Countries. *Public Choice* 83: 173–184.

———. 2006. The Paradox of Power Reconsidered: A Theory of Political Regimes in Africa. *Journal of African Economies* 15: 26–58.

Barro, R. 1991. Economic Growth in a Cross Section of Countries. *Quarterly Journal of Economics* 106 (2): 407–443.

Berman, J. 2000. Boardrooms and Bombs: Strategies of Multinational Corporations in Conflict Areas. *Harvard International Review* 22 (3): 28–32.

Björkman, M., and J. Svensson. 2009. Power to the People: Evidence from a Randomized Field Experiment on Community-Based Monitoring in Uganda. *Quarterly Journal of Economics* 124 (2): 735–769.

Campbell, J. Y., A. W. Lo, and A. C. MacKinlay. 1997. *The Econometrics of Financial Markets*. Princeton, N.J.: Princeton University Press.

Collier, P., and A. Hoeffler. 1998. On the Economic Causes of Civil War. *Oxford Economic Papers* 50: 563–573.

———. 2004. Greed and Grievance in Civil War. *Oxford Economic Papers* 56: 563–595.

Collier, P., A. Hoeffler, and M. Soderböm. 2004. On the Duration of Civil War. *Journal of Peace Research* 41 (3): 253–274.

Corrado, C. 1989. A Nonparametric Test for Abnormal Security-Price Performance in Event Studies. *Journal of Financial Economics* 23: 385–395.

Corrado, C., and T. Zivney. 1992. The Specification and Power of the Sign Test in Event Study Hypothesis Tests Using Daily Stock Returns. *Journal of Financial and Quantitative Analysis* 27: 465–478.

DellaVigna, S., and E. La Ferrara. 2007. Detecting Illegal Arms Trade. NBER working paper 13355.

Djankov, S., and M. Reynal-Querol. 2007. The Colonial Origins of Civil War. ⟨http://www.econ.upf.edu/docs/papers/downloads/1038.pdf⟩.

Duggan, M., and S. Levitt. 2002. Winning Isn't Everything: Corruption in Sumo Wrestling. *American Economic Review* 92: 1594–1605.

Fearon, J. 2004. Why Do Some Civil Wars Last So Much Longer than Others? *Journal of Peace Research* 41 (3): 275–302.

———. 2005. Civil War Since 1945: Some Facts and a Theory. Paper presented at the 2005 Annual Meeting of the American Political Science Association. Washington, D.C.

Fearon, J., and D. Laitin. 2003. Ethnicity, Insurgency, and Civil War. *American Political Science Review* 97: 75–90.

Grossman, H. 1995. Insurrections. In *Handbook of Defense Economics*, ed. K. Hartley and T. Sandler. Vol. 1, 191–212. Amersterdam: Elsevier.

———. 2004. Constitution or Conflict? *Conflict Management and Peace Science* 21: 29–42.

Grossman, H., and M. Kim. 1995. Swords or Plowshares? A Theory of the Security of Claims to Property. *Journal of Political Economy* 103 (6): 1275–1288.

Guidolin, M., and E. La Ferrara. 2005a. The Economic Effects of Violent Conflict: Evidence from Asset Market Reactions. Working paper 2005-066. Federal Reserve Bank of St. Louis.

———. 2005b. Firm Value and Political Tension Intensity in High-Conflict Environments: Evidence from Angola. Working paper 2005-066A. Federal Reserve Bank of St. Louis.

———. 2007. Diamonds Are Forever, Wars Are Not. Is Conflict Bad for Private Firms? *American Economic Review* 97 (5): 1978–1993.

Hirshleifer, J. 1991. The Technology of Conflict as an Economic Activity. *American Economic Review* 81 (2): 130–134.

Horowitz, D. L. 1985. *Ethnic Groups in Conflict.* Berkeley: University of California Press.

Jacob, B. A., and S. Levitt. 2003. Rotten Apples: An Investigation of the Prevalence and Predictors of Teacher Cheating. *Quarterly Journal of Economics* 118: 843–877.

Klare, M. T. 2001. *Natural Resource Wars: The New Landscape of Global Conflict.* New York: Metropolitan Books.

La Ferrara, E., and R. H. Bates. 2001. Political Competition in Weak States. *Economics and Politics* 13 (2): 159–184.

La Porta, R., F. Lopez-de-Silanes, A. Shleifer, and R. Vishny. 1999. The Quality of Government. *Journal of Law, Economics and Organization* 15: 222–279.

Le Billon, P. 2001. The Political Ecology of War: Natural Resources and Armed Conflicts. *Political Geography* 20: 561–584.

Mehlum, H., K. Moene, and R. Torvik. 2003. Predator or Prey? Parasitic Enterprises in Economic Development. *European Economic Review* 47 (2): 275–294.

———. 2006. Institutions and the Resource Curse. *Economic Journal* 116: 1–20.

Miguel, E., S. Satyanath, and E. Sergenti. 2004. Economic Shocks and Civil Conflict: An Instrumental Variables Approach. *Journal of Political Economy* 112 (4): 725–753.

Montalvo, J. G., and M. Reynal-Querol. 2005. Ethnic Polarization, Potential Conflict and Civil War. *American Economic Review* 95: 796–816.

———. 2007. Ethnic Polarization and the Duration of Civil Wars. WPS 4192. World Bank.

Posner, D. N. 2005. *Institutions and Ethnic Politics in Africa.* Cambridge: Cambridge University Press.

Reinikka, R., and J. Svensson. 2004. The Power of Information: Evidence from a Newspaper Campaign to Reduce Capture. WPS 3239. World Bank.

Reno, W. 1998. *Warlord Politics and African States.* Boulder, Colo.: Lynne Rienner.

Rigobon, R., and B. Sack. 2005. The Effects of War Risk on U.S. Financial Markets. *Journal of Banking and Finance* 29: 1769–1789.

Ross, M. 2004. How Do Natural Resources Influence Civil War? Evidence from Thirteen Cases. *International Organization* 58 (1): 35–67.

Skaperdas, S. 1992. Cooperation, Conflict, and Power in the Absence of Property Rights. *American Economic Review* 82: 720–739.

Slantchev, B. 2004. How Initiators End Their Wars: The Duration of Warfare and the Terms of Peace. *American Journal of Political Science* 48: 813–829.

Svensson, J. 1998. Investment, Property Rights, and Political Instability: Theory and Evidence. *European Economic Review* 42: 1317–1341.

Weinstein, J. 2005. Resources and the Information Problem in Rebel Recruitment. *Journal of Conflict Resolution* 49 (4): 598–624.

Wolfers, J., and E. Zitzewitz. 2009. Using Markets to Inform Policy: The Case of the Iraq War. *Economica* 76 (302): 225–250.

Wood, B. 2006. Strengthening Compliance with UN Arms Embargoes: Key Challenges for Monitoring and Verification. Amnesty International Report.

World Bank. 2003. *Breaking the Conflict Trap: Civil War and Development Policy.* Washington, D.C.

4 Liberalization Meets Investment Climate

Robin Burgess

The last three decades have witnessed a departure from the model of planned industrialization that dominated development policy in the postwar period. The emphasis on planning as a means of engendering industrial development was replaced by an emphasis on liberalization and competition. In their quest for growth many developing countries abandoned central planning, dismantled government controls over industry, and liberalized trade. This shift from government control to the promotion of competition represents a key paradigm shift in development policy over the past fifty years.

A parallel shift has been the growing focus on institutional factors as a key driver of economic growth. This reflects a heightened awareness that political, legal, and social institutions surrounding economic production fundamentally affect the investment and growth prospects of countries. Four sets of factors, over which governments exercise some control, are considered to be important in this respect: Stability and security, regulation and taxation, finance and infrastructure, and human capital and labor markets (World Bank 2005). Collectively these factors, which try to capture the domestic institutional and policy conditions relevant to economic growth (and hence go well beyond a narrow "rules of the game" definition of institutions) are referred to as the investment climate of a country or region of a country. Much effort has been devoted to trying to quantify the factors that make up investment climate. The Doing Business indicators produced by the World Bank (2009a), for example, have been a powerful tool for attracting attention to the deficiencies of the investment climate in different countries. And there is evidence that countries are responding by taking steps to improve their rankings. The World Bank (2009b) has also produced investment climate indicators within countries using firm-level surveys that seek to identify constraints to investment and growth.

An important question is whether the impact of liberalization (for example, dismantling planning controls or liberalizing trade) on economic performance is magnified or dampened by the domestic policies and institutions that determine investment climate in a country or region. This question does not focus on the direct effect of either liberalization or investment climate on economic performance but rather on whether liberalization and investment climate are complements or substitutes when present together. If they interact in a meaningful manner, then domestic institutional and policy reforms may play a central role in determining whether a country or region benefits from, or is harmed by, liberalization. This approach brings the spotlight back onto local policy and institutional reforms as determinants of the impact of liberalization reforms on economic outcomes. Indeed, the strong interest shown by policymakers in improving their investment climate can be understood as an attempt to ensure that they benefit in a relative sense from the liberalization process.

Although there are large separate literatures on liberalization and on investment climate, the literature that looks at how they interact is still embryonic. It is important to fill this gap. The cross-country regression literature has failed to establish a consensus on whether and how liberalization affects economic performance. One potential reason for this ambiguity could be that the impact of liberalization is heterogeneous depending on investment climate in different regions of a given country. It seems entirely plausible that different parts of a country may respond differently to the same liberalization experiment. A natural way to make progress on this issue is to exploit subnational heterogeneity in investment climate to investigate whether the response of industries, located in different regions, to the same nationwide liberalization episode is mediated by local policies and institutions. These types of studies can generate important policy insights because current debates have tended to focus on average effects of liberalization on economic outcomes using cross-country data that are not particularly suited to this purpose. Our ability to make effective policy recommendations hinges on understanding whether liberalization and investment climate interact as complements or substitutes. Understanding whether the impact of a liberalization episode has heterogeneous effects depending on policy and institutional conditions in different regions, and identifying precisely which conditions are important, therefore represents a research agenda ripe for exploitation.

This chapter, which is intended to stimulate research in this area, is structured as follows. First, I examine how the literatures on liberalization and investment climate separately evolved and are now beginning to overlap. The next section contains a case study, based on the work of Aghion et al. 2008, of how liberalization (in the form of industrial delicensing) and investment climate in the major Indian states (along the dimensions of labor regulation, access to finance, human capital, and infrastructure) interacted during the 1980–1997 period.

Liberalization Meets Investment Climate

In the postwar period, planned industrialization became a major doctrine for tackling economic backwardness in developing countries. The theoretical argument was that massive state investment would help kick-start development, and state coordination of economic activities would ensure the rapid and sustained growth of domestic industries (Rosenstein-Rodan 1943; 1961; Rostow 1952). Policymakers translated these principles into a variety of policies. In countries where private initiative was not altogether suppressed, a cornerstone of the development strategy was the requirement for firms to obtain a license to begin or expand production. The goal of this policy was to place industrial development under the control of central governments, allowing them to allocate plan targets to firms and to address inequities across regions. Trade restrictions were also part of the same package. Tariffs would shelter nascent domestic industries from foreign competition, and help promote the industrialization process according to the objectives of the plan. The bulk of developing countries engaged in some form of planned industrialization in the postwar period.

These views remained influential among policymakers during the 1950s, 1960s, and 1970s. However, amidst growing dissatisfaction with its results, the consensus shifted in the 1980s from planned industrialization to liberalization and laissez-faire. Many developing countries progressively abandoned central planning, dismantled government controls over industry, and liberalized trade. This paradigm change has spurred a passionate debate regarding the relationship between liberalization and economic performance. Advocates argued that by increasing the size of markets and fostering product market competition, liberalization enhances growth (e.g., Dollar and Kray 2002; 2004; Frankel and Romer 1999; Sachs and Warner 1995; World Bank 2001). Critics pointed out that liberalization can be detrimental to growth by inhibiting infant industries and learning-by-doing (Krugman 1981; Hausman and Rodrik 2002; Young 1991; Stiglitz 2002; Acemoglu, Aghion, and Zilibotti 2006).

The evidence gathered so far on this issue is mainly at the country level and does not arrive at any clear consensus (see Rodriguez and Rodrik 2001). This partly reflects the deficiencies of trying to look at this issue in a cross-country setting. Liberalization episodes may not be comparable across countries, and it is difficult to control for all the factors that might affect the relationship between liberalization and economic performance. Indeed, it is arguable that it is next to impossible to establish a causal effect of liberalization on economic performance in this setting (see Rodrik 2005).

Prompted by these deficiencies, recent work has moved in a microeconomic direction (see Tybout 2000 for an early and influential review). A host of new studies track manufacturing firms or plants across trade liberalization episodes within single countries. This precludes evaluation of the economywide impacts of liberalization but nonetheless greatly enhances the ability to make causal inferences. These studies tend to find evidence of a positive average effect of trade opening on aggregate productivity in manufacturing (see, e.g., Pavcnik 2002 on Chile; Trefler 2004 on Canada; Bernard, Jensen, and Schott 2006 on the United States; Topalova 2004 on India).

A key insight from this literature is that the response to the same liberalization shock is highly heterogeneous across firms and plants. Firm characteristics such as relative productivity have a key role to play here. Pavcnik (2002), for example, found that two-thirds of the 19 percent increase in industry productivity in Chile following the trade liberalization of the late 1970s and early 1980s was due to expansion of higher-productivity plants and exit of low-productivity plants. The remaining one-third came from within-plant productivity gains as firms adapted to the more competitive environment. Trefler (2004), studying the Canadian tariff reductions that resulted from the creation of the North American Free Trade Agreement (NAFTA), found that about two-thirds of industry productivity increases were due to reallocation of production from low- to high-productivity plants, with the remaining one-third coming from within-plant productivity improvements. In a similar vein, Bernard, Jensen, and Schott (2006) found that low-productivity firms in the United States were more likely to exit when trade costs fall.

This microeconomic literature has brought to the fore the idea that liberalization has heterogeneous effects depending on firm/plant characteristics. This idea was formalized in the influential model of Melitz (2003). What may be a boon for a high-productivity plant may be anathema for a low-productivity plant. Much less attention, however, has been paid to whether heterogeneity in the institutional environment in which firms and industries are embedded has a bearing on postliberalization industrial performance. It is on this interaction between liberalization and institutional environment that I focus on in this chapter. Put simply, I examine whether cross-regional heterogeneity in factors like labor regulations, access to finance, human capital, and infrastructure affects how firms and industries located in different regions respond to the same liberalization reform.

In the investment climate literature, recent studies from the cross-country literature have played an important role in bringing attention to the fact that deficiencies in economic, legal, and political institutions are a key constraint to economic expansion in developing countries (see, e.g., Hall and Jones 1999; Acemoglu, Johnson, and Robinson 2001). Translating these key insights into concrete and comparable indicators of investment climate for different countries and regions of countries has been a major challenge. Whereas the bulk of these indicators (such as the risk-of-expropriation measure used by Acemoglu, Johnson, and Robinson 2001) have tended to be measured at the country level, this literature is moving resolutely in a subnational direction.

The challenge is now seen as identifying measures of investment climate that vary across regions of a country and across time and that allow some degree of causal inference with regard to the impact of investment climate on economic performance. Holmes (1998), for example, looked at how the passage of right-to-work laws in U.S. states affected manufacturing activity at the borders of adopting and non-adopting states (where labor markets were common). Bertrand and Kramarz (2002) examined how the actions of regional zoning boards, which had different propensities to accept applications for large retail stores, affected regional employment in the retail sector. Besley and Burgess (2004) presented evidence that pro-worker labor regulation is strongly positively correlated with measures of industrial disputes in the registered sector, such as workdays lost through strikes and lockouts. They also found that states that moved in a pro-worker direction experienced lower output growth in the registered manufacturing sector. In contrast, output in unregistered manufacturing increased. This suggests that labor regulation is picking up something about the policy environment facing registered firms as opposed to the overall investment climate facing all firms. In a similar vein, Sanyal and Menon (2005) demonstrated that new industrial plants in the registered sector in India tended to open more in pro-employer states, which suffered less from industrial disputes.

This literature does not, however, consider how investment climate in a region interacts with the broader liberalization process that might be occurring in a country. A number of theoretical models highlight how conditions in the labor market affect the impact of product market deregulation such as trade liberalization (Rama 1997; Rama and Tabellini 1999; Blanchard and Giavazzi 2003; Cuñat and Melitz 2005; Banerjee and Newman 2005). These theoretical studies make contradictory predictions on how liberalization and investment climate interact (that is, whether they are complements or substitutes), highlighting the need for empirical work in this area.

Such work, however, is extremely sparse. Topalova (2005) found that trade liberalization was associated with less poverty reduction in Indian districts located in states with inflexible labor laws. This suggests that rigid labor markets fostered by state-specific labor regulations prevented the reallocation of labor in the face of trade liberalization, thus retarding the pull out of poverty for the poorest subsistence farmers. In contrast, in flexible labor areas, where reallocation was easier and growth was faster, the impact of trade liberalization on poverty was negligible. This highlights how the impact of trade liberalization may be heterogeneous depending on the functioning of labor institutions in different parts of a single country. Domestic policies pursued by state governments clearly have a bearing on how trade liberalization impacts the welfare of citizens under their jurisdiction. In particular, labor mobility is emerging as a key theme in understanding why the impact of a common trade liberalization reform varies across different regions of a country like India. In a similar vein, Hanson (2004) found that the response of wages of Mexican workers to NAFTA was more pronounced in those parts of the country that were more exposed to trade liberalization. The location of Mexican workers turned out to be an important determinant of the extent to which workers benefited from trade liberalization.

A Case Study of India

To illustrate how investment climate may mediate the impact of liberalization, I focus on one country, India. India is an interesting case because it has gone through a number of nationwide liberalization reforms and is a large federal democracy. This implies that there is considerable heterogeneity across states as regards the local institutional environment in which liberalization reforms were implemented. I focus, in particular, on the findings from the study by Aghion et al. (2008), which examined how the nationwide industrial delicensing reforms of the 1980s and 1990s interacted with the investment climate in different Indian states.

The postwar period in India was characterized by a strong focus on planned industrialization, and industrial licensing was extensively used to control the pace and pattern of industrial development across the country. By controlling who could begin or expand production in narrow product categories, the central government was able to allocate five-year production targets to firms. This system of central control came to be known as the License Raj (Bhagwati and Desai 1970).

Failure of the system to deliver sustained industrial growth, however, led it to be progressively abandoned. At particular dates different three-digit industries were no longer required to obtain a license to begin or expand production or to change product line or location. On these dates barriers to entering these sectors were effectively lowered, and more intense competition between firms ensued. As their measure of liberalization Aghion et al. (2008) coded when each three-digit manufacturing industry in India was delicensed (see figure 4.1).

The figure shows two key delicensing waves. One was in 1985, when Rajiv Gandhi became Prime Minister following the assassination of his mother, Indira Gandhi. Rajiv Gandhi was an unknown quantity—an airline pilot with no political experience—who turned out to be a fervent reformer and was responsible for moving India in a pro-business direction (Rodrik and Subramaniam 2004). In 1985, 30 percent of three-digit manufacturing industries were delicensed. The second delicensing wave occurred in 1991, following the assassination of Rajiv Gandhi in an election campaign that subsequently carried his Congress Party to victory. The new prime minister, Narasimha Rao, under pressure from the International Monetary Fund, implemented a wide-ranging liberalization drive. As with Rajiv Gandhi, the depth of the reformist tendencies of the Rao government had been largely unanticipated (Rodrik and Subramaniam 2004; Topalova 2005). In 1991 industrial delicensing occurred for a further 52 percent of the three-digit manufacturing industries.

In the 1980–1997 period, only 8 percent of three-digit industries were delicensed in years other than 1985 and 1991, and 10 percent of industries were still licensed at the end of the period in 1997. A small

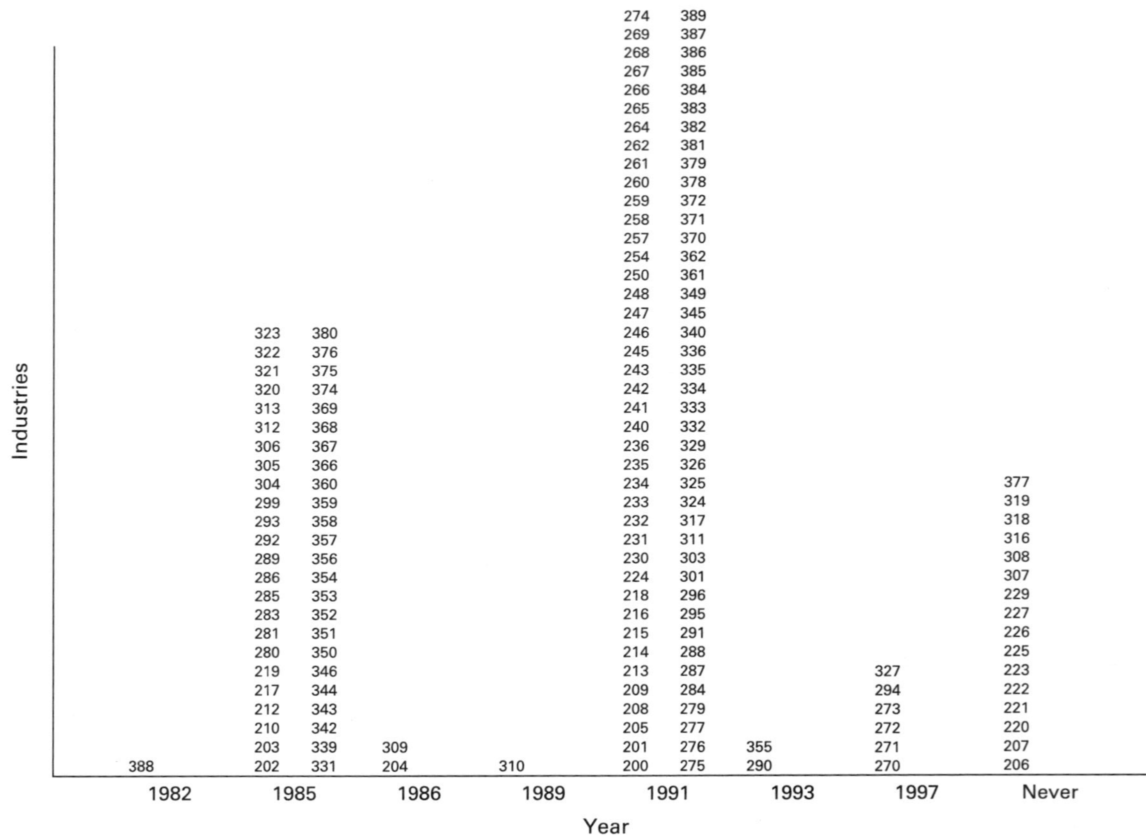

Figure 4.1
Delicensing of registered manufacturing industries in India, 1980–1997. Industries in the "Never" column had not been delicensed as of 1997. Numbers are three-digit registered manufacturing codes from the Indian National Industrial Classification 1987. From Aghion et al. (2008).

number of industries remained subject to the licensing requirements "for reasons related to security and strategic concerns, social reasons, problems related to safety and over-riding environmental issues, manufacture of products of hazardous nature and articles of elitist consumption" (Government of India 1991).

The question posed in Aghion et al. (2008) is whether the impact of the same nationwide delicensing reforms differs according to the policy and institutional conditions extant within different Indian states. They were interested in studying whether delicensing had a heterogeneous impact depending on the local investment climate. This is an important question from a policy standpoint because it will indicate whether engaging in policy and institutional reforms that improve the investment climate in an Indian state will generate higher industrial growth after delicensing, that is, whether liberalization makes state-level investment climate reforms more pressing.

Which areas of investment climate might be important and at least partly under the control of government? The World Development Report entitled *A Better Investment Climate for Everyone* (World Bank 2005, 1) states, "While governments have limited influence on factors such as geography, they have more decisive influence on the security of property rights, approaches to regulation and taxation (both at and within the border), the provision of infrastructure, the functioning of finance and labor markets, and broader governance features such as corruption." Because India is a federal democracy, these factors will vary across states. And if one can construct proxies, one can examine whether state-level policy and institutional conditions mediate the impact of nationwide liberalization reforms.

Aghion et al. (2008) looked at a number of factors that captured, albeit crudely, some of these dimensions of investment climate. The first was a state-specific labor regulation measure from Besley and Burgess (2004). Under the Indian constitution, central and state governments share responsibility for industrial relations. The key piece of central legislation is the Industrial Disputes Act of 1947, which sets out the conciliation, arbitration, and adjudication procedures to be followed in the case of an industrial dispute. It was extensively amended by state governments during the post-Independence period. Besley and Burgess (2004) coded all state-level amendments to this Act as pro-worker (+1), neutral (0), or pro-employer (−1) and cumulated these scores over time to get a picture of the evolution of state-level labor regulations. (States classified as neutral did not experience any amendment activity in a pro-worker or pro-employer direction over the 1958–1997 period.) This is shown in figure 4.2, which is drawn from Aghion et al. (2008) for the 1980–1997 period.

Labor regulations exhibit significant variation across states and time. Figure 4.2 shows six neutral states, whose lines lie on the zero line: Assam, Bihar, Haryana, Jammu and Kashmir, Punjab, and Uttar Pradesh. Among those that have passed amendments, six states are classified as pro-employer (lines lying below zero): Andhra Pradesh, Karnataka, Kerala, Madhya Pradesh, Rajasthan, and Tamil Nadu. This leaves four pro-worker states (lines lying above zero): Gujarat, Maharashtra, Orissa, and West Bengal. This measure captures legislated as opposed to implemented labor regulations; caution is therefore required in interpreting results obtained using this measure.

To capture the level of financial development in a state, Aghion et al. (2008) used the instrumented state-level bank branch expansion measure from Burgess and Pande (2005). This captures the expansion of commercial bank branch networks into rural, unbanked locations across Indian states driven by the introduction (in 1977) and removal (in 1990) of a branch licensing rule. The licensing rule stipulated that for each branch opened in a banked (typically urban) location, four branches had to be opened in unbanked (typically rural) locations. The imposition of the 1:4 licensing rule in effect forced commercial banks to open more branches in rural, unbanked locations, thus expanding access to finance in these areas. The Burgess-Pande (2005) measure can thus be viewed as a state-level measure of access to finance.

Human capital is often pointed to as a key element of investment climate. Aghion et al. (2008) divided up per capita state development expenditure into three separate variables: education expenditure, health expenditure and other development expenditure. The education and health expenditure variables can be viewed as crude proxies of state-level investment in human capital. It is possible that states with higher investment in human capital may respond differently to delicensing relative to states that have invested less in these areas.

The "other development expenditure" variable mainly captures spending on infrastructure and can be treated as a rough proxy of state-level investment in this area. Poor infrastructure is often identified as a key bottleneck to economic expansion in India. And because infrastructure largely remains in the public sphere, state spending in this area may be related to the quality of infrastructural environment in which economic production is embedded. It is therefore interesting

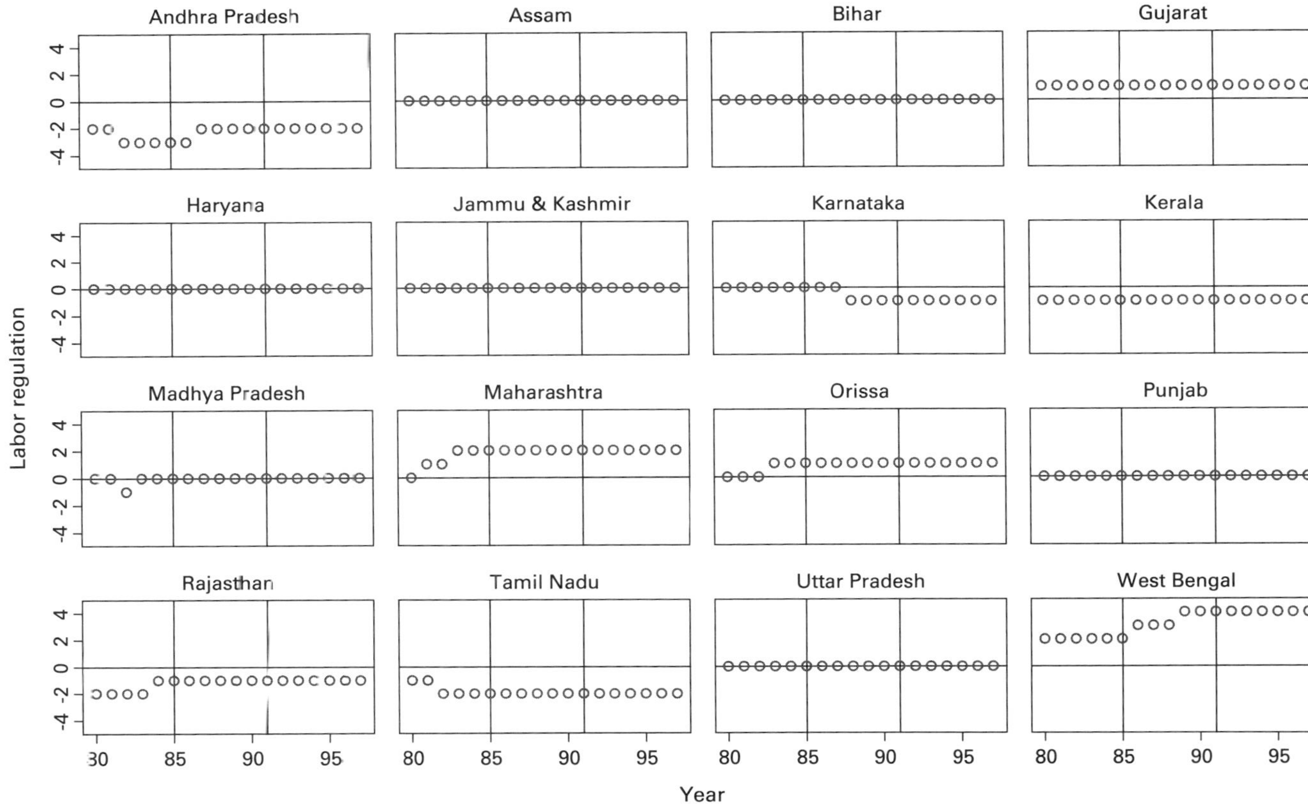

Figure 4.2
Labor regulation in India, 1980–1997. State amendments to the Industrial Disputes Act, cumulated from 1947 to 1997, are coded 1 = pro-worker, 0 = neutral, −1 = pro-employer. From Aghion et al. (2008). Vertical lines denote the two waves of delicensing in 1985 and 1991.

to see whether higher per capita spending in this area confers any advantage when industries are delicensed in India.

These five variables provide a crude characterization of the investment climate in the Indian states. They cover four areas (regulation, access to finance, human capital, and infrastructure) that are typically viewed as central elements of investment climate both globally and within the Indian context (World Bank 2005). They are also areas of policy over which state governments exert some influence, and because India is a federal democracy, there is significant heterogeneity both across states and across time in these variables. It is this heterogeneity that Aghion et al. (2008) exploited in examining whether nationwide delicensing has unequal effects depending on the investment climate in the Indian states.

To link delicensing to investment climate Aghion et al. (2008) used data from the Annual Survey of Industries to track output in sixty-four three-digit industries across the years 1980–1997. This covers the period when delicensing took place in India (see figure 4.1). They denoted the year when each three-digit industry was delicensed and then interacted this delicense variable with investment climate variables. In their preferred specification Aghion et al. (2008) included state-industry fixed effects (to control for time-invariant characteristics of state industries), industry-year fixed effects (to control for time-varying industry effects), and state-year fixed effects (to control for time-varying state effects). Inclusion of these latter two sets of fixed effects precludes estimation of the level effects of delicensing (which varies by industry and year) or of the investment climate variables (which vary by state and year). The focus instead is on the interaction between delicensing and state investment climate measures, which enables the authors to discern whether the effect of delicensing is heterogeneous depending on the investment climate in an Indian state.

Delicensing–investment climate interaction results obtained using this specification are displayed in table 4.1. Column 1 shows the results of the interaction between delicensing and labor regulation. The coefficient is negative and significant. This tells us that when delicensing occurred, industries in states with pro-employer regulation experienced larger increases in output relative to those located in pro-worker states. This is the key result in Aghion et al. (2008). Delicensing magnifies the negative impact of pro-worker labor regulation on industrial performance suggesting, in this case, that liberalization and investment climate are complements.[1] This has two key implications. First, policies

Table 4.1
The Unequal Effects of Liberalization: Evidence from India, 1980–1997

	(1) Log Real Output	(2) Log Real Output	(3) Log Real Output	(4) Log Real Output
Delicense × Labor regulation	−0.054**			0.050**
	(.024)			(.023)
Delicense × Financial development		0.035***		0.025*
		(.014)		(.015)
Delicense × Log education expenditure			−0.194	−0.083
			(.123)	(.135)
Delicense × Log health expenditure			0.125	0.120
			(.129)	(.134)
Delicense × Log other development expenditure			0.244***	0.131*
			(.091)	(.080)
No. of observations	18,324	18,324	18,324	18,324
R-squared	0.92	0.92	0.93	0.93
State-industry fixed effects	yes	yes	yes	yes
State-year fixed effects	yes	yes	yes	yes
Industry-year fixed effects	yes	yes	yes	yes
Standard errors	Cluster State × ydel	Cluster State × ydel	Cluster State × ydel	Cluster State × ydel

Notes:
Robust standard errors adjusted for clustering on state-year delicensed are in parentheses.
*significant at 10% level; **significant at 5% level; ***significant at 1% level.
"Log real output" is log real registered manufacturing output. "Delicense," a dummy variable, = 1 if all or part of a three-digit industry is delicensed in a particular year, 0 otherwise. State amendments to the Industrial Disputes Act are coded 1 = pro-worker, 0 = neutral, and −1 = pro-employer and cumulated over 1947–1997 to generate the labor regulation measure. "Financial development" is from Burgess and Pande (2005), who used the number of bank branches per capita in 1961 interacted with (i) a post-1976 time trend, and (ii) a post-1989 time trend as instruments for state-level bank branch expansion for 1961–2000. I use predicted financial development from this state-year regression interacted with "Delicense." The *F*-statistic for the significance of excluded instruments in the first-stage state-year regression is 16.87. Standard errors in columns 2 and 4 have been adjusted to take account of the fact that predicted financial development is generated in a first-stage regression. "Log of development expenditure" is real per capita state spending on social and economic services; it has been split into three components: education expenditure, health expenditure, and other development expenditure (mainly infrastructure expenditure). The data set is a balanced panel of three-digit state industries that are present in the data in all 18 years, and it includes an average of 64 three-digit industries in 16 states over the period 1980–1997. See Aghion et al. (2008) for further information on variable definitions and data sources.

that are (partly) under state government control (like labor regulation) become a natural target of reform efforts. Put simply, the state of the investment climate is a major determinant of whether, in a relative sense, a state will benefit from, or be harmed by, the nationwide delicensing experiment. Second, because liberalization magnifies the disadvantage of having anti-business labor regulations, the need for reform of the investment climate becomes all the more pressing after delicensing occurs.

Column 2 turns to the delicensing–financial development interaction. The coefficient is positive and significant. This tells us that when delicensing occurred, states that had opened more bank branches in rural, unbanked locations grew more quickly than states with fewer openings.[2] This is a signal that the government-led penetration of the commercial bank network in a state may affect postdelicensing industrial development. This result makes sense. If, in order to expand, firms need to have access to the borrowing and saving facilities offered by commercial banks, then having less access may act like a brake on expansion when delicensing occurs. In effect, firms in states with less access to finance may be put at a disadvantage relative to states with more access when competition intensifies following delicensing. Again, this result places the spotlight on state-level institutions and policies as key determinants of postdelicensing industrial performance.

In column 3 each of the elements of development expenditure (education, health, and other) is interacted with delicensing. The delicensing–education expenditure interaction is statistically insignificant, as is the delicensing–health expenditure interaction. Greater investment in human capital by a state as captured by these two variables did not seem to confer an advantage with regard to postdelicensing rates of industrial growth. This is somewhat surprising but may reflect that these very broad measures do not capture the type of human capital that is relevant to generating growth in manufacturing (e.g., supply of skilled workers).

In contrast, the delicensing–other development expenditure interaction, also shown in column 3, is positive and significant. This tells us that when delicensing occurred, industrial output increased more in states that had invested more in infrastructure. This is an interesting result because it suggests that infrastructural bottlenecks were a key impediment to manufacturing growth in the postdelicensing period. Infrastructure remains largely under government control, and state governments are major providers of all key types of communication, transportation, and power infrastructure, so this result suggests that improving the infrastructural environment in which manufacturing firms are embedded may be a major means for encouraging industrial growth in the postdelicensing period.

Conclusion

The key insight that emerges from this chapter is that liberalization magnifies policy and institutional disadvantages. Parts of a country with policy and institutional conditions that are less conducive to investment and growth are going to do even worse, in a relative sense, after competition-enhancing reforms take place. Firms and industries located in these places do worse than their competitors precisely because they are exposed to less business-friendly labor regulations, have less access to finance, and have weaker infrastructures. Having a better investment climate along these dimensions is clearly complementary with liberalization in terms of achieving higher rates of industrial growth.

The focus of reform should therefore be on the local policy and institutional environment in thinking about how to encourage industrial growth during periods of economic liberalization. And the need for reform of the investment climate becomes all the more pressing after competition-enhancing reforms are introduced.

The challenge for the future is to identify precisely which elements of the industrial environment are important for encouraging industrialization and growth in a changing world. Part of this challenge will have to be met with better measurement of investment climate. The India case study makes it clear that some of the investment climate measures being used were not specific enough to the sector (registered manufacturing) being examined. However, the challenge cannot be fully met without more studies that exploit liberalization episodes in different countries to illuminate the institutional and policy conditions that constrain economic expansion in these different settings. Only in this way can one begin to build up a body of evidence to accurately guide investment climate reform efforts in different countries.

Notes

I am grateful to Oriana Bandiera, Tim Besley, Pranab Bardhan, David Donaldson, Raji Jayaraman, Imran Rasul, and Anthony Venables for useful comments, and to CESifo for financial support. This chapter is based on joint work with Philippe Aghion, Stephen Redding, and Fabrizio Zilibotti (see Aghion et al. 2008).

1. Both Besley and Burgess (2004) and Aghion et al. (2008) demonstrated that moving in a pro-worker direction is associated with falls in industrial output. The negative interaction result in table 4.1 tells us that delicensing magnifies the disadvantage of being a pro-worker state.

2. The variation exploited in obtaining this estimate comes from bank expansion into previously unbanked areas, as driven by the imposition and removal of the 1:4 branch licensing rule (Burgess and Pande 2005).

References

Acemoglu, D., P. Aghion, and F. Zilibotti. 2006. Distance to Frontier, Selection, and Economic Growth. *Journal of the European Economic Association* 4 (1): 37–74.

Acemoglu, D., S. Johnson, and J. A. Robinson. 2001. The Colonial Origins of Comparative Development: An Empirical Investigation. *American Economic Review* 91 (5): 1369–1401.

Aghion, P., R. Burgess, S. Redding, and F. Zilibotti. 2008. The Unequal Effects of Liberalization: Evidence from Dismantling the License Raj in India. *American Economic Review* 94 (4): 1397–1412.

Attanasio, O., P. K. Goldberg, and N. Pavcnik. 2004. Trade Reforms and Income Inequality in Colombia. *Journal of Development Economics* 74 (2): 331–366.

Banerjee, A., and A. Newman. 2005. Inequality, Growth and Trade Policy. Unpublished paper. Massachusetts Institute of Technology.

Bernard, A. B., J. B. Jensen, and P. K. Schott. 2006. Trade Costs, Forms, and Productivity. *Journal of Monetary Economics* 53 (5): 917–937.

Bertrand, M., and F. Kramarz. 2002. Does Entry Regulation Hinder Job Creation? Evidence from the French Retail Industry. *Quarterly Journal of Economics* 117 (4): 1369–1413.

Besley, T., and R. Burgess. 2004. Can Labor Regulation Hinder Economic Performance? Evidence from India. *Quarterly Journal of Economics* 19 (1): 91–134.

Bhagwati, J., and P. Desai. 1970. *India Planning for Industrialization: Industrialization and Trade Policies Since 1951.* New Delhi: Oxford University Press.

Blanchard, O., and F. Giavazzi. 2003. Macroeconomic Effects of Regulation and Deregulation in Goods and Labor Markets. *Quarterly Journal of Economics* 118 (3): 879–909.

Burgess, R., and R. Pande. 2005. Do Rural Banks Matter? Evidence from the Indian Social Banking Experiment. *American Economic Review* 95 (3): 780–795.

Cuñat, A., and M. J. Melitz. 2005. Labor Market Flexibility and Comparative Advantage. ⟨www.crei.cat/activities/crei_seminar/05-06/cu%F1at.pdf⟩.

Dollar, D., and A. Kray. 2002. Growth Is Good for the Poor. *Journal of Economic Growth* 7 (3): 195–225.

———. 2004. Trade, Growth and Poverty. WPS 2615. World Bank.

Frankel, J., and D. Romer. 1999. Does Trade Cause Growth? *American Economic Review* 89 (3): 379–399.

Government of India. 1991. Statement of Industrial Policy. New Delhi.

Hall, R., and C. Jones. 1999. Why Do Some Countries Produce So Much More Output per Worker than Others? *Quarterly Journal of Economics* 114: 83–116.

Hanson, G. 2004. What Has Happened to Wages in Mexico Since NAFTA? In *FTAA and Beyond: Prospects for Integration in the Americas*, ed. T. Estevadeordal, D. Rodrick, A. Taylor, and A. Velasco. Cambridge, Mass.: Harvard University Press.

Hausman, R., and D. Rodrik. 2002. Economic Development as Self-Discovery. NBER working paper 8952.

Holmes, T. J. 1998. The Effect of State Policies on the Location of Manufacturing: Evidence from State Borders. *Journal of Political Economy* 106 (4): 667–705.

Krugman, P. 1981. Trade, Accumulation and Uneven Development. *Journal of Development Economics* 8 (2): 149–161.

Melitz, M. J. 2003. The Impact of Trade on Intra-Industry Reallocations and Aggregate Industry Productivity. *Econometrica* 71: 1695–1725.

Pavcnik, N. 2002. Trade Liberalization, Exit, and Productivity Improvement: Evidence from Chilean Plants. *Review of Economic Studies* 69 (1): 245–276.

Rama, M. 1997. Organized Labor and the Political Economy of Product Market Distortions. *World Bank Economic Review* 11 (2): 327–355.

Rama, M., and G. Tabellini. 1999. Endogenous Distortions in Product and Labor Markets. WPS 1413. World Bank.

Rodriguez, F., and D. Rodrik. 2001. Trade Policy and Economic Growth: A Skeptic's Guide to the Cross-National Evidence. In *NBER Macroeconomics Annual 2000*, ed. B. Bernanke and K. S. Rogoff. Vol. 15, 261–338. Cambridge, Mass.: MIT Press.

Rodrik, D. 2005. Why We Learn Nothing from Regressing Economic Growth on Policies. Working paper. Harvard University.

Rodrik, D., and A. Subramanian. 2004. From "Hindu Growth" to Productivity Surge: The Mystery of the Indian Growth Transition. NBER working paper 10376.

Rosenstein-Rodan, P. 1943. Problems of Industrialization of Eastern and South-Eastern Europe. *Economic Journal* 53: 202–211.

———. 1961. Notes on the Theory of the "Big Push." In *Economic Development for Latin America: Proceedings of a Conference Held by the International Economic Association*, ed. H. S. Ellis with H. C. Wallich. New York: St. Martin's Press.

Rostow, W. W. 1952. *The Process of Economic Growth*. New York: W.W. Norton.

Sachs, J., and A. Warner. 1995. Economic Reform and the Process of Global Integration. *Brookings Papers on Economic Activity* 26 (1): 1–118.

Sanyal, P., and N. Menon. 2005. Labor Disputes and the Economics of Firm Geography: A Study of Domestic Investment in India. *Economic Development and Cultural Change* 53: 825–854.

Stiglitz, J. E. 2002. *Globalization and Its Discontents.* New York: W.W. Norton.

Topalova, P. 2004. Trade Liberalization and Firm Productivity: The Case of India. WP/04/28. International Monetary Fund.

———. 2005. Factor Immobility and Regional Impacts of Trade Liberalization: Evidence on Poverty and Inequality from India. Economic Growth Center, Yale University. ⟨www.isid.ac.in/~planning/Topalova.pdf⟩.

Trefler, D. 2004. The Long and Short of the Canada-U.S. Free Trade Agreement. *American Economic Review* 94: 870–895.

Tybout, J. 2000. Manufacturing Firms in Developing Countries: How Well Do They Do, and Why? *Journal of Economic Literature* 38 (March): 1–44.

Young, A. 1991. Learning by Doing and the Dynamic Effects of International Trade. *Quarterly Journal of Economics* 106: 369–406.

World Bank. 2001. *Globalization, Growth and Poverty: Building an Inclusive World Economy.* Washington, D.C.

———. 2005. *A Better Investment Climate for Everyone. World Development Report 2005.* Washington, D.C.

———. 2009a. Doing Business database. ⟨http://www.doingbusiness.org⟩.

———. 2009b. Enterprise Surveys database. ⟨http://enterprisesurveys.org⟩.

5 Local Democracy and Ethnic Diversity: A Review, a New Framework, and Some Evidence from Indonesian Villages

Oriana Bandiera and Gilat Levy

During the past decade several developing countries have undertaken extensive decentralization programs entailing the devolution of political decision-making power to small local entities. Concurrently, the World Bank and international aid donors have redirected funds toward programs over which local communities hold direct management and control rights.

In both cases, the presumption is that giving decision-making power to local communities is good for the poor because it gives them a voice, thus improving the fit between policies and their needs. This notwithstanding, if village elites dominate the decision-making process, granting decision-making power to local communities might fail to bring the poor's interests to the fore.

To assess whether the devolution of political decision making to local communities keeps its promise of giving the poor a voice, it is important to understand how local democracies aggregate citizens' preferences to decide the size of the local budget and the allocation of funds among different public goods, infrastructure projects, and transfer programs.

For this purpose, one should note that the interests of individuals in a local community differ along several dimensions. Therefore, different types of conflicts interact with governance institutions to determine public choices. This chapter reviews findings on the effects of different governance systems and the two main sources of social conflict, class and ethnic identity, on poverty-related outcomes. It brings together two strands of the literature. The first analyzes the effects of decentralization, local democracy, and community participation to assess whether giving more voice to the poor results in a more favorable allocation of resources. The second analyzes the effects of ethnic diversity on various outcomes of public interest.

We then combine insights from both strands to assess how ethnic and class conflicts interact with governance institutions to determine the allocation of public resources and the welfare of the poor. We do so in the context of a new theoretical framework, illustrated with evidence on the provision of public goods in Indonesian villages characterized by different levels of ethnic diversity and different governance systems.

We analyze a society comprising three groups whose interests clash along two dimensions: the poor and the rich disagree on the extent of redistribution, and people from different ethnic groups disagree on the allocation across different types of public goods because of different preferences.

The principal aim of the analysis is to assess how ethnic diversity affects public finance outcomes under democracy and oligarchy. The key theoretical insight is that the power of elites in local democracies is endogenously determined by the distribution of income and the cohesiveness of the lower classes. In particular, when ethnic divisions within the lower classes create differences in their preferences for public goods, and the share of the ethnic minority is sufficiently large, decision-making power can be seized by a coalition of elites and the ethnic minority, and the policies implemented by the coalition are closer to those that maximize the welfare of elites as ethnic diversity increases.

We complement our theoretical analysis with empirical evidence on local governments' outcomes in Indonesian villages. The institutional and geographical context of Indonesia offers two sources of variation that are ideal for the analysis at hand. First, customary (*adat*) laws create natural differences in the extent of village democracy, ranging from centralized elite decision making to decisions being taken democratically in village meetings. Second, Indonesia is one of the world's most ethnically diverse countries, and the extent of ethnic diversity varies across villages.

This study exploits both features to investigate whether ethnic diversity is associated with elite capture in the sense that spending patterns and infrastructure provisions in an ethnically diverse democracy resemble those of an oligarchy. We find that whenever there is a difference between democratic and oligarchic villages, the difference is decreasing in the level of ethnic diversity. In particular, compared to oligarchic villages, ethnically homogeneous democratic villages devote more resources to education and health and less to public security. In contrast, ethnically heterogeneous democracies are indistinguishable from oligarchies. Finally, democratic and oligarchic villages do not differ in the provision of utilities such as sewage systems, regardless of ethnic diversity.

Local Democracies and Ethnic Diversity in the Developing World

Local Democracy and the Welfare of the Poor

Several developing countries have recently undergone processes of decentralization and democratization, effectively transferring political decision-making powers to local community organizations. The popularity of these reforms naturally raises the question of whether and how the devolution of power to local democracies keeps its promise to give a voice to the poor and improve their welfare.

Theoretical analyses of the political economy of decentralization (Bardhan and Mookherjee 2000) highlight that the answer depends on the balance of two forces. The poor might benefit from the fact that compared to the central government, local governments are better informed of the needs of their citizens and hence likely to be more responsive and offer better service delivery. This notwithstanding, local governments might be more likely to be captured by local elites and hence favor these at the expense of the poor.

Bardhan and Mookherjee (2006a) showed that whether the first, good, effect prevails depends on the degree of fiscal autonomy of local governments and on the severity of elite capture at the local level, which in turn depends on local wealth inequality and other underlying institutional factors. Ultimately, theory indicates that whether giving a voice to the poor effectively helps improve their welfare depends on the specific circumstances of the setting under study and, as such, the question begs empirical investigation.

Empirical analyses of the effect of democracy and decentralization are still in their infancy, mostly because of the lack of adequate data and proper counterfactuals. The earliest contributions exploited cross-country differences in governance structure and found that compared to dictatorships, democracies grow faster and have higher income levels (Barro 1996). Governance institutions, however, are not randomly assigned to different countries, so that the comparison between democracies and dictatorships is inevitably polluted by unobservable country characteristics that determine the choice of governance structures and also affect economic performance.

Four recent studies have tackled the question by exploiting variation at the local government level within the same country. This methodology has the clear advantage of identifying the effect of democracy and community participation by comparing similar units and, as such, provides estimates that are not confounded by country-specific unobservables, although location-specific unobservables might still bias the estimates.

Of the four studies, described below, the first three exploit variation in the level of voice the poor have in different local democracies to assess whether more voice results in a more favorable allocation of resources. The fourth explicitly compares resource allocation in villages with democratically elected local governments and villages traditionally ruled by elites.

Exploiting the variation in institutional arrangements across more than 500 Indian villages, Besley, Pande, and Rao (2005) showed that greater community participation improves service delivery to the poor. Indian law requires local governments to hold villagewide meetings to discuss resource allocation in the village. While meetings are compulsory throughout the country, the frequency at which they are held is at the discretion of the elected local governments. The evidence indicates that holding village meetings improves resource targeting toward the landless and the illiterate.

In line with these findings, Chattopadhyay and Duflo (2004) showed that giving a voice to weaker groups in society improves targeting toward those groups. The evidence from 265 villages in West Bengal and Rajasthan indeed indicates that when the local council leadership is randomly assigned to a woman, the council invests more in infrastructure that relates to rural women's concerns, such as water.

Bardhan and Mookherjee (2006b) shed light on the role of land inequality in determining elite capture and pro-poor targeting. Using a twenty-year panel from eighty West Bengal villages, they showed that inequality does not affect the targeting of publicly provided private goods (working capital credit and agricultural kits) but it does worsen the allocation of local public goods, such as infrastructure projects generating employment for the poor.

Foster and Rosenzweig (2004) exploited cross-time and cross-sectional variation in democracy in a twenty-year panel of 250 Indian villages. They compare resource allocation in villages where the group which makes decisions is democratically elected to villages where elites rule. The findings indicate that in villages with democratic governance, an increase in the share of landless laborers is associated with higher spending on road construction. Since construction projects increase the wage of laborers and thus benefit the landless, the finding is consistent with the hypothesis that giving a voice to the poor does indeed change the allocation of resources in their favor.

Evidence from Community-Based Development Programs

Parallel to the decentralization and democratization of governance, international development institutions and donors have redirected funds toward programs that give local communities direct control over key project decisions, such as management and allocation of funds. The World Bank increased its lending to community-based projects more than sixfold from 1996, reaching $2 billion in 2003 (Mansuri and Rao 2004).

Like decentralized democracy, community-based development initiatives have the potential to give a voice to the poor, exploit the information advantages of local communities, and ultimately improve targeting and service delivery to the poorest segments of the population. Not surprisingly, however, community-based initiatives are also exposed to the risk of elite capture, which can prevent funds from reaching the intended beneficiaries.

A few studies present evidence on the practical relevance of this issue. Gugerty and Kremer (2004) showed that providing financial assistance to eighty rural women's groups in western Kenya did not improve participation rates, assistance to members, or assistance to other community projects. The funding did, however, skew the composition of the groups toward the less needy. Younger, more educated women, women employed in the formal sector, and men joined, and better educated and wealthier women replaced existing leaders.

In a similar vein, Platteau (2004) presented detailed descriptive evidence from sub-Saharan Africa showing how elites are attracted by donations to community projects and manage to capture a large share, sometimes on the grounds of being able to keep accounting books and negotiate with donors.

While empirical evidence on the comparison of community-based initiatives with other ways of funding is lacking, two studies shed some light on the conditions that reduce elite capture and hence improve pro-poor targeting in community-based programs.

Galasso and Ravallion's (2005) analysis of Bangladesh's Food for Education program showed that in villages where income distribution is more unequal pro-poor targeting is less effective, namely, the share of poor households receiving targeted benefits is lower.

Olken's (2006) study of community-based infrastructure projects in Indonesia also showed evidence of elite capture and clear-cut corruption through missing expenditures for materials and labor. Experiments with alternative accountability mechanisms showed that increases in attendance of project meetings by a large segment of the population reduces missing labor expenditures, but audits are more effective at reducing missing expenditures for materials and labor.

The effectiveness, or lack thereof, of community-based initiatives has been discussed in several case studies. Mansuri and Rao's (2004) review of these showed that evidence on success and pro-poor targeting is mixed; effects in different communities are heterogeneous. While the case studies highlighted the link between elite dominance and the strength of the class conflict, the decision-making process at the local level is still not fully understood.

Ethnic Diversity and Public Policies

Studies have uncovered a solid link between the level of social diversity, public finance, and the management of common property resources.[1] In their seminal contribution, Easterly and Levine (1997) showed that ethnic diversity explains cross-country differences in public policies and, through these, in economic growth. Strikingly, ethnic diversity alone explains about 30 percent of the growth differential between the countries of Africa and East Asia.

Theoretical contributions have highlighted four mechanisms through which diversity might affect the choice of public policies, the provision of public goods, and the management of common resources. First, different ethnic groups are likely to have different preferences over the characteristics of the common good (Alesina et al. 1999; Esteban and Ray 1999; Fernandez and Levy 2005). To the extent that ethnically heterogeneous communities find it difficult to agree on the characteristics of the common good, they would be less likely to cooperate in its provision.

Second, individuals of different ethnicity might simply dislike working with each other, thus making cooperation less likely in heterogeneous communities (Alesina and La Ferrara 2000).

Third, the different groups in heterogeneous communities might disagree on how to share the private benefits associated with collective action, or value less the benefits accruing to members of the other groups (Banerjee, Iyer, and Somanathan 2005).

Finally, social heterogeneity might undermine the ability to devise mechanisms that sustain cooperation. For instance, if social sanctions are effective within but not across different groups, heterogeneous communities are less likely to be able to use sanctions as an enforcement mechanism (Gugerty and Miguel 2005).

On the empirical front, Banerjee, Iyer, and Somanathan (2005) showed that in Indian districts heterogeneity along caste and religious lines is associated with a different allocation of resources across local public goods. More heterogeneous districts have a lower share of villages with schools, public transport, and electricity; the provision of communication and health facilities is uncorrelated to the level of heterogeneity; and water facilities, such as wells and hand pumps, are more likely to be found in heterogeneous districts. The latter finding might be a symptom of social disunity to the extent that people do not want to share water with others outside their own social group.

Evidence from more disaggregated data also indicates that heterogeneity is correlated with lower contributions to local public goods. Using cross-sectional data on eighty-four schools in Kenya, Gugerty and Miguel (2005) showed that in areas that are more fragmented along ethnic lines, voluntary monetary contributions to the local school are up to 20 percent lower, and this has a real impact on school quality. Ethnic heterogeneity is indeed negatively correlated with several measures of infrastructure quality and with the availability of textbooks.

Exploiting variation in ethnic diversity across Indonesian villages, Olken (2005) explored the link between diversity and corruption in a government transfer program. He found that the gap between the amount of rice given to local village governments for redistribution to poor households and the amount effectively received by the listed beneficiaries was larger in more diverse communities.

Finally, a related strand of the literature analyzes the effects of community characteristics on the management of common property resources and the maintenance of common assets.

Baland et al. (2007) found that extraction of firewood from common Nepalese forests was up to 17 percent higher in villages that are more heterogeneous along the lines of caste and ethnicity. Dayton-Johnson (2000) showed that social heterogeneity is negatively correlated with the maintenance status of irrigation systems in Mexico. Similarly, Khwaja (2003) showed that heterogeneity along clan, political, and religious lines is negatively correlated with the maintenance status of common infrastructure projects in Pakistan.

Overall, the existing empirical evidence provides some support to the idea that heterogeneity along ethnic, but also religious and economic lines, hampers cooperation in the provision of local public goods and in the management and maintenance of common property resources. More evidence, however, is needed to shed light on the institutional features that can ameliorate the negative consequences of diversity.

Local Decision Making with Class and Ethnic Conflicts: Theoretical Insights

Setup

Our starting point is that the interests of individuals in a local community differ along several dimensions and that the different types of conflicts interact with governance institutions to determine public choices.

To make matters concrete, we focused on two sources of diversity and on two types of governance. In Bandiera and Levy (2006) we modeled the political economy of public decision making when society is divided into groups that differ by income and ethnicity. We compared public finance outcomes under oligarchy—when the rich elites choose public policies to maximize their interests—to decision making under democracy—when decisions are taken by whoever wins a majority vote. Our principal aim was to assess how ethnic diversity affects outcomes under democracy and oligarchy.

The key contribution of our analysis is that it combines the study of the effects of ethnic diversity and of the comparison between democracy and oligarchy to highlight the interplay between the two. We assume there are three groups in society, R, P, and E, where R denotes the rich elites belonging to the dominant ethnic group, P denotes the poor of the dominant ethnic group, and E denotes the poor ethnic minority.

Society chooses the size of the budget (financed via income tax or labor contributions) and how to allocate it between different public goods. Naturally, income heterogeneity makes the optimal budget size differ across agents; the elites prefer a smaller budget than either of the two poor groups.

Following Alesina et al. (1999), we assume that ethnic heterogeneity generates different preferences over different public goods. In particular, we assume there is a general public good, which is enjoyed by all groups, and an "ethnic" public good, which only provides utility to the ethnic minority. We focus on the case of pure public goods, which implies that the cost of providing the good is not related to the number of people using it and that the good must be financed via general taxation.

The Political Process

We compare two governance structures: oligarchy and democracy. In oligarchy, the rich elites choose the size of the local government and how to allocate funds between the general and the ethnic public goods to maximize the utility of their group. Oligarchy is thus an extreme form of elite capture, whereby the interests of other groups in society are ignored altogether.

In democracy there is a political process that translates the economic preferences of the three groups into a policy outcome. To analyze the democratic political process we adopt the model with endogenous political parties developed by Levy (2004). We assume that the three groups, R, P, and E, are represented in the political process by politicians. Politicians care about the implemented policy and can join other politicians to form parties. These parties offer policies on which the voters vote. We assume that each party can only offer credible policies, that is, policies in the Pareto set of its members. This captures the idea that parties allow different factions to reach (efficient) internal compromises.

The political outcome is the policy that receives the largest number of votes. It satisfies three requirements. First, it has to belong to the Pareto set of one of the parties. Second, there is no other party that can win against it while increasing the utility of all its members. Finally, we focus on stable political outcomes, namely, winning policies that are immune to politicians changing their party membership. Parties are therefore endogenous in the model in the sense that we identify the array of political parties and political outcomes such that no group of politicians wish to quit their party.

Ethnic Diversity and the Power of Elites

The characterization of stable political outcomes allows us to determine the composition of the winning coalitions, their tax policies, and the suggested division of tax revenues between the general and the ethnic public goods.

We use this to analyze how the allocation changes with ethnic diversity, captured by the size of the ethnic minority and the extent to which preferences differ across ethnic groups. Our main aim is to assess how changes in these parameters affect outcomes in democracy and oligarchy.

The main result of the model is that the difference between outcomes in democracy and oligarchy is decreasing in the level of ethnic diversity, so that public finance outcomes in ethnically diverse democracies are more similar to the outcomes that emerge when the elites rule. Ethnic diversity thus increases the degree of elite capture in the sense that in an ethnically diverse democracy, the elites manage to obtain an outcome that is closer to their optimum.

The intuition behind the result is as follows. If the share of voters belonging to the ethnic minority is low, P (the poor of the dominant ethnic group) is more likely to have the majority of votes and hence choose the equilibrium policy. As the share of voters belonging to the ethnic minority increases to the point that no group alone has the majority, a unique stable coalition is formed by R (the rich elites) and E (the poor ethnic minority). This follows from the fact that in the absence of parties, the unique winner of the election is P (the poor of the ethnic majority) because E and R disagree with one another on both dimensions but agree with P on one dimension each. Therefore, parties with P are not stable because P can split the party and win by itself. However, the coalition of R and E can win against P if they offer policies in their Pareto set that are better for both than the ideal policy of P.

In this setting, when the preferences of P and E become more disparate, the ethnic minority gets lower utility from the ideal policy of P and is happy to settle for lower public spending in exchange for a positive level of the ethnic good. This implies that the set of policies that can be offered by the coalition of R and E is more favorable to the elites.[2]

The theoretical framework thus illustrates that the effectiveness of democracy in fostering the interests of the poor crucially depends on whether the poor are a cohesive class or whether they are split along ethnic lines. In the former case, democratic outcomes differ substantially from those that would maximize the welfare of the elites. When there is a large enough ethnic minority whose preferences are sufficiently different from those of the majority however, the difference between democracy and oligarchy falls as the elites' policy influence endogenously increases.

Evidence from Indonesian Villages

The Context: Law and Governance in Indonesian Villages

With 700 living languages and over 1,000 ethnic groups, Indonesia is one of the most diverse countries in the world (Gordon 2005). Ethnic diversity dates centuries back and is accompanied by diversity in the traditional laws that regulate life in the 69,000 villages scattered throughout the Indonesian archipelago.

Law scholars and anthropologists describe the Indonesian legal system as pluralistic, whereby modern postindependence Indonesian codes coexist with Dutch colonial law, Islamic law, and traditional *adat* law. Especially in the rural sector, many Indonesians follow the diverse native legal systems known as *adat* laws, which have been used to regulate their territories since well before the arrival of the European colonizers (Lindsey 1999).

Adat laws were first formally mapped by Dutch legal scholars to provide the basis of the legal system used to rule over the indigenous people of Indonesia. *Adat* laws were applicable to all indigenous people in all spheres of life, with a few exceptions to protect the Dutch commercial interests in transactions involving Europeans and Indonesians.

In this spirit, Dutch colonial rule recognized village governments as lawful entities and encouraged self-rule according to *adat* laws. This state of affairs continued after independence until Soeharto took over in 1978. Soeharto's Law 5/79 aimed to make village governance homogeneous throughout the country by imposing uniform local government structures consisting of a headman and a village assembly (LMD). The headman was elected every eight years but was only accountable to the district government, and he appointed the members of the village assembly.

Development projects and assistance were managed by community resilience boards (LKMD). The main purpose of these was to allocate development grants across households and projects within the village and to act as a forum to collect villagers' opinions. Members of the LKMD were also appointed by the headman. Following the demise of Soeharto and the extensive decentralization process, village governments were reformed by Law 22/99, fully enacted by January 2001.

Law 22/99 introduced three main changes. First, it replaced the appointed village assembly with an elected village council (BPD). Elections for both the headman and the council take place every five years, and the headman is directly accountable to the council. Second, the new law gave villages more autonomy in raising local revenues. Third, it encouraged regional diversity by allowing governance structures to follow local *adat* laws.

Evidence from case studies indicates that village headmen belong to the elites and that prior to decentralization, power resided entirely with these.[3] The headmen and the elites could choose whether and how to involve citizens in village governance, ranging from pure oligarchy to participatory democracy (Antlov 2003).

Prior to decentralization, the village government was already responsible for several infrastructure projects, such as maintaining and or building sewage systems, water pipes, health posts, and schools. The village government was also in charge of administering various income and food transfer programs. Village expenditures were financed by a central government grant, combined with villagers' donations and in-kind labor contributions (*gotong royong*). Following decentralization, village governments were also allowed to raise local funds via taxation and the establishment of village enterprises.

Data Description: Governance Institutions and Public Goods

Our main data source is the village modules of the 1997 Indonesian Family Life Survey (IFLS 2). These contain detailed information on public goods, ethnic composition, and *adat* laws at the village level for 259 villages, located in 35 out of the 241 Indonesian districts.

The *adat* laws module provides information on village governance, namely, on the systems employed to take decisions of communitywide importance, such as construction and maintenance of infrastructure. Figure 5.1 shows that governance systems vary considerably across villages. The most common system is consensus building (*musyawarah*), by which citizens in assembly engage in a process of group deliberation leading to consensus. At the other end of the spectrum, there are villages in which local elites or the headmen are solely responsible for making decisions. We categorize the latter as oligarchy, whereas consensus building is combined with majority voting and categorized as democracy. Overall, democratic rule prevails in 73 percent of the sample villages.

Figure 5.2 shows that there is considerable variation in governance systems across villages in the same district. The share of democratic

According to *adat* law, how are decisions of community importance (e.g. construction, celebrations) made?

	Number of Villages (percentage of total)	
consensus building	177 (68.3%)	democracy
voting	12 (4.63%)	democracy
village elites decide	35 (13.5%)	oligarchy
village head + assembly decide	35 (13.5%)	oligarchy

Figure 5.1
Village governance structures.

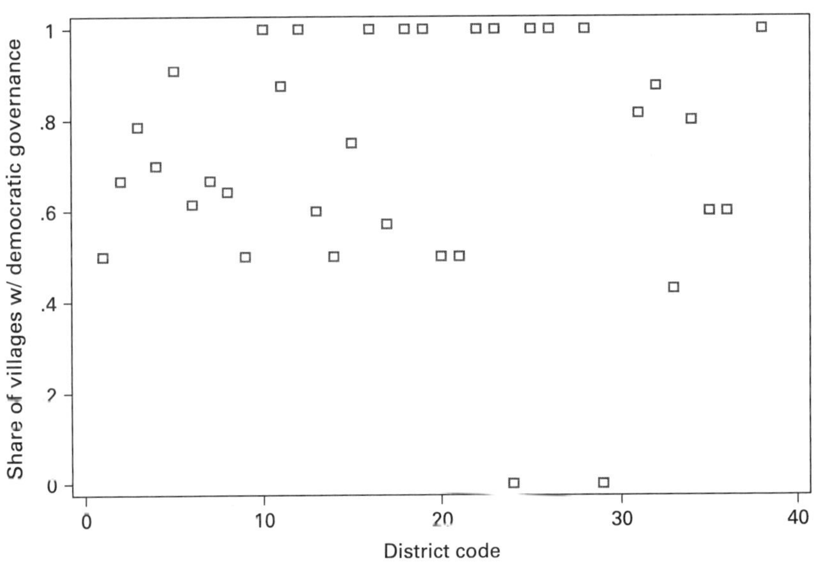

Figure 5.2
Governance structure by district.

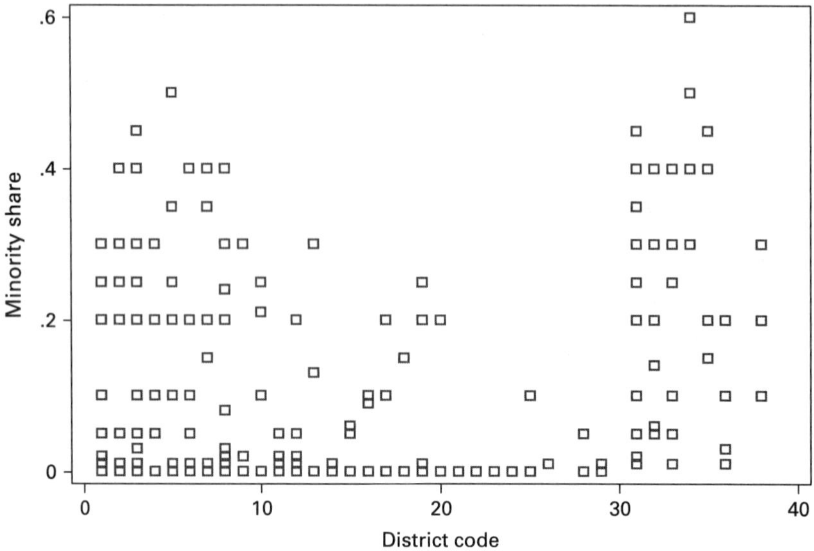

Figure 5.3
Ethnic diversity by district.

villages within a district typically lies between 0 and 1, indicating that democracy and oligarchy coexist in most districts.

During Soeharto's New Order, power resided solely with the headman in every village. Throughout we rely on the assumption that these headmen respected democratic institutions where these traditionally existed according to *adat* law. Obviously, if twenty years of regime managed to successfully erase centuries of *adat* practice, our measure of democracy would only capture the effect of democracy before the 1979 reform rather than current governance structures. This in turn would make it more difficult to find that governance systems affect outcomes.

Our survey contains information on the population shares of the three main ethnic groups in each village. Throughout we measure ethnic diversity with the minority share, namely, the combined population share of the smallest groups. With three groups, only this measure is highly correlated with the fragmentation and polarization indexes used in the literature. Figure 5.3 shows that there is considerable variation in ethnic diversity both across and within districts. At one extreme, 28 percent of villages are ethnically homogeneous; at the other, the dominant group barely constitutes a majority.

Table 5.1
Village Characteristics, by Governance Structure

	Democracy	Oligarchy	difference = 0 p-value
Minority share	.126	.141	.466
	(.011)	(.018)	
Ethnic fragmentation	.190	.211	.456
	(.015)	(.026)	
Population	7221.5	7073.1	.883
	(522.8)	(866.7)	
Rural villages share	.460	.557	.167
	(.036)	(.060)	
IDT villages share	.238	.228	.873
	(.031)	(.050)	
Post office (= 1 if in village)	.208	.186	.686
	(.030)	(.047)	
Public phone (= 1 if in village)	.473	.406	.336
	(.036)	(.059)	
Bus stop (= 1 if in village)	.217	.357	.495
	(.030)	(.053)	
Bank (= 1 if in village)	.367	.328	.568
	(.035)	(.056)	

Note: Standard errors are in parentheses.

Table 5.1 shows that there is no correlation between democracy and ethnic diversity, namely, the average minority share or ethnic fragmentation is identical in democratic and elite-dominated villages. This indicates that there is no endogenous sorting of different ethnicities by governance structure and that it is possible to test whether outcomes in democracy and oligarchy depend on the level of ethnic diversity.

Table 5.1 also shows that democratic and elite-dominated villages are of similar size and have similar communication, transport, and financial facilities. As a proxy for development, we report the share of villages in each category that received IDT (Inpres Desa Tertinggal) funds in 1997. IDT was the main antipoverty program at the time and was targeted to the poorest villages. Governance systems thus do not appear to be correlated with the state of development.

Table 5.2 reports data on a set of public services, ranging from education to health and village security. The data indicate that there is no significant difference by governance structure.

Table 5.2
Public Services and Facilities, by Governance Structure

	Democracy	Oligarchy	difference = 0 p-value
Elementary schools per 1000 inhabitants	.953	.900	.603
	(.059)	(.057)	
Average teacher/student ratio	.049	.045	.063
	(.001)	(.001)	
Health posts per 1000 inhabitants	1.30	1.16	.172
	(.059)	(.062)	
Community security program (= 1 if yes)	.849	.800	.352
	(.048)	(.026)	
Security program members per capita	.135	.120	.558
	(.015)	(.017)	
Village has sewage (= 1 if yes)	.598	.543	.427
	(.036)	(.059)	

Note: Standard errors are in parentheses.

Empirical Analysis

The principal aim of the analysis is to establish whether ethnic diversity affects public goods provision in democracy and oligarchy. We estimate the following model:

$$y^{vd} = \alpha^d + \beta D^v + \gamma D^v \times M^v + \delta M^v + \varepsilon^{vd},$$

where y^{vd} is the outcome of interest, α^d is the district fixed effect, D^v equals 1 if governance is democratic, and M^v is the logarithm of the minority share.

The coefficient of interest throughout is γ, which measures how the outcomes in democracy and oligarchy vary with ethnic diversity. β captures the difference in outcomes between ethnically homogeneous democracies and autocracies. If the difference between democracy and oligarchy is smaller in ethnically diverse communities, we expect γ and β to have opposite signs.

Naturally, the level effect of democracy β cannot be interpreted as the causal effect of democracy on outcomes. Indeed, even if the difference in governance structure dates centuries back, the effect of democracy on outcomes might be proxying for correlated unobservables that have a persistent effect on the outcome of interest.

Likewise, α cannot be interpreted as the causal effect of diversity because variation in diversity might be correlated to unobservables that affect the outcome of interest.

The problem of correlated unobservables is partially ameliorated by the fact that the coefficients of interest are estimated by exploiting the within-district variation. Namely all district-specific omitted characteristics that might create a spurious correlation between the outcome of interest and the right-hand-side variables are absorbed by the district fixed effect α.

Results

Table 5.3 presents estimates of the model for a subset of public services and facilities in the areas of education, health, security, and infrastructure. The outcomes of interest are the number of elementary schools per capita, the teacher/student ratio, the number of community health posts per capita, the existence of public security services, and the presence of a sewage system. The village government and the local community are responsible for the maintenance of school buildings and the constructions of new classrooms, both of which are likely to affect the education measures. In addition, the village government and the local community are directly responsible for establishing and managing health posts, security services, and sewage systems.

Columns 1 and 2 of table 5.3 indicate that ethnically homogeneous democratic villages have more elementary schools per capita and higher average teacher/student ratio compared to ethnically homogeneous oligarchic villages. The interaction term between democracy and diversity is negative and significantly different from zero in both columns, suggesting that ethnic diversity reduces the difference between democracy and oligarchy. For instance, in ethnically homogeneous villages, democracy is associated with a 16 percent increase in schools per capita. An increase in minority share from zero to the mean of 0.12 reduces the difference between democracy and oligarchy to 6 percent. Similarly, in ethnically homogeneous villages, democracy is associated with a 0.7 percent increase in teacher/student ratio. An increase in the minority share from zero to the mean, however, halves the difference between democracy and oligarchy.

Column 3 presents estimates for the number of community health posts (*posyandu*) per thousand inhabitants.[4] The coefficient of the democracy dummy is positive, and the interaction between democracy and diversity is negative and significant at conventional levels. The evidence thus suggests that compared to oligarchic villages, democratic villages have more health posts and the difference is smaller when there is more diversity. An increase in the minority share from zero to the mean halves the effect of democracy.

Table 5.3
Democracy, Diversity, and Public Services

	(1) Elementary Schools per capita × 1000	(2) Teacher/ Student Ratio	(3) Community Health Posts per capita × 1000	(4) Community Security Program	(5) Security Program Members/ Population	(6) Sewage System
Democracy	0.158***	0.007***	0.120**	−0.073	−0.039**	0.041
	(.053)	(.002)	(.054)	(.064)	(.015)	(.126)
Democracy × Minority share	−1.040***	−0.033**	−0.511**	0.772**	0.374***	0.098
	(.344)	(.014)	(.265)	(.366)	(.109)	(.488)
Minority share	0.715***	0.015	−0.001	−1.140***	−0.364***	0.230
	(.241)	(.014)	(.256)	(.377)	(.069)	(.541)
Adjusted R-squared	0.1402	0.0989	0.1418	0.1656	0.2799	0.1445
No. of observations	258	252	255	254	201	258

Notes:
Linear regression with district fixed effects. Standard errors, clustered by district, are in parentheses.
* = significant at 10% level; ** = significant at 5%; *** significant at 1%.
Dependent variables are (1) log of number of elementary schools per thousand inhabitants; (2) log of average teacher/student ratio in the three main elementary schools in the village; (3) log of number of community health posts per thousand inhabitants; (4) dummy variable = 1 if community security program exists, 0 otherwise; (5) log of the ratio of the number of villagers who participate in the security program/village population; (6) dummy variable = 1 if there is a sewage system in the village, 0 otherwise.

Columns 4 and 5 show results for the provision of security services. The survey contains information on whether the community organizes a neighborhood security service and, if so, how many villagers participate. Community security programs are rather widespread; on average 80 percent of villages have one, and the participation rate is around 15 percent.

Columns 4 and 5 show that in contrast to education and health facilities, security services are *less* common and have a lower participation rate in democratic, compared to elite-dominated, villages. In line with previous findings, increase in ethnic diversity reduces the difference between the two systems.

Finally, Column 6 shows that the provision of utilities, in this instance community-operated sewage systems, does not differ by governance structure or level of ethnic diversity.

Overall, the findings are consistent with the interpretation that the difference between democracy and oligarchy depends on the characteristics of the public good in question, namely, on whether the benefits are skewed toward the poor or toward the elites. Goods that benefit both classes equally, such as sewage, are equally provided under both systems. However, democracies have more education and health facilities but devote fewer resources to public security.

Intriguingly, ethnic diversity reduces the difference between the two governance systems, so that outcomes in ethnically diverse democracies resemble those achieved in elite-dominated communities.

Conclusion

To assess whether the devolution of decision-making power to local communities keeps its promise of giving the poor a voice, it is important to know how local democracies aggregate citizens' preferences. This, in fact, determines the size of the local budget and the allocation of funds between different public goods, infrastructure projects, and transfer programs.

We reviewed recent findings and discussed a new theoretical framework designed to analyze the interplay of two-dimensional conflict with governance structure.

The key insight that forms the basis of the theoretical analysis is that the interests of individuals in a local community differ along several dimensions and that therefore the different types of conflicts interact with governance institutions to determine public choices. To highlight conflicts that are practically relevant in most communities, we focused on diversity along the lines of income and ethnic (or religious) identity.

Using an extended citizen candidate model, we showed that the extent of elite capture and hence the effectiveness of democracy in fostering the interests of the poor crucially depend on whether the poor are a cohesive class or are split along ethnic lines. In the former case, democratic outcomes differ substantially from those that would maximize the welfare of the elites. When ethnic diversity increases, however, the elites' policy influence endogenously increases.

We presented evidence on local governments' outcomes in Indonesian villages, exploiting variations in both the extent of democracy and ethnic diversity. We found that ethnic diversity is associated with elite capture in the sense that public policy outcomes in an ethnically diverse democracy resemble those of an elite-dominated oligarchic regime. In particular, compared to oligarchies, ethnically homogeneous democracies have more education and health facilities but devote fewer resources to public security. The difference between oligarchies and ethnically diverse democracies is considerably smaller.

In future work, we plan to apply this theoretical framework to analyze the effects of changes in income inequality and in the characteristics of relevant public goods, allowing for congestion and user fees. Moreover, we plan to extend the empirical analysis to present evidence on the allocation of the village budget and the targeting of pro-poor transfer programs.

These results have important implications for understanding decision making in local democracies and for the design of political institutions in village economies.

Notes

1. See Alesina and La Ferrara (2005) for an exhaustive review of recent studies on the effect of ethnic fragmentation and social heterogeneity on public goods provision in the United States and economic performance across countries.

2. In this setting, the size of the ethnic minority matters only to the extent that the coalition of R and E can win a majority vote. Given that the ethnic good is a pure public good, the size of E does not affect the coalition policies.

3. The cost of running for office effectively acts as a barrier to entry.

4. Community health posts (*posyandu*) are community-sponsored health posts that offer family planning and maternal and child health services. These are run by volunteers from the community with supervision from staff from a government health center (Frankenberg and Thomas 2000).

References

Alesina, A., R. Baqir, and W. Easterly. 1999. Public Goods and Ethnic Divisions. *Quarterly Journal of Economics* 114: 1243–1284.

Alesina, A., and E. La Ferrara. 2000. Participation in Heterogeneous Communities. *Quarterly Journal of Economics* 115: 847–904.

———. 2005. Ethnic Diversity and Economic Performance. *Journal of Economic Literature* 63: 762–780.

Antlov, H. 2003. Village Government and Rural Development in Indonesia: The New Democratic Framework. *Bulletin of Indonesian Economic Studies* 39: 193–214.

Baland, J., P. Bardhan, S. Das, D. Mookherjee, and R. Sarkar. 2007. Inequality, Collective Action, and the Environment: Evidence from Firewood Collection in Nepal. In *Inequality, Cooperation, and Environmental Sustainability*, ed. J. Baland et al. New York: Russell Sage Foundation.

Bandiera, O., and G. Levy. 2006. Diversity, Democracy, and Elite Power. Unpublished paper. London School of Economics.

Banerjee, A., L. Iyer, and R. Somanathan. 2005. History, Social Divisions, and Public Goods in Rural India. *Journal of the European Economic Association* 3 (2-3): 639–647.

Banerjee, A., D. Mookherjee, K. Munshi, and D. Ray. 2001. Inequality, Control Rights, and Efficiency: A Study of Sugar Cooperatives in Western Maharashtra. *Journal of Political Economy* 109: 138–190.

Banerjee, A., and R. Somanathan. 2001. Caste, Community, and Collective Action: The Political Economy of Public Goods Provision in India. Unpublished paper. Department of Economics, Massachusetts Institute of Technology.

Bardhan, P., and D. Mookherjee. 2000. Capture and Governance at Local and National Levels. *American Economic Review* 90 (2): 135–139.

———. 2006a. Decentralization and Accountability in Infrastructure Delivery in Developing Countries. *Economic Journal* 116 (1): 101–127.

———. 2006b. Pro-Poor Targeting and Accountability of Local Governments in West Bengal. *Journal of Development Economics* 79 (2): 303–327.

Barro, R. 1996. Democracy and Growth. *Journal of Economic Growth* 1: 1–27.

Besley, T., and S. Coate. 1997. An Economic Model of Representative Democracy. *Quarterly Journal of Economics* 112: 85–114.

Besley, T., R. Pande, and B. Rao. 2005. Participatory Democracy in Action: Survey Evidence from India. *Journal of the European Economics Association* 3: 648–657.

Bowen, J. R. 2003. *Islam, Law, and Equality in Indonesia: An Anthropology of Public Reasoning*. Cambridge: Cambridge University Press

Chattopadhyay, R., and E. Duflo. 2004. Women as Policy Makers: Evidence from a Randomized Policy Experiment in India. *Econometrica* 72 (5): 1409–1443.

Dayton-Johnson, J. 2000. Determinants of Collective Action on the Local Commons: A Model with Evidence from Mexico. *Journal of Development Economics* 62: 181–208.

Easterly, W., and R. Levine. 1997. Africa's Growth Tragedy: Policies and Ethnic Divisions. *Quarterly Journal of Economics* 112 (4): 1203–1250.

Edmonds, E. 2002. Government-Initiated Community Resource Management and Local Resource Extraction from Nepal's Forests. *Journal of Development Economics* 68: 89–115.

Esteban, J., and D. Ray. 1999. Conflict and Distribution. *Journal of Economic Theory* 87: 379–415.

Fernandez, R., and G. Levy. 2005. Diversity and Redistribution. NBER working paper 11570.

Foster, A. D., and M. R. Rosenzweig. 2004. Democratization and the Distribution of Local Public Goods in a Poor Rural Economy. ⟨adfdell.pstc.brown.edu/papers/democ.pdf⟩.

Frankenberg, E., and D. Thomas. 2000. The Indonesian Family Life Survey (IFLS): Study Design and Results from Waves 1 and 2. RAND Corporation. DRU-2238/Vols 1–7 NIA/NICHD.

Galasso, E., and M. Ravallion. 2005. Decentralized Targeting of an Anti-Poverty Program. *Journal of Public Economics* 85: 705–727.

Gordon, R. G., Jr., ed. 2005. *Ethnologue: Languages of the World.* 15th ed. Dallas, Tex.: SIL International. ⟨http://www.ethnologue.com/⟩.

Gugerty, M. K., and M. Kremer. 2004. The Rockefeller Effect. Paper presented at the Fourth Conference on Development Economics, Bureau for Research and Economic Analysis of Development (BREAD).

Gugerty, M. K., and E. Miguel. 2005. Ethnic Diversity, Social Sanctions, and Public Goods in Kenya. *Journal of Public Economics* 89 (11/12): 2325–2368.

Khwaja, A. 2003. Can Good Projects Succeed in Bad Communities? Collective Action in the Himalayas. RWP 01-043. Kennedy School of Government, Harvard University.

La Ferrara, E. 2002. Inequality and Group Participation: Theory and Evidence from Rural Tanzania. *Journal of Public Economics* 85: 235–273.

Levy, G. 2004. A Model of Political Parties. *Journal of Economic Theory* 115 (2): 250–277.

Lindsey, T. 1999. An Overview of Indonesian Law. In *Indonesia: Law and Society*, ed. T. Lindsey. Leichardt, New South Wales: Federation Press.

Mansuri, G., and V. Rao. 2004. Community-Based and -Driven Development: A Critical Review. *World Bank Research Observer* 19 (1): 1–39.

Olken, B. 2005. Monitoring Corruption: Evidence from a Field Experiment in Indonesia. NBER working paper 11753.

———. 2006. Corruption and the Costs of Redistribution: Micro Evidence from Indonesia. *Journal of Public Economics* 90 (4-5): 853–870.

Osborne, M., and A. Slivinski. 1996. A Model of Political Competition with Citizen Candidates. *Quarterly Journal of Economics* 111: 65–96.

Platteau, J.-P. 2004. Monitoring Elite Capture in Community-Driven Development. *Development and Change* 35 (2): 223–246.

6 Local Accountability Improves Health Services

Martina Björkman, Ritva Reinikka, and Jakob Svensson

As policymakers in developing countries search for ways to improve health and education for the poor—which, in turn, would boost economic and social development—it is becoming clear that more is required than just additional funds. A key obstacle to better public services looks to be the weak incentives that providers face. Schools and health clinics are not open when they should be. Teachers and health care workers are frequently absent from schools and clinics, and even when there, they spend a significant amount of time not serving the intended beneficiaries. Equipment, even when working, is not used. Drugs are misused, and public funds are expropriated.[1]

As some observers argue, this evidence reflects failures in street-level institutions and governance, that is, in the relationships of accountability for providers. Although these failures directly hinder economic and social development, they have until recently received much less attention in the literature than weaknesses in macroeconomic institutions. In public service delivery, there are two vital relationships of accountability: provider-to-state and provider-to-citizen/clients.

In the provider-to-state relationship, the policymaker provides resources and delegates power and responsibility for collective objectives to the service providers. Enforceability and answerability (getting information about performance) come into play when the policymaker specifies the rewards (and possibly the penalties) for the service provider's actions and outputs. In practice, enforceability and answerability are achieved through delegation. Someone in the institutional hierarchy is assigned to monitor, control, and reward or penalize agents further down the hierarchy (the providers). The tacit assumption is that more and better enforcement of rules and regulations will strengthen the providers' incentives to increase both the quantity and quality of service provision.

Delegation and central monitoring is by far the most common approach to holding providers accountable. But in many poor countries the institutions assigned to monitor providers are weak and malfunctioning, and they may act in a system that provides few incentives to effectively monitor the providers. As a result, the relationship of accountability between provider and state is ineffective.[2]

Partly in response to the failures of these traditional mechanisms of enforceability and answerability, a growing number of experts argue that more emphasis must be placed on strengthening beneficiary control, that is, strengthening providers' accountability to citizens/clients.[3] How best to do this in practice and whether it works remain open questions, which until recently have been little researched.

To shed more light on this issue, a major study was recently undertaken in Uganda to assess the impact of one possible type of intervention: community-based monitoring. This chapter discusses the results of the study, a randomized field experiment in the primary health care sector (Björkman and Svensson 2009). The encouraging news is that a properly designed intervention can greatly improve both the quality and quantity of health care provision. In Uganda's case, there were new or stronger practices and processes, better treatment practices, a better use of services, and better health outcomes, such as a lower mortality rate for children under five years of age.

Value of Community Monitoring

How is accountability achieved in the public sector? To begin to answer this question, consider how accountability is achieved in the market contexts. In the private market dissatisfied consumers can use the exit option—if the price is too high or the quality too low, consumers can choose not to buy the good or to buy from another producer. If many consumers act in the same way, this will influence the producer's profitability and, in the end, its survival in the market. But the exit mechanism may not work well in the public sector. In some cases there may be no easily available alternative to the local public provider, say, a primary health clinic. More important, the link between the public provider's performance and its financial position (or its staff's remuneration) is often weak or nonexistent. Typically, public wages are not based on the number of patients treated and the performance of the treatment, and hiring, salaries, and promotions are determined largely by seniority and educational qualifications.[4]

Governments have tried to compensate for the lack of a well-functioning exit mechanism or competition effect by increasing control and supervision. Indeed, the political agency literature shows that when individuals and households are well informed and have mechanisms to sanction politicians, for example, the right to vote them out of office, politicians have potentially strong incentives to monitor and pressure public institutions to do what individuals and households want.[5] But the mounting evidence of failure in street-level institutions across the developing world suggests that this mechanism alone is not enough.

Why doesn't the political system generate demand for stronger supervision and control of providers? There are at least three explanations. First, supervision and control are not performed solely by politicians but instead are delegated to various institutions and agencies. And given that many poor countries lack the trustworthy machinery and institutions (judges, court personnel, police, and auditors) to supervise and enforce rules, politicians, even if so inclined, are restricted in supervising and controlling providers.

Second, while well-functioning legal and financial systems can curtail obvious mismanagement, they only partly constrain the discretionary powers of public sector managers and employees. The complexity of the tasks performed by a typical public sector unit and its informational advantage relative to users make it nearly impossible to design legal and accounting measures for all types of misuse and thus to curtail less obvious cases of mismanagement (such as shirking, political considerations, and budget priorities in favor of staff).

Third, campaigning for a crackdown on poorly performing health staff may not be a winning strategy (Chaudhury et al. 2006). Providers are an organized interest group; clients, particularly in health, are diffuse. Those poor enough to use public clinics may have less political power than the better organized and middle-class health workers. In many countries, including Uganda, people who are moderately well off use private clinics. This pattern may create a self-reinforcing cycle of low quality, exit of the politically influential from the public sector, and further deterioration (Chaudhury et al. 2006; Hirschman 1970). This effect is compounded by the users' lack of information on service delivery outcomes.

As studies have shown, people have private information about health outcomes and whether the provider did anything to help them, but they are unlikely to hold a distant politician accountable for this experience (see, e.g., Khemani 2007). They typically do not have information on aggregate development outcomes, such as how many children in their community did not survive beyond age five, where citizens on average seek care, and the extent of immunization of children in the community. Even if people can guess that others in their neighborhood are suffering similar tragedies, they might be skeptical about using these estimates as an indicator of politicians' performance, focusing instead on actions they can directly observe, such as announcements of a price subsidy, job provision, or infrastructure construction. Politicians respond accordingly: they will focus attention on inefficient, and sometimes ineffective, policies of targeted transfers, in the process shifting efforts and resources away from supervision and reform of the public sector (Keefer and Khemani 2005). The public in turn understands these incentives and expects little from providers meant to serve them.

In response to these constraints, it has been argued that more emphasis must be placed on strengthening beneficiary control. In theory, beneficiary control or community monitoring has at least three advantages:

- It is likely to be cheaper for beneficiaries to monitor providers because they are better informed about the staff's behavior (at least as a group) than an external agent assigned to supervise the provider.
- Beneficiaries may have means to punish providers who are not available to others, such as verbal complaints or social opprobrium (Banerjee and Duflo 2005).
- To the extent that the service is valuable to them, beneficiaries should have strong incentives to monitor and reward or punish the provider—incentives that an external agent may lack.

But there can also be large problems in community-based monitoring:

- Compiling information about performance (answerability) and acting on this information are subject to (possibly large) free-riding problems. In other words, the community would like to ensure that the provider performs, but everyone would prefer that someone else collect information and monitor performance.
- Beneficiary control is unlikely to work if citizens do not have a high demand for the service or have easy access to available and affordable alternatives (private providers). If so, the expected relative return for monitoring the public provider will be low.

- The community must have some direct or indirect way of sanctioning or rewarding the provider (or some higher arm of the state).
- Any project, and perhaps any community-based intervention, may be subject to capture. That is, the elite may corrupt the collection or dissemination of information or prevent citizens from speaking out or putting pressure on the provider.

In the end, whether provider accountability to citizens/clients can be strengthened and whether this type of local accountability reform improves outcomes are empirical questions. In the following sections we discuss a recent attempt to address the question: a randomized field experiment on community-based monitoring in the primary health care sector in Uganda by Björkman and Svensson (2009).

Novel Elements of the Field Experiment

What are the challenges in establishing whether strengthening providers' accountability to citizen-clients can improve outcomes? The first is that an intervention has to be designed and implemented so that it enhances the ability of citizens/clients to monitor and control the provider.

In an effort to deal with the first challenge, the recent Ugandan study by Björkman and Svensson (2009) was designed to improve access to information and boost local participation and organizational capacity. Access to reliable and structured information about the beneficiaries' experiences and entitlements (as a group) improves users' ability to challenge abuses because reliable quantitative information is more difficult for service providers to brush aside as anecdotal, incomplete, or irrelevant. Enhanced participation and local organizational capacity, by contrast, mitigate collective action problems and get citizens to act on the information provided.

A citizen report card is one type of intervention that gives these elements a central focus. It collects feedback from users (and potential users) of public services (in this case primary health care providers). The findings are disseminated back to the citizen-users so that they have reliable information on how their community views the quality and efficacy of service delivery. The report cards also provide the community with an opportunity to compare service delivery in their community with service delivery in other communities or across districts and municipalities in the country. The methodology emphasizes the active dissemination of information through participatory approaches where the community actively interprets and analyzes the information. The participatory methodology is aimed at creating awareness and nurturing community engagement.

The second challenge is evaluating the impact of the intervention, which involves establishing a credible comparison group—a group of observational units (communities) that would, in the absence of the intervention, have had outcomes similar to those exposed to it.

Björkman and Svensson's study deals with this challenge by relying on a randomized design. That is, by randomly assigning communities to a treatment group (communities in which the citizen report card project was implemented) and a control group (communities in which the citizen report card project was not implemented), we can be fairly confident about the absence of confounding factors. In addition, the intervention that the study evaluates was run on a large scale—about 5,000 households from fifty communities covering nine districts in Uganda, surveyed in two rounds of about 110,000 households in the treatment and control communities. This large scale increases confidence in the external validity of the results.

Shape of Uganda's Health Sector

Uganda, like many newly independent African countries, had fairly accessible and affordable health care in the early 1960s. But government services collapsed in the 1970s and 1980s as the country underwent political upheaval, and health indicators fell dramatically until peace was restored in the late 1980s. Since then, the government has carried out a major rehabilitation of the public health sector's infrastructure, improving some health indicators but not others. For example, the infant mortality rate stagnated at 88 deaths per 1,000 live births in the second half of the 1990s (Möller 2002). Maternal mortality has remained high, and immunization rates have stagnated since the late 1990s. All this despite GDP growth of 64 percent and a dramatic (about 40 percent) drop in poverty in the 1990s (Appleton 2001).

Since 2001, public health services have been free of charge. But anecdotal and survey evidence suggests that users still encounter costs that deter many users, especially the poor.

Uganda's health sector comprises four types of facilities: hospitals, health centers, dispensaries (health center III), and aid posts or subdispensaries. These facilities can be government, private for-profit, or private not-for-profit. The focus of the impact evaluated in the Ugandan study is on dispensaries, which are closest to the users. Most dispensaries in Uganda are rural (89 percent), and they are staffed by a clinical officer (typically a medical doctor), nurses (including midwives), and nursing aides or other assistants. The standard for dispensaries includes preventive, promotional, outpatient, maternity, and general ward care and laboratory services, according to the government health sector strategic plan (Republic of Uganda 2000).

In Uganda's decentralized health sector, dispensaries are supervised and controlled at the district level, where several actors such as the Health Sub-district and the Director of District Health Services are responsible for their functioning. The most important local actor is the Health Unit Management Committee (HUMC), the main link between the community and the health facility. Each dispensary has an HUMC comprising members from the health facility staff (those in charge) and community representatives.

The Health Sub-district monitors funds, drugs, and service delivery at the dispensary. Supervision meetings by the Health Sub-district are supposed to be quarterly, but monitoring, in practice, is infrequent (Björkman and Svensson 2009). The Health Sub-district and the Director of District Health Services have the authority to reprimand health facility staff for indiscipline but cannot dismiss. The District Service Commission is the appointing authority for the district with authority to suspend or dismiss staff. Another important actor in local health service delivery is community-based organizations (CBOs).

Using Citizen Report Cards

The citizen report card project evaluated by Björkman and Svensson (2009) was carried out by staff from the World Bank and Stockholm University in cooperation with Ugandan practitioners, eighteen community organizations, and the Uganda Ministry of Health's Planning Division. The project was initiated at the end of 2004 and was evaluated in early 2006.

The fifty project facilities (all in rural areas) were drawn from nine districts. With the catchment area (or the community) of each dispensary defined as the households and villages residing within a 5 km radius, about 110,000 households reside in the communities supposedly served. The facilities were stratified first by location (district) and then by the number of households in the catchment areas. From each group twenty-five facilities, with corresponding catchment areas, were randomly assigned to the treatment group, and the remaining twenty-five facilities were assigned to the control group. Each district thus had both treatment and control groups.[6]

The citizen report card project had four components:

- Collecting quantitative information from users (citizens) and service providers using microsurvey techniques.
- Presenting this information in report cards easily accessible to the community.
- Disseminating the report cards using a participatory approach to users and providers to create awareness and invoke participation.
- Encouraging communities to develop a plan that identified steps that the providers and the community should take to improve service provision and get the community more actively involved in monitoring the providers.

The report card project and the final evaluation drew heavily on two surveys, one of health care providers and one of health care users. Both surveys were implemented prior to the intervention and one year after the project had been initiated. For the household survey a stratified random sample of roughly 5,000 households was interviewed within the catchment areas of the fifty project facilities.[7]

The data from the two preintervention surveys were analyzed, and a subset of the findings was assembled in report cards for the treatment localities.[8] The data in the report cards covered key areas for improvement, including use, services, drugs, user charges, and comparisons with other health facilities in the district and country. Each treatment facility and its community had a unique report card summarizing, in a format easily accessible to the communities, the findings of the survey conducted in their area.

The report cards were translated into the main local languages. To support the illiterate community members, posters were designed and painted by a graphic artist so that otherwise complex information and concepts would be easily understood. Because the information in the report cards was largely statistical, the posters conveyed the main ideas, such as where people go to seek medical care and why they do so.

The report card information was disseminated to citizens and providers by staff from local CBOs, who used a "participatory rural appraisal" approach.[9] The facilitators were perceived to be a good conduit for delivering the citizen report cards because they constantly interacted with the communities and had a mandate drawn from a long-term presence on the ground.[10]

The objective of dissemination was threefold:

- Allow community members to analyze and draw conclusions from the summary findings in the report cards.
- Develop a shared view on how to monitor the health service provider by debating the various elements of accountability in the primary health sector (who is accountable to whom, what a particular actor is accountable for, how these actors can account for their actions, and how these elements are reflected in the report card findings).
- Ensure that the process was not captured by the elite or any other subgroup of the community.

To achieve these objectives, a variety of methods were used, including maps, diagrams, role play, focus group discussions, and action planning.[11] The process of information dissemination and participation was initiated through three separate meetings: a community meeting, a staff meeting, and an interface meeting.

The community meeting was a two-day (afternoon) event with typically more than 150 participants invited from the surveyed villages in the health facility's catchment area. The participants included representatives from all walks of life (young, old, disabled, women, mothers, leaders). And the facilitators mobilized the villagers by cooperating with local council representatives in the catchment area.

During the meeting, facilitators shared the report card information and presented information on patients' rights and entitlements, using methods that aimed to solve the collective action problem. Because the objective was not only to inform but also to encourage people to participate in developing a shared view on how to improve service delivery and monitor the provider, the facilitators structured the discussions through a series of questions on the various elements of accountability in the primary health sector (*Who* is accountable to *whom*? *What* is a particular actor accountable *for*? *How* can these actors account for their actions? How are these elements reflected in the report card findings?). The participants were divided into focus groups (women, men, old, leaders, youth) so that each group could discuss issues specific to them.

At the end of the meeting, community members drew up their own appraisals and action plan, assuming no additional resources. The plan focused on health issues and services that had been identified as the most important and urgent, on how these issues could be addressed, and on how the community could monitor progress. Participants were given posters and copies of the report card to take back to their villages and share with other villagers.

The health facility staff meeting was a one-day (afternoon) event held at the health facility, with all staff present. Facilitators used the report card to contrast the information on service provision as reported by the provider with the findings from the household survey. The meeting enabled providers to review and analyze their performance and compare their performance with other health clinics in the district and country.

The interface meeting brought participants (chosen at the community meeting) from villages in the catchment area together with the health facility staff. Drawing on the action plan developed in the community meeting and the discussions from the health facility meeting, the group devised a joint strategy (a shared action plan) for better health care provision, including what needed to be done, how it would be done, when it would be done, by whom, and how the community would monitor the process. In the process of devising the consensus plan there was a role-playing exercise, with community participants and staff reversing roles to better understand their rights and responsibilities as patients or medical staff.

After the initial three meetings, the communities were left alone to monitor the providers, as agreed on in the action plan. The CBOs were asked to support the communities in their continuing monitoring, with follow-up meetings as part of the CBOs' ordinary work in the villages.

Six months later the communities and health facilities were revisited for a midterm review, a repeat engagement on a smaller scale. The review, which included a one-day community meeting and a one-day interface meeting, tracked implementation of the action plan, identified new areas of concern (if any), and came up with a new set of recommendations for improvement. Health facility staff and community members then jointly discussed suggestions on actions for sustaining or improving progress. Where improvements had not been made, new recommendations were agreed on and noted in an updated action plan. Where improvements had been made, suggestions for sustainability were recorded.

Better Incentives Pay Off

What did the citizen report card study show? Björkman and Svensson's (2009) study showed that overall there were improvements in a variety of outcomes, both in the quantity and quality of health service provision.[12]

New or Stronger Practices and Processes

Although the citizen report card project was a structured intervention, it left plenty of room for the communities to choose whether and how to react to the information disseminated. As discussed earlier, one of the obstacles with community monitoring is the problem of collective action. That is, everybody in the community wants to see a change, but everyone would rather see someone else exert the effort of monitoring the providers. In the citizen report card project in Uganda, the information and the applied participatory approaches were aimed at not only sparking community action but also providing citizens with hard data and encouragement to monitor and evaluate the health facility.

To avoid influencing local initiatives, the evaluation team decided not to have enumerators spend time in the field after the first round of meetings. Even so, the team was able to glean information on how processes in the community had changed. To begin with, the CBOs submitted reports on changes observed. The evidence from these reports suggests that the project influenced the way providers were monitored. This evidence is supported by facility and household survey data as well as data assembled through a local council survey.

According to the CBO reports, the community monitoring that followed the first set of meetings (community, facility, and interface meetings) was a joint effort managed mainly by the village local councils, the Health Unit Management Committee, and the community members. The performance of the health facility was discussed during village meetings. The local council surveys confirm this claim. A typical village had, on average, six meetings in 2005. In those meetings 89 percent of the villages discussed specific issues concerning the project health facility and the action plan.

The CBOs report that concerns raised by the village members were carried forward by the local council to the health facility or the HUMC. Although the HUMC was viewed as an entity that should monitor the provider, it was often viewed as ineffective. As a result, mismanaged HUMCs were dissolved, and others felt pressure from the community to actively follow up on the issues covered in the action plan. Once again, these reports are confirmed in the survey data: more than one-third of the HUMCs in the treatment communities were dissolved and received new members following the initial intervention. Further, the CBOs report that the community also monitored health facility staff during health visits to the clinic, questioning issues in the action plan that had (or had not) been addressed.

In addition, tools such as suggestion boxes (for comments on changes supposed to have taken place), numbered waiting cards (to ensure first-come, first-served), and duty rosters were established in several treatment facilities. The facilities posted more information about free services and patient's rights and obligations.[13] And they held more discussions about their own performance in village meetings.

Better Treatment Practices

Drawing on several quantitative indicators, Björkman and Svensson (2009) showed that treatment practices and staff behavior improved.

One measure of treatment practices is *examination procedures*. This indicator showed that, about half of the patients in the treatment community reported that equipment (such as a thermometer or blood pressure equipment) was used during the examination. But in the control communities, only 41 percent reported that equipment was used the last time the respondent (or respondent's child) visited the project clinic.[14]

A second measure is *patient waiting time*, defined as the difference between the time the user left the facility and the time the user arrived at the facility minus the examination time. On average, the waiting time was 119 minutes in the treatment facilities, a marked improvement over the 131 minutes in the control facilities.

A third measure is *staff absenteeism*. On average, the absence rate—defined as the ratio of workers not physically present at the time of the postintervention survey to the number of workers employed—was 13 percentage points lower in the treatment facilities (compared to the 47 percent absenteeism rate in the control facilities).

A fourth measure is *information sharing*. For this indicator, households in the treatment communities were better informed about various aspects of service provision following the intervention. For example, a significantly larger number of households received information about the dangers of self-treatment and the importance of visiting a health clinic for medical treatment and family planning.

A final measure is *immunization coverage*. The household survey collected information on how many times (doses) each child had been immunized against polio, DPT, BCG, and measles. To the extent possible, these data were collected from immunization cards, then compared with the national immunization schedule put out by the Uganda National Expanded Program on Immunization. Next, mean outcomes—the share of children for each age group (0–12 months, 13–24 months, 25–36 months, 37–48 months, and 49–60 months) that received the required doses of measles, DPT, BCG, and polio vaccines—were compared.

The results showed that the treatment communities had significantly higher immunization rates than the control communities for all four vaccines. For example, in the treatment group, twice as many newborns received vitamin A supplements, and for BCG and polio, the difference was positive (46 and 42 percent, respectively) and significant in the youngest age group. But the differences were not significant in all age groups.

Better Use of Services

For this indicator, Björkman and Svensson (2009) exploited two sources of information on the use of services. First, detailed information on the outpatients, deliveries, antenatal care patients, and people seeking family planning services was assembled from the health facility's records. These data were collected by counting the number of patients from the health facility's daily patient records, maternity unit records, the antenatal care register, and the family planning register. Second, detailed information on each household member's decision of where to seek care in case of illness that required treatment was collected in the household survey.

Based on facility records, the study shows improved use in all of the service areas for the treatment group. One year into the program, use (for general outpatient services) was 20 percent higher in the treatment facilities. The number of deliveries at the facility was up 58 percent (albeit from a low level). And the number of patients seeking antenatal care (19 percent) and family planning (22 percent) also rose, and these estimates are jointly significantly different from zero.

A similar pattern of better use of services is evident from the household data. The increase, 11–13 percent higher in the treatment group than in the control group, is similar to that found using facility records. The use pattern from the household data also reveals that households in the treatment group reduced visits to traditional healers and the extent of self-treatment following the intervention, although there were no statistically significant differences across the two groups in the use of other providers (not-for-profit and for-profit facilities). Thus, households in the treatment communities switched from traditional healers and self-treatment to the project facility in response to the intervention.

Better Health Outcomes

In the ex-post evaluation survey, data were collected on whether the household suffered from the death of a child (under five years of age) in 2005, the first year of the community monitoring project. The average under-five mortality rate in the treatment community was 97 per 1,000, markedly lower (about 33 percent) than the average rate of 144 in the control community. With about 55,000 households residing in the treatment communities, the treatment effect corresponds to 550 averted under-five deaths following the intervention, with children younger than two years driving this reduction in under-five mortality.

As for infant weight, the study focused on weight-for-age *z* scores for all infants (under 18 months) and children (18–36 months).[15] The difference in mean *z* scores was 0.14, which corresponds to a reduction in average risk of mortality of about 7 percent.

Going Forward

Identifying and implementing incentives that strengthen accountability between service providers and beneficiaries is critical for better service delivery. How to best do this in practice and whether it works remain open questions. This chapter discussed the pros and cons of one type of intervention—community monitoring—and illustrated the potential impact using recent evidence from a randomized field experiment of a Ugandan citizen report card project in primary health care (Björkman and Svensson 2009).

The citizen report card project evaluated by Björkman and Svensson (2009) was successful in many dimensions, with both the quality and quantity of health service provision improving significantly in the treatment communities. One year into the program, average use was 20 percent higher in the treatment communities, the weight of infants was higher, and the number of deaths among children under five years was markedly lower. Treatment communities had become more involved in monitoring the providers, and the health unit staff had responded by trying harder to serve the community.

But while the initial outcomes of the project are promising, several outstanding issues remain. One issue is sustaining the processes initiated by the citizen report card project. Since the project is ongoing—scaled up to involve an additional twenty-five health facilities—the process can be studied over time. It is also possible that even better results can be achieved by combining bottom-up monitoring (community monitoring) with a top-down approach (supervision and possibly sanctions or rewards from someone in the institutional hierarchy assigned to monitor and control the primary health care providers).

Another issue is subjecting the project to a cost-benefit analysis and relating the cost-benefit outcomes to other possible interventions. This would require putting a value on the improvements documented in the Ugandan study. To provide a flavor of such analysis, consider the findings on averting the death of a child under five years. A back-of-the-envelope calculation suggests that the cost per death averted, $300, must be considered cost-effective. Compare that with the cost of averting a child death by increasing public expenditures on health ($47,112–$100,927) or by making more conventional treatments ($1,000–$10,000 for diarrheal diseases, $379–$1,610 for acute respiratory infections, $78–$990 for malaria, and $836–$3,967 for pregnancy complications).[16]

The bottom line is that experimentation and evaluation of new tools to enhance accountability should be an integral part of the research agenda for improving social service outcomes. And research on what works and what doesn't is clearly lagging behind policy.

Notes

1. For anecdotal and case study evidence, see *World Development Report 2004* (World Bank 2004). Chaudhury et al. (2006) provided systematic evidence on the rates of absenteeism in primary schools and health clinics in seven developing countries. The absenteeism rates are based on surveys in which enumerators made unannounced visits to the schools and clinics. Averaging across countries, 35 percent of health care workers were found absent. Banerjee, Deaton, and Duflo (2004) and Duflo and Hanna (2005) confirm these findings. On misappropriation of public funds and drugs, see Reinikka and Svensson (2004) and McPake et al. (1999).

2. As an example, most anticorruption programs rely on legal and financial institutions—judiciary, police, and financial auditors—to enforce and strengthen accountability in the public sector. But in many poor countries, these legal and financial institutions are often corrupt. Not surprisingly, there is scant evidence that devoting additional resources to existing legal and financial government monitoring institutions reduces corruption (Svensson 2005).

3. See, for example, the *2004 World Development Report* (World Bank 2004).

4. This is the case not only in Uganda's health sector but also in developing countries more generally. See, for example, Chaudhury et al. (2006).

5. For references and textbook treatment of the literature, see Persson and Tabellini (2000).

6. See Björkman and Svensson (2009) for details on the sampling procedure.

7. See Björkman and Svensson (2009) for a detailed explanation of the design and implementation of the surveys.

8. The design and size of the surveys were largely driven by the second objective—to evaluate impact.

9. "Participatory rural appraisal" is a label given to a growing family of participatory approaches and methods with the common aim of enabling people to make their own appraisal, analyses, and plans. It evolved from a set of informal techniques used by development practitioners in rural areas to collect and analyze data.

10. As noted in Björkman and Svensson (2009), the various CBOs (including some participating in the project) also operate in the control districts. Thus, the presence (and numbers) of CBOs in the project communities is similar across treatment and control groups.

11. See Björkman and Svensson (2009) for a more detailed description of the various methods.

12. Here, it should be noted that thanks to the randomized design of the project, causal effects can be determined by comparing means across treatment and control groups.

13. These data were collected through visual checks by the enumerators. See Björkman and Svensson (2009) for more details on the data collection procedure.

14. There is no easily measured indicator to evaluate whether patients in the project facilities receive better treatment. Naturally, the relevant treatment is conditional on illness and the condition of the patient. But since the project was randomly allocated across communities, there is no reason to believe that the type of illness and the condition of the patients should be systematically different across groups. It is possible that due to the intervention, patients with more severe illnesses sought care at the project facilities in the treatment area and that this in turn impacted treatment practices. However, the evidence found in Björkman and Svensson (2009) does not support this claim.

15. See Björkman and Svensson (2009) for details. The *z*-score is a normally distributed measure of growth defined as the difference between the weight of an individual and the median value of weight for the reference population (2000 CDC Growth Reference in the United States) for the same age, divided by the standard deviation of the reference population.

16. These numbers should be viewed with caution. For the cost-benefit estimates of the citizen report card project, it should be noted that the sample is, by construction, not fully representative of the population (since villages closer to the facility were oversampled). Naturally, the 95 percent confidence interval would also include a much smaller estimate of program impact than the estimate used here. Moreover, since the largest cost item was the collection of data, and these data were used partly in the intervention and partly to evaluate impact, the cost is a rough estimate. Filmer and Pritchett's (1999) estimates of

the cost of averting a child death derived from increasing public expenditures on health are subject to a variety of estimation problems and the health interventions–based cost-effectiveness estimates of the minimum required cost to avert a death are, as noted by Filmer and Pritchett, at best suggestive.

References

Appleton, S. 2001. The Rich Are Just Like Us, Only Richer: Poverty Functions or Consumption Functions? *Journal of African Economies* 10 (4): 433–469.

Banerjee, A., A. Deaton, and E. Duflo. 2004. Wealth, Health, and Health Service Delivery in Rural Rajasthan. *American Economic Review* 94 (2): 326–330.

Banerjee, A., and E. Duflo. 2005. Addressing Absence. *Journal of Economic Perspectives* 20 (1): 117–132.

Björkman, M., and J. Svensson. 2009. Power to the People: Evidence from a Randomized Field Experiment on Community-Based Monitoring in Uganda. *Quarterly Journal of Economics* 124 (2): 735–769.

Chaudhury, N., J. Hammer, M. Kremer, K. Muralidharan, and F. H. Rogers. 2006. Missing in Action: Teacher and Health Worker Absence in Developing Countries. *Journal of Economic Perspectives* 20 (1): 91–116.

Duflo, E., and R. Hanna. 2005. Monitoring Works: Getting Teachers to Come to School. NBER working paper 11880.

Filmer, D., and L. Pritchett. 1999. The Impact of Public Spending on Health: Does Money Matter? *Social Science and Medicine* 49 (10): 1309–1323.

Hirschman, A. O. 1970. Exit, Voice, and Loyalty: Responses to Decline in Firms, Organizations, and States. Cambridge, Mass.: Harvard University Press.

Keefer, P., and S. Khemani. 2005. Democracy, Public Expenditures, and the Poor: Understanding Political Incentives for Providing Public Services. *World Bank Research Observer* 20 (1): 1–27.

Khemani, S. 2007. Can Information Campaigns Overcome Political Obstacles to Serving the Poor? In *The Politics of Service Delivery in Democracies: Better Access for the Poor*, ed. S. Devarajan and I. Widlund. Stockholm: Expert Group on Development Issues, Ministry for Foreign Affairs.

McPake, B., D. Asiimwe, F. Mwesigye, M. Ofumbi, L. Ortenblad, P. Streefland, and A. Turinde. 1999. The Economic Behavior of Health Workers in Uganda: Implications for Quality and Accessibility of Public Health Services. *Social Science and Medicine* 49 (7): 849–865.

Möller, C. 2002. Infant Mortality in Uganda, 1995–2000: Why the Non-improvement? *Uganda Health Bulletin* 8 (3-4): 211–214.

Persson, T., and G. Tabellini. 2000. *Political Economics: Explaining Economic Policy*. Cambridge, Mass.: MIT Press.

Reinikka, R., and J. Svensson. 2004. Local Capture: Evidence from a Central Government Transfer Program in Uganda. *Quarterly Journal of Economics* 119 (2): 679–705.

Republic of Uganda. Ministry of Health. 2000. Health Sector Strategic Plan 2000/01–2004/05. Kampala.

Samuel, P. 2002. *Holding the State to Account: Citizen Monitoring in Action.* Bangalore: Books for Change.

Svensson, J. 2005. Eight Questions about Corruption. *Journal of Economic Perspectives* 19 (3): 19–42.

World Bank. 2004. *Making Services Work for Poor People. World Development Report 2004.* Washington, D.C.

7 Extended Family Networks in Rural Mexico: A Descriptive Analysis

Manuela Angelucci, Giacomo De Giorgi, Marcos A. Rangel, and Imran Rasul

Economists usually focus on the household as the key unit of analysis from which to study household behavior. There are good reasons for this. Theories of household behavior, such as the unitary model (Becker 1981), bargaining models (Manser and Brown 1980; McElroy and Horney 1981), collective choice models (Chiappori 1988), and noncooperative models (Chen and Woolley 2001) all emphasize the interplay among the preferences and resources of individuals within the household in shaping household outcomes. In addition, household data are typically constrained in the sense that it is not possible to identify the familial ties between surveyed households.

However, every household is actually embedded within a wider network of its extended family members, and these related households may exert important influences that determine the behavior of any given household within the family network. Indeed, if the institution of the extended family shapes the objectives and constraints relevant for each household, then analyzing household behavior in isolation from the presence and characteristics of its extended family members may lead to an incomplete understanding of the forces driving household choices. The divergence between what may be optimal for a single household acting in isolation and what is actually optimal for the family network as a whole can be expected to increase in economic environments characterized by missing markets, correlated income shocks, the prevalence of informal institutions that enforce contracts, and widespread policy interventions that affect many households in the local economy.

This chapter begins to fill this void in the literature by providing descriptive evidence from household data used to evaluate the Progresa social assistance program in rural Mexico on the presence and characteristics of each member of a household's extended family in the same village. This environment has all the features just described in which there may be significant influences of the extended family on household behavior.

Two key aspects of data and context lie at the heart of this analysis. First, to build data on the existence of extended family links between households, we exploit information in the Progresa data on the paternal and maternal surnames of heads of households and their spouses. Second, we combine this information with the patronymic naming convention in Mexico to build intergenerational and intragenerational extended family links outside of the household but within the village.

We also use information from the household roster to build equivalent measures of extended family links that co-reside within the household. Taken together, these two sources of information provide an almost complete mapping of extended family structures across 506 villages in rural Mexico, covering about 24,000 households and over 130,000 individuals.

In this chapter we use this information to provide evidence on (1) whether husbands and wives differ in the extent to which members of their extended families are located in geographic proximity; (2) the characteristics that predict the existence of each type of extended family link; and (3) the similarity of households within the same family network in terms of their poverty, and how this differs within and between generations of the extended family.

Family networks may influence household behavior through a number of mechanisms. First, there is scope for insurance or redistribution within families because, as highlighted in the descriptive analysis, the correlation in poverty of households within the same family network varies considerably between intergenerationally and intragenerationally linked households. Much of the existing literature has focused on the determinants of transfers along such intergenerational links, and whether they are crowded in or crowded out by publicly provided transfers (Altonji, Hayashi, and Kotlikoff 1992; 1997; Jensen 2003; Albarran and Attanasio 2004; Raut and Tran 2005). Understanding how flows of private transfers across households respond to the provision of public transfers can ultimately reveal whether private transfers are motivated by altruistic concerns (Becker 1981; Cox and Jakubson 1995) or the exchange of goods and services (Bernheim, Shleifer, and Summers 1985).

Second, households within the same family network may learn about, or revise their expectations of, outcomes on the basis of each other's experiences. Relatedly, there may be peer pressure from parents, and rivalry, cooperation, conformity, or imitation among siblings. Evidence from similar rural settings shows the quantitative importance of learning from others in agriculture (Foster and Rosenzweig 1995; Conley and Udry 2005; Bandiera and Rasul 2006). However, little is known about learning or peer effects in general, within the same extended family.

Third, inside and outside options in marital bargaining between husbands and wives may be shaped by the presence of each partner's extended family. Much of the literature has explored the effects of the resources controlled by husbands and wives, and other factors shaping spouses' outside options, on marital bargaining (Schultz 1990; Thomas 1990; Lundberg, Pollak, and Wales 1997; Attanasio and Lechene 2002; Rubalcava, Teruel, and Thomas 2004; Rangel 2005; Behrman and Rosenzweig 2006; Qian 2006). A more recent literature has begun to explore the allocation of resources within the household when there are more than two relevant actors present, such as the parents of one of the spouses (Rangel 2006). However, little is known about the presence of extended family members outside the household driving within-household bargaining.

We view the construction of extended family networks as being a first step in a broader research agenda in which the challenge lies in understanding whether and how such networks shape household behavior. The experimental research design of the Progresa evaluation data also opens up the possibility of overcoming some of the econometric concerns that have affected earlier studies and thus identifying the causal effect of extended family links on household behavior. In the conclusion, we discuss particular issues that the constructed data on extended family networks can be used to explore.

The emphasis throughout this research agenda is on the influence of the extended family on household behavior, and not the influence of others, such as friends of the family or those that are similar on observable characteristics per se. While undoubtedly other households outside the extended family network also influence behavior, there are a number of theoretical, empirical, and sociologically founded justifications for focusing on extended family links.

First, evolutionary biology suggests preferences may be defined over the family dynasty. This aspect of behavior is commonly modeled within an overlapping-generations framework. Moreover there are specific intergenerational investments—such as those in children's education, bequests, transfers to parents, and the choice of marriage partners—that have no counterpart in the relationships between friends.

Second, the extended family provides a well-defined reference group from which to empirically identify social influences on behavior (Manski 1993). Third, social ties between family members may differ from those with friends because the former are strong in the sense that they are long-term, embody mutual trust and reciprocity, and are not easily undone (Granovetter 1985). This may, for example, make it easier to enforce implicit contracts within families than among friends, especially when formal legal institutions are weak. In addition, the process underlying the formation of family networks is different from that underlying the formation of friendship networks. For example, households have less scope to strategically place themselves within a family network, and family ties are necessarily bidirectional.

In this chapter, we first describe the Progresa program and evaluation data and discuss how we exploit information on paternal and maternal surnames to identify family links outside of the household. We then describe the data on family networks. We conclude with a discussion of how the constructed information on extended families can be utilized in future research.

The Progresa Program and Evaluation Data

Progresa is an ongoing publicly funded social assistance program in Mexico, aimed toward poor households. The program began in 1997 and was initially offered to 140,544 households in 3,369 villages. The program provides grants to households in the form of conditional cash transfers related to their children's school attendance, and attendance at local health clinics. By the end of 1999 the program had expanded to cover more than 2.6 million recipient households throughout rural Mexico (Skoufias 2005).[1]

To determine a household's entitlement to Progresa transfers, in 1997 households were classified as either being eligible (poor) or noneligible (nonpoor) according to a household poverty index. This index is calculated as a weighted average of household income (excluding children), household size, durables, land and livestock, education, and other physical characteristics of the dwelling. The index is designed to give relatively greater weight to correlates of permanent, rather than current, income.[2] In October 1997, 52 percent of households were classified as being eligible for Progresa.

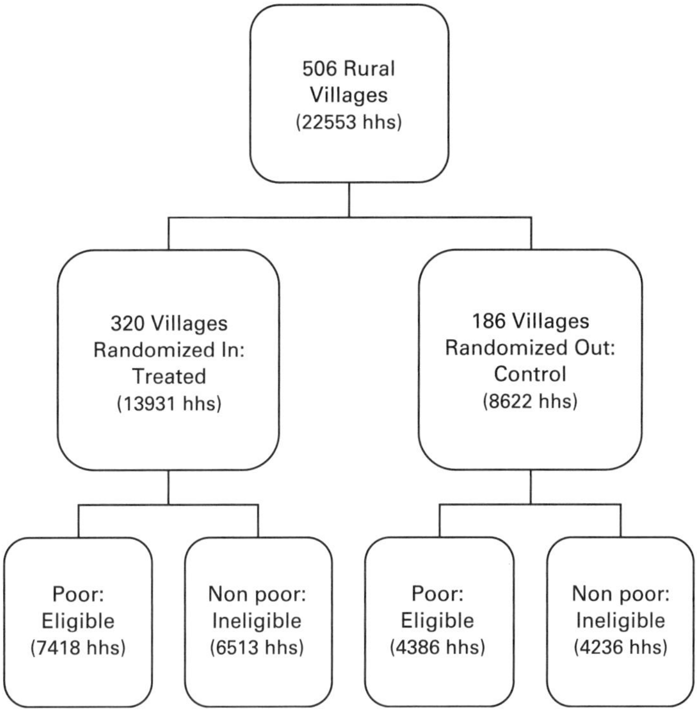

Figure 7.1
Progresa research design. The sample is restricted to the 22,553 households that could be tracked for the first and third waves of the Progresa data, in the baseline survey in October 1997 (wave 1) and the first postprogram survey in October 1998 (wave 3).

To evaluate the effectiveness of Progresa, an experimental research design was implemented, and household data were collected on a panel of about 24,000 households every six months in 506 villages between March 1998 and November 1999.[3] Of the 506 villages, 320 were randomly assigned to the treatment group, namely, locations where Progresa would later be implemented, and 186 villages were assigned to be control villages. Figure 7.1 summarizes the research design.

The first two waves of household panel data were collected in October 1997 and March 1998, before any cash transfers from Progresa had been distributed. The remaining waves, collected in October 1998, May 1999, and November 1999, all correspond to the postprogram period. We restrict our analysis to the 22,553 households that were surveyed in the first and third waves of the data. As we aim to compare and contrast the extended family links of heads and their spouses, we focus attention on the 85 percent of households that are couple-headed, where the head is always defined to be male.

Construction of Extended Family Links

Information on Surnames and the Matching Algorithm

To build data on the existence of extended family links between households in the same village, we exploit information on surnames provided in the third wave of the evaluation data. We combine this information with the patronymic naming convention in Mexico to build two types of extended family link for each household: (1) intergenerational family links, such as those from the head of household to his parents, from the spouse of the head of household to her parents, and from the head and spouse of the household to their adult sons and daughters; and (2) intragenerational family links, such as those from the head of household to his brothers and sisters, and similarly those for his spouse.[4]

It is important to note that Mexicans have *two* surnames: the first is inherited from the father's paternal lineage and the second from the mother's paternal lineage. For example, former Mexican president Vicente Fox Quesada would be identified by his given name (Vicente), his father's paternal name (Fox), and his mother's paternal name (Quesada).

In the evaluation data, respondents were asked, "Tell me the complete/full name with all surnames for all the members of this household, starting with the head of household." Respondents were then asked to provide the given name, paternal surname, and maternal surname for each member of the household.[5] Hence a household headed by a husband and wife, has four associated surnames: the paternal and maternal surnames of the head, and the paternal and maternal surnames of his wife.[6]

To define each inter- and intragenerational link, we use information on two of these four surnames. Figure 7.2 provides an illustration of the matching algorithm used to build each family link. Consider household A at the root of the family tree. The head of household has paternal and maternal surnames F1 and f1, respectively. His wife has paternal and maternal surnames *F2* and *f2*, respectively.[7]

The children of the couple in household A will adopt the paternal surnames of their father (F1) and mother (*F2*). Hence we define there to be a parent-son relationship between households A and B if (1) the

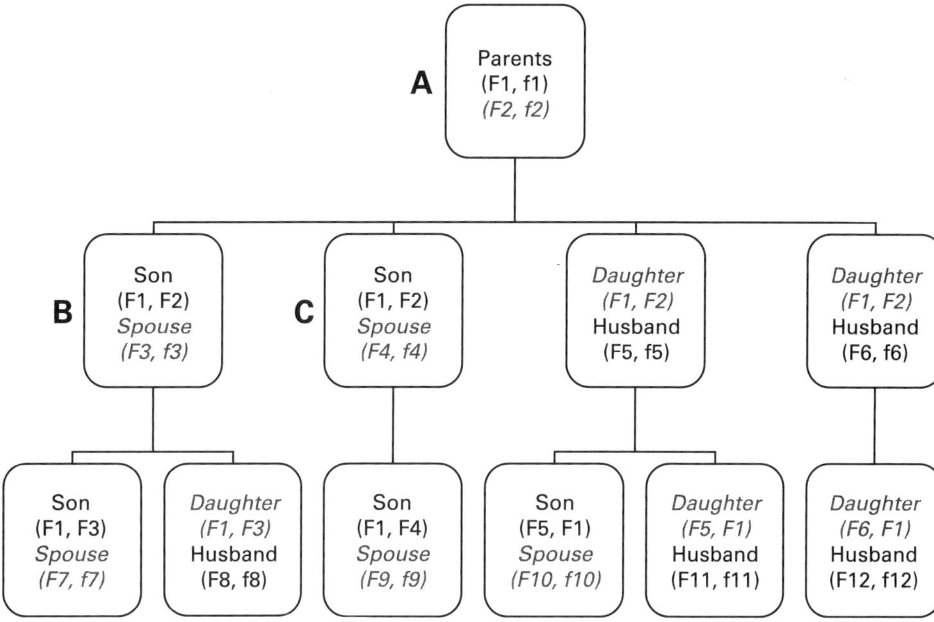

Figure 7.2
Family tree. Head's surname in Roman font, wife's surname in italic font; paternal surname uppercase, maternal surname lowercase. Households are assumed to be couple-headed.

paternal surname of the head of household B is the same as the paternal surname of the head of household A (F1); and (2) the maternal surname of the head of household B is the same as the paternal surname of the spouse in household A (*F*2). Clearly, parent-daughter extended family relationships can be similarly defined. In addition, intragenerational family ties between siblings can be identified. For example, the heads of households B and C are identified to be brothers if they share the same paternal and maternal surnames. This relationship can be identified even if the parents of B and C themselves are not heading their own household but are perhaps co-residing with one of their adult children.

While in figure 7.2 we assume all households are couple-headed, this need not be the case. In order to deal with this issue, we combine our matching algorithm with information on whether households are couple-headed or not, and the gender of the head if they are single-headed, to precisely define each extended family link.

There are some limitations on the extent to which information on paternal and maternal surnames can be used to accurately measure the presence and number of extended family links. We now make clear the limits of our matching algorithm and some refinements we employ to address these concerns. In the next section we discuss in more detail the possible forms of measurement error in family links we identify, and provide evidence on the prevalence of each type of error in the data.

We only define extended family links that exist within the same village. There are three reasons for this: (1) families that are in close geographic proximity are more likely to influence household behavior; (2) villages were partly selected into the evaluation data because they were geographically remote; hence there is a relatively low probability of extended families residing in neighboring villages; and (3) the number of households reporting a member to have permanently migrated away is less than 4 percent, so within-village family transfers are likely to be more important that those from other locations.[8]

Next, consider links from household *i* to household *j*, where household *j* is single-headed. As shown in figure 7.2, the fact that household *j* is single-headed does not affect the construction of links from the head and spouse of household *i* either to their children or to their siblings. However, links from the head (spouse) of household *i* to the household of his (her) parents can only be identified if *both* his (her) parents are alive and live together. This is because this particular family link definition relies on information from household *j* on the paternal surnames of both head and spouse.[9]

Support for the accuracy of the matching algorithm can be found using the following intuition. By definition, household *i* cannot have parental links to more than two other households (the parents of the head and the parents of the spouse), conditional on the parents not being present within the household. Reassuringly, this is true for 97 percent of households in the Progresa data using our matching algorithm. On the other hand, there is no upper bound on the number of links that household *i* may have to their children or siblings. To reduce potential errors, we therefore combine our matching algorithm with the following information when defining family links: (1) we limit intergenerational links (parent-child, child-parent) to exist when the relevant individuals have at least 15 years' age difference and no more than 60 years' age difference between mother and child; and (2) we limit intragenerational links (siblings) to exist when the relevant individuals have at most 30 years' age difference.

Measurement Error in Family Links

There are a number of potential sources of measurement error in the recorded surnames data that can be checked for. The first arises from the convention that women change their maternal surname to that of their husband's at the time of marriage. To address this concern, we note that the precise wording of the question specifically asks respondents to name the paternal and maternal surnames of each household member. Furthermore, in only 6.9 percent of households do we observe the spouse's maternal surname to be the same as that of her husband. These data therefore provide an upper bound on the extent to which measurement error of this form occurs.

Next, if the male head is the respondent, he might not recall his wife's maternal surname and might simply replace it with her paternal surname. This is plausible given that his children would actually receive his wife's paternal surname as their second surname. Reassuringly, this occurs in only 5.9 percent of households.

Also, the accuracy of the surname data may be questioned in households where the paternal and maternal surnames of both the head and spouse are all reported to be identical. In 1.7 percent of households this is the case, although the percentage drops to 0.5 percent if we exclude households with the most common surname in the data.

With these caveats and concerns in mind, we note finally that there are potential forms of measurement error in family links that simply cannot be addressed. The first arises from any remaining typos in the surname data. Second, there might be two identical families in the village who share the same paternal and maternal surnames of head and spouse but are genuinely unrelated. The matching algorithm then assigns the number of family links to be double what they actually are. As mentioned before, one indication that this problem may not be first-order is that 97 percent of households are matched to two or fewer parental households. Third, consider a scenario in which a woman's brother marries someone with the same maternal surname as himself. Then the woman's niece will be identified as her sister, and although the households are in the same family network, we may overestimate the closeness of the family tie.

Descriptive Evidence

Surnames Data

Table 7.1 provides descriptive evidence on surnames, split according to each surname type—the paternal and maternal surnames of the head

Table 7.1
Descriptive Statistics on Surnames, by Surname Type

	Head's Paternal Surname (F1)	Head's Maternal Surname (f1)	Spouse's Paternal Surname (*F2*)	Spouse's Maternal Surname (*f2*)
Number of surnames	1696	1996	1912	2025
Number [percentage] of surnames mentioned more than once	1064 [62.7%]	1188 [59.5%]	1088 [56.9%]	1100 [54.3%]
Probability of same surname in population	9.50×10^{-6}	7.54×10^{-6}	8.60×10^{-6}	8.33×10^{-6}
	(5.48×10^{-6})	(4.16×10^{-6})	(4.95×10^{-6})	(4.95×10^{-6})
Expected number of same surname matches in population	13.3	11.2	9.92	9.26
	(1.66)	(1.36)	(1.25)	(1.19)
Probability of same surname in the village	.042	.021	.022	.020
	(.0005)	(.0004)	(.0004)	(.0004)
Expected number of same surname matches in the village	7.55	5.31	5.42	4.98
	(.039)	(.036)	(.036)	(.040)
Odds ratio	355.7	344.8	345.4	353.0
	(8.26)	(7.47)	(7.55)	(8.18)

Notes:
Mean, standard errors in parentheses. For the matching probabilities and expected number of same surname matches in the population, the standard errors are clustered by surname for each surname type. The sample is restricted to the 22,553 households that could be tracked for the first and third waves of the Progresa data, in the baseline survey in October 1997 (wave 1) and the first postprogram survey in October 1998 (wave 3).

(F1, f1) and spouse (*F2, f2*). For both head and spouse, fewer paternal than maternal surnames are reported. As figure 7.2 shows, this reflects the fact that given the patronymic naming convention, paternal surnames have a greater survival rate across generations than maternal surnames.

There are 1,696 different paternal surnames reported by heads (F1), lower than for the other types of surname, including those reported as the spouse's paternal surname (*F2*). This is because the patronymic naming convention implies spouses' paternal surnames have a lower survival rate across generations than those of male heads of household, and also because spouses move into the 506 villages in the data from villages outside of the evaluation sample.

The majority of surnames are mentioned at least twice. Figure 7.3 shows the frequency distribution of surnames for the most frequently mentioned names. For each surname type, one particular name covers about 9 percent of households. For the head's paternal surname, the median household has the fifty-fifth most common surname.

Table 7.1, rows 3 and 4, highlights that the probability (without replacement) of two randomly matched households in the sample having the same surname type is close to zero and that the expected number of households with the same head's paternal surname is 13.3. This is higher than the expected number of households with the same spouse's paternal surname, again suggestive of women moving into Progresa villages from other locations, perhaps at the time of marriage.[10]

The next two rows of table 7.1 report the same information but at the village level. The probability (without replacement) of two randomly chosen households in the village having the same surname type is orders of magnitude larger than in the population. The fact that the expected number of households in the village with the same surname is smaller than in the population implies households do not perfectly sort into villages by surname. On the other hand, the expected number of same surname matches in the village is orders of magnitude higher than if households were randomly allocated by surname types into villages.[11]

Note that this expected number of matches in the village is based on the use of only one surname and so provides an upper bound on the total number of specific extended family links we define, which are always based on two name matches.

Figure 7.4 shows how the probability and expected number of same surname matches in the village vary by village size, as defined by the

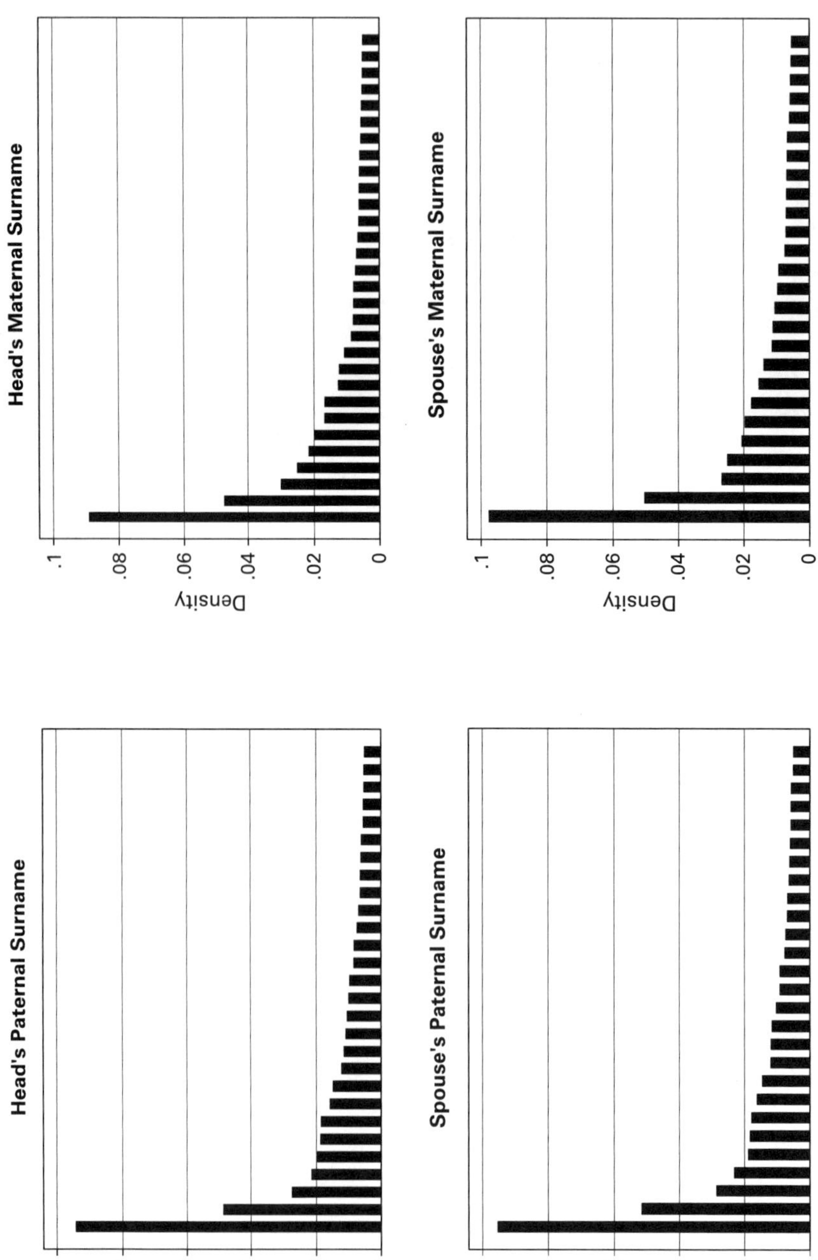

Figure 7.3
Distribution of surnames, by surname type, for the most common surnames. Plotted for surnames covering at least 0.5% of the population.

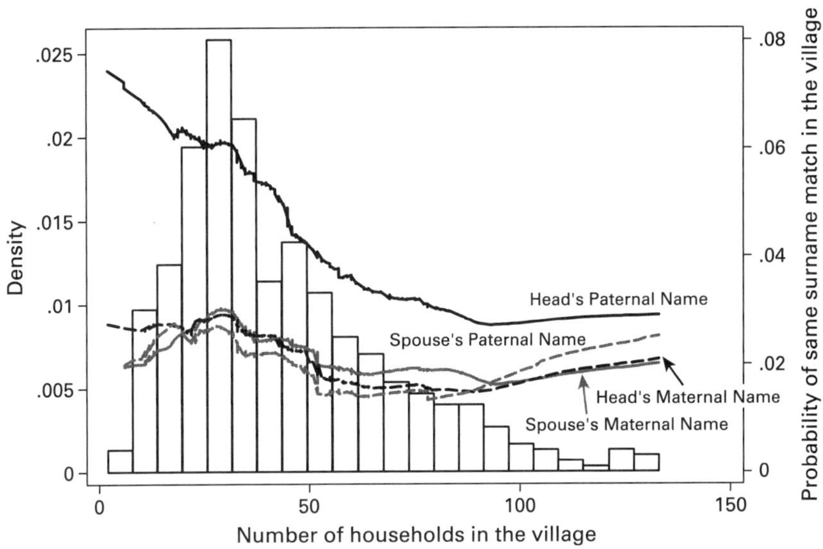

(A) Prob (same surname in locality) by surname type and number of households in the village

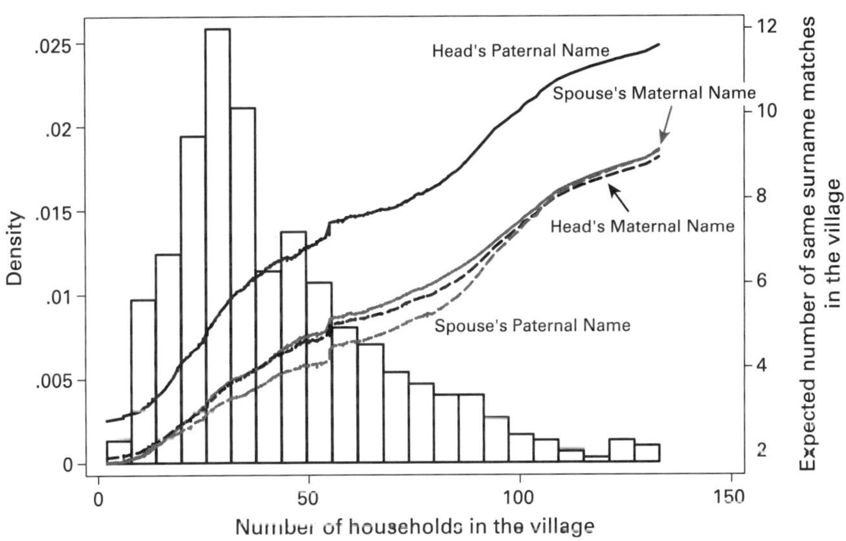

(B) Expected number of same surname matches by surname type and number of households in the village

Figure 7.4
Surnames and village size. *Upper graph*: locally weighted regression of probability of the same surname match in the village on the village size, defined as the number of households in the village; *lower graph*: locally weighted regression of expected number of same surname matches on the village size. Backgrounds of graphs show histograms of village size. Both regressions were estimated using a bandwidth of 0.8. The largest 0.5% of villages were omitted.

number of households in the village. We see that the probability of a same surname match declines with village size but not at the same rate as the increase in village size. Hence, the expected number of same surname matches increases with village size overall. This again suggests some degree of sorting by each surname into villages.

The final row in table 7.1 sheds more light on the degree of sorting of households into villages by the surname type, as measured by the odds ratio. This is defined as the ratio of the probability that two randomly chosen households from within the same village have the same surname, divided by the probability that two randomly chosen households from the population of Progresa villages have the same surname. The odds ratio suggests that households are, for example, 356 times more likely to match within a village on their head's paternal surname than if they were randomly allocated by this surname across villages.[12]

The Number of Family Links

The upper panel of table 7.2 provides information on the number of family links each household has to other households in the village, as generated by the matching algorithm previously described. The columns of the table split family links into intergenerational links, namely, those to parents of the head or spouse and those to the adult children of the head and spouse; and intragenerational links, namely, those to siblings of the head and spouse. Each row in the table splits each type of extended family link into those from the head of the household and those from his spouse. The sample is limited to couple-headed households that have at least one extended family link in the village. About 81 percent of couple-headed households have at least one extended family member heading their own household in the village.

The lower panel of table 7.2 uses information from the household roster from wave 3 of the data to construct information on the corresponding family links that co-reside inside the household. Again, using information on the relationship of each person to the household head, we can decompose these family links inside the household into those from the head and those from his spouse.

Consider links to parents. Table 7.2 shows that parents are more likely to reside outside the household than inside the household of their adult children. The number of parents present is higher for the head than for his spouse, and this is true for parents inside and outside the household. This is consistent with the spouse's migrating to the village or moving in with her husband's family within the same village.

Table 7.2
Number of Family Links, by Family Tie

	Outside the Household and in Village				
	Parent	Children Aged 0–16	Adult Children	Siblings	All
From head of household to	0.461 (.094) [0.837]	–	0.652 (.487) [2.09]	2.23 (.601) [3.00]	3.34 (1.01) [3.93]
From spouse of household to	0.250 (.083) [0.656]	–	0.652 (.487) [2.09]	1.63 (.611) [2.90]	2.54 (1.01) [3.90]
	Inside the Household				
	Parent	Children Aged 0–16	Adult Children	Siblings	All
From head of household to	0.062 (.033) [0.271]	3.23 (.223) [2.20]	0.821 (1.83) [3.00]	0.033 (.037) [0.256]	4.15 (.310) [2.92]
From spouse of household to	0.018 (.049) [0.139]	3.23 (.223) [2.20]	0.821 (1.83) [3.00]	0.013 (.019) [0.131]	4.09 (.299) [2.90]

Notes:
The sample is restricted to couple-headed households that could be tracked in the first and third waves of Progresa and that have at least one extended family tie present in the village. We define the head of a couple-headed household to be male.
Means, standard deviation between villages in parentheses; standard deviation within village in brackets. Standard deviations between and within villages are calculated taking account of the fact that there are unequal numbers of households across villages. By construction, the number of family links to parental households is always two, conditional on such a family link existing. By construction, the numbers of children of the couple inside and outside the household are identical for the head and the spouse. Adult children are defined to be at least 17 years of age.

On links to adult children, by construction, the number of family links to children are identical for head and spouse. Given the age of respondents, there are many more young children inside than adult children outside the household. On links to siblings, we find that these are more likely to be outside than inside the household, which is again as expected given the age of respondents. The number of siblings is higher for the head than his spouse, and this is again true for family links both inside and outside the household.

Overall, the data emphasize that the extended family networks of male heads of households are considerably greater than those of their spouses. This is true for family links that co-reside within the same household and for family links that reside in other households in the same village. The source of this difference may arise from women moving households and potentially villages at the time of marriage. In support of this we note that in wave 4 of the data, wives were asked about where they went to live after marriage; 49.3 percent stated that they went to live with their in-laws after marriage, and only 6.5 percent reported living with their own parents after marriage. Moreover, 85 percent of spouses with their parents present in the village reported remaining in the same village at the time of marriage. The corresponding figure for spouses with no parental links in the village is only 59 percent.

Along other dimensions, women with and without parents in the village are similar. For example, age at marriage is not significantly different between women with and without parents, and the proportion of women reporting that their in-laws originally proposed the marriage is 56 percent for both groups.

These results are in the same spirit as the findings of Rosenzweig and Stark (1989), who examined marital arrangements in rural India. They found that women move to distant villages at the time of marriage, and they argued that in an economy characterized by information costs and spatially covariant risks, such marriages can be viewed as a consumption-smoothing device. Indeed, they found that marriages accompanied by migration of the daughter significantly reduced the variance of food consumption in the household of origin. We leave for future research a more complete analysis of the relationship between the marriage market and consumption smoothing in rural Mexico.

Finally, in table 7.2 we also decompose the overall variation in each statistic into that arising from variation between villages and that arising from variation across households in the same village. Reassuringly, in each case we find that the within-village variation is around ten times as great as the between-village variation. This highlights that variations in family structure occur within the same village, and that there are not systematically different types of family structures in each village.[13]

Correlates of Family Links

The presence of extended family members is unlikely to be exogenously determined. The earlier literature explored a number of mechanisms that drive the presence of extended family members, such as the need for insurance and the choice of marriage partners for children

(Rosenzweig and Stark 1989), the value of services provided by social networks (Munshi and Rosenzweig 2009), inheritance of land and other household assets (Foster 1993), and the nature of household production (Foster and Rosenzweig 2002). Here, we present correlations between three types of factors and the presence of extended family ties.

First, there is a somewhat mechanical correlation between the ages of the head and spouse and the likelihood that their parents and adult children are in close proximity.

Second, wealthier family dynasties may enjoy higher fertility and lower mortality, and so are more likely to have extended family members present, other things equal. Wealthier families may also be more likely to own land. As rural land markets are typically missing, the ability to inherit land or to acquire land-specific human capital may lead adult children to be more likely to remain within the village than otherwise.

A third mechanism behind why households may partition and form larger extended family networks is through the need to insure against idiosyncratic income shocks. Such insurance can be gained through the strategic marriage of daughters into families with less correlated income shocks, or through the migration of some family members to other locations.

To shed light on these channels, we estimate a conditional logit regression where the dependent variable, L_{jh}, is a dummy equal to 1 if extended family link type j exists for household h in the village, and zero otherwise. We consider the following extended family links: (1) intergenerational links such as the parents of the head (spouse) and links to adult children; (2) intragenerational links such as the brothers and sisters of the head and spouse; and (3) whether household h has any extended family link.

For each link type, L_{jh}, we control for the ages of the head and spouse, and dummy variables for whether they are working, literate, and speak an indigenous language. At the household level, we control for whether the household owns its home, whether any land is owned, whether any member of the household temporarily migrated in the last year, the eligibility status of the household, the household poverty index, and the household size as measured at baseline.[14]

We group the conditional logit regression by village to take account of differences across villages that drive the formation of extended family networks. For example, if some villages are differentially subject to climatic shocks, that alters the need for households to insure each other against village-level shocks and may cause alternative patterns of extended networks to form.

Standard errors are clustered by village, and we report log odds ratios throughout. Hence tests of significance are relative to the log odds ratio being equal to 1. All continuous variables are divided by their standard deviation, so the corresponding coefficients can be interpreted as the effect of a one standard deviation change in the continuous variable. The results, reported in table 7.3, highlight the following.

First, the mechanical correlations with age are as expected, with older heads and spouses being significantly less likely to have their parents outside the household and resident in the village (the log odds ratio is significantly less than 1) and significantly more likely to have their adult children in other households in the village. Older heads and spouses are more likely to have brothers present and less likely to have sisters present, presumably because women move villages at the time of marriage.

Second, literate heads and spouses are more likely to have their parents present. If such correlations persist across generations, then parents who educate their children increase the likelihood of their children remaining geographically proximate, other things equal.

Third, home and land ownership are positively correlated with the likelihood that children and siblings reside in the same village, other things equal. The coefficients are of similar magnitude for brothers and sisters as well as for the adult children of the head and spouse (not shown). This pattern of coefficients is consistent both with inheritance norms in rural Mexico that do not favor men over women, and with a dynastic wealth effect such that wealthier families accumulate greater assets and have higher rates of fertility. Households in which at least one member has temporarily migrated in the last year—18.5 percent of all households—are more likely to have adult children present.

Fourth, although there is a slight positive correlation between the household poverty index and the presence of adult children, there is no discontinuous effect of eligibility status on the presence of any extended family ties. Whether the head and spouse speak an indigenous language also does not predict the presence of extended family ties. This is reassuring because the number of extended family ties, for each type of tie, is no different for indigenous and nonindigenous households.

Fifth, households with a greater number of individuals within them are also significantly more likely to have a greater number of extended family members residing in the same village. There are at least three explanations for this: (1) there may be persistent differences in fertility levels within the same family dynasty across generations; (2) the presence of extended family members reduces the costs of having and raising children because extended family members are able to supply time, labor, and other resources to the household; and (3) there may be pressure for households to partition once they become sufficiently large.

A comparison across the columns of table 7.3 is also informative. Consider first the presence of the parents of the head and spouse. In general, the control variables have a differential effect on the likelihood that the parents of the head are present, vis-à-vis the parents of the spouse being present. This is in line with the earlier evidence suggesting that the process that drives the presence of parents is very different for the head and his spouse. In contrast, most of the controls have similar effects on the likelihood of brothers or sisters of the head and spouse being present.[15]

Family Networks

Having described the construction of family links between any given pair of households in the same village, and the characteristics that correlate with the existence of such a link, we now describe the characteristics of the family network as a whole. Consider the following scenario in which the heads of households i and j are linked because they are brothers. Household j may itself be linked to household k, say, because the parents of the spouse of household j reside in household k. Households i and k then lie within the same family network, even though they do not have a *direct* family link between them. Following the terminology in Wasserman and Faust (1994), households i and j are said to be of distance 1 from each other, and households i and k are of distance 2 from each other. Two households i and j are then defined to be within the same family network if the distance between them, d_{ij}, is finite.

We use tools from the analysis of social networks to describe family networks in Progresa villages. For this analysis we do not consider households that are single nodes, namely, those unconnected to any other household in their village. We consider family networks with at least two members. There are 2,196 such family networks, covering 17,030 households.[16]

Figure 7.5 shows the number of family networks in a village. There are about five to ten different family dynasties within the same village.

Table 7.3
Determinants of Extended Family Links

Type of Family Link:	Intergenerational Family Links			Intragenerational Family Links				
	Parents of Head	Parents of Spouse	Adult Child	Brothers of Head	Sisters of Head	Brothers of Spouse	Sisters of Spouse	Any Link
Head age (years)	0.373***	0.307***	1.48***	0.953	0.805***	0.792***	0.841***	0.768***
	(.023)	(.024)	(.079)	(.041)	(.037)	(.034)	(.041)	(.041)
Spouse age (years)	0.755***	1.02	2.97***	0.872***	0.941	1.20***	0.969	1.18***
	(.043)	(.072)	(.166)	(.037)	(.041)	(.052)	(.047)	(.063)
Head literate (yes = 1)	1.45***	1.13	0.911*	1.07	1.13***	0.966	0.993	1.05
	(.099)	(.095)	(.049)	(.046)	(.056)	(.041)	(.046)	(.052)
Spouse literate (yes = 1)	1.14**	1.30***	0.785***	1.11**	1.03	1.08	0.956	1.13**
	(.074)	(.100)	(.039)	(.047)	(.046)	(.048)	(.049)	(.062)
Head speaks indigenous language (yes = 1)	1.01	0.843	1.16	0.963	1.02	0.967	1.02	0.911
	(.186)	(.138)	(.167)	(.107)	(.125)	(.102)	(.105)	(.115)
Spouse speaks indigenous language (yes = 1)	0.854	1.05	1.02	0.936	0.998	1.33	1.17	0.998
	(.144)	(.148)	(.145)	(.094)	(.133)	(.175)	(.151)	(.154)
House is owned (yes = 1)	1.03	1.08	1.34**	1.54***	1.38***	1.26***	1.33***	1.43***
	(.094)	(.122)	(.200)	(.112)	(.112)	(.107)	(.133)	(.126)
Any land is owned (yes = 1)	0.846***	1.00	1.26***	1.14***	1.19***	1.11***	1.14***	1.14**
	(.046)	(.069)	(.077)	(.050)	(.059)	(.047)	(.056)	(.062)
Any member temporarily migrated in last year (yes = 1)	1.09	0.993	1.15**	0.937	0.967	1.05	0.993	1.01
	(.066)	(.071)	(.071)	(.044)	(.044)	(.051)	(.050)	(.064)
Eligible (yes = 1)	0.963	1.07	1.02	1.01	1.03	1.03	1.05	1.02
	(.069)	(.091)	(.070)	(.051)	(.056)	(.055)	(.059)	(.064)
Poverty index	1.02	1.03	1.19***	1.08**	1.05	0.975	1.02	1.00
	(.042)	(.052)	(.048)	(.035)	(.036)	(.031)	(.036)	(.042)

Type of Family Link:	Intergenerational Family Links			Intragenerational Family Links				
	Parents of Head	Parents of Spouse	Adult Child	Brothers of Head	Sisters of Head	Brothers of Spouse	Sisters of Spouse	Any Link
Household size	0.967	1.18***	1.11***	1.10***	1.11***	1.07***	1.11***	0.992
	(.030)	(.040)	(.028)	(.021)	(.022)	(.021)	(.024)	(.023)
Mean of Dependent Variable	.187	.101	.217	.485	.332	.306	.274	.811
No. of observations	18,309	17,046	18,634	18,907	18,686	18,740	17,648	18,611

Notes:
Odds ratio significantly different from 1: *significant at 10%; **significant at 5%; ***significant at 1%. In each column a conditional logit specification is estimated, grouped by village, where the standard errors are clustered by village, and the log odds ratios are reported.
The underlying sample is restricted to couple-headed households that could be tracked over the first and third Progresa waves. The sample varies across the columns because villages in which all or no households have the given type of family link are dropped when the conditional logit regression is estimated. All characteristics are measured in the third wave (October 1998) except household size, which is measured at baseline. A higher household poverty index implies the household has a higher level of permanent income and so is less poor.

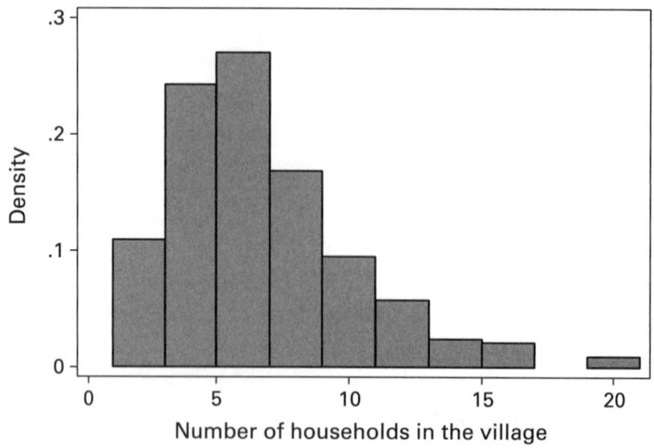

(A) Number of Family Networks in the Village

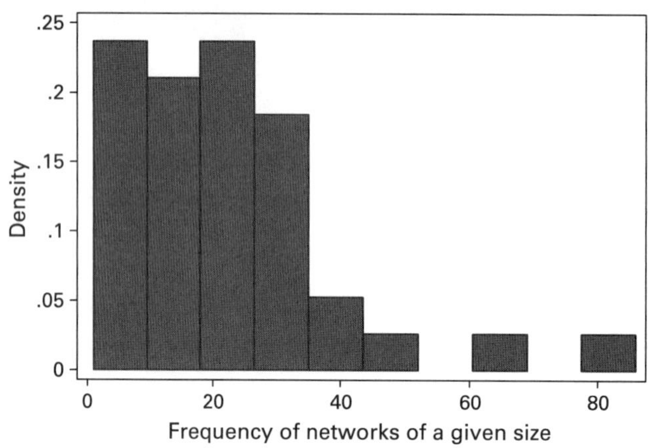

(B) Size Distribution of Family Networks

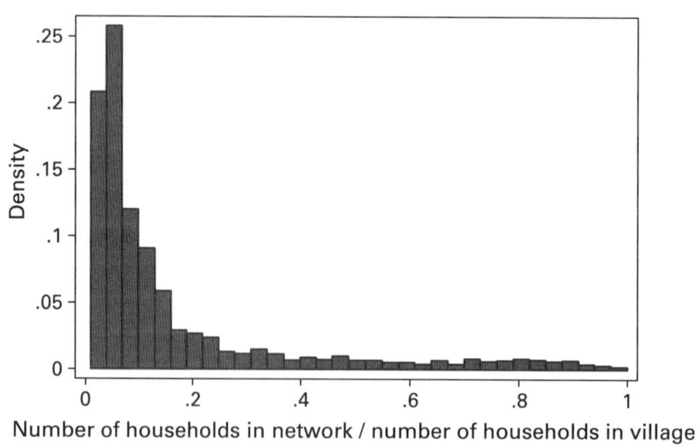

(C) Family Network Size as a Ratio of Number of Households in the Village

Table 7.4
Family Network Descriptives

Network Level	Size of Family Network	Network Size/ Number of Households in Village	Diameter
Mean	7.76	0.167	2.45
Standard deviation between villages	(9.65)	(0.149)	(1.18)
Standard deviation within village	[11.3]	[0.153]	[2.11]
Household Level	**Degree**	**Mean Distance**	**Central Closeness**
Mean	4.39	2.93	0.507
Standard deviation between networks	(2.05)	(0.686)	(0.205)
Standard deviation within network	[4.02]	[1.11]	[0.189]

Notes: Means, standard deviation between villages in parentheses; standard deviation within village in brackets.
The upper panel reports descriptive statistics on the family network as a whole. There is one observation per family network, so that each network has the same weight irrespective of the number of households within it. The size of the network is the number of households in the network. The diameter of the networks is the longest distance between two households that exists in a network. We define two households that are directly connected to be of distance 1 to each other.
The lower panel reports descriptive statistics on the family network at the household level. There is one observation per household, so family networks that are larger will have more weight associated to them. The degree of a household is the number of family links a household has. The mean degree is the mean of degrees across all network members. The central closeness is the inverse of the sum of the distances from household *i* to all other households in the locality, multiplied by the number of members of the network minus 1. This index ranges from 0 to 1.

It also shows the size distribution of family networks. On average, there are 7.8 households within the same family network. On average, 17 percent of households within a given village are part of the same family network.

The upper panel of table 7.4 provides precise information on these statistics.[17] In addition we provide information on the diameter of the network. This is the largest distance d_{ij} between any two households in the family network. This is about 2.5, and one implication of this is that family networks in Progresa are unlikely to span across more than

◀ **Figure 7.5**
Family network descriptives. Constructed from family networks with at least two households. Of the baseline sample of 22,553 households, 17,030 (75.5%) were within family networks with at least two households.

three generations. Finally, there is considerable variation in each statistic, both within family networks in the same village and between family networks in different villages.

To emphasize how the structure of family networks can differ between villages, figure 7.6 provides a graphical representation of family networks in two villages of median size (thirty-six households). The upper panel shows a village with a relatively dispersed set of family networks. There are five families with only two households present, one large family network of ten households, and sixteen households that have no family ties to any other household in the village. In contrast, the lower panel shows another village, which is of the same size but in which there exists one large family network containing thirty households, and six single-node households.

The lower panel of table 7.4 provides statistics at the household level for households in family networks. The first statistic is the degree of the household, which is simply the number of family links the household has to other households in the village. The average household in a family network is linked to 4.39 other households in the same village. The second column shows that the mean distance between any two households in the same family network is 2.93.

The last statistic, on central closeness, is a function of the inverse of the mean distance between household i and other households in its family network. To understand the intuition behind this measure, consider the network shown in the lower panel of figure 7.6. In this family, some households are in denser parts of the network in the sense that households linked to them are also more likely to be linked to each other and so have lower central closeness. In contrast, other households are at the periphery of the network and so have higher central closeness. In order for the statistic to be comparable across networks of different size, the inverse of the mean distance between household i is multiplied by the size of the network minus 1. The index ranges from 0 to 1. We see that for the average household this index is close to 0.5, although it varies considerably within households in the same family network.

Although the descriptive evidence opens up the possibility of differential impacts of Progresa depending on the presence of the extended family, this section has highlighted another potential dimension of heterogeneous responses arising from the position of the household in the family network.[18]

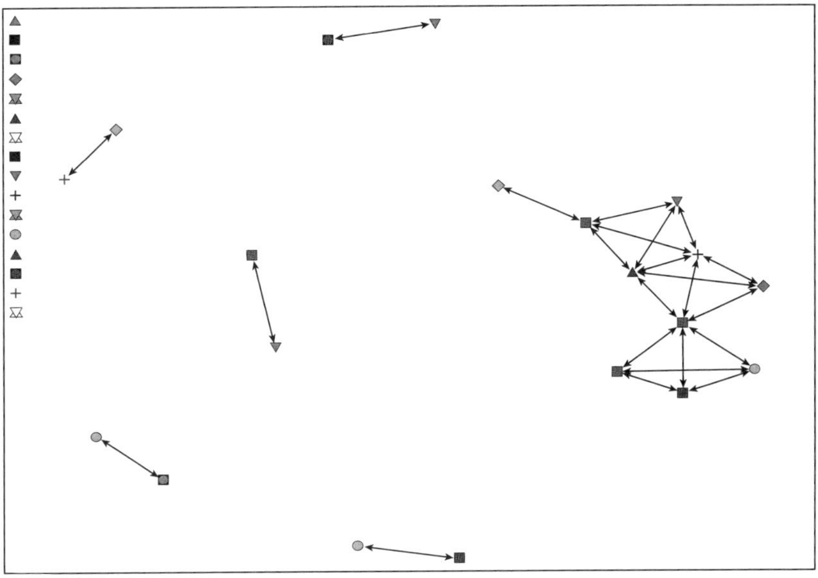

(A) Dispersed Village

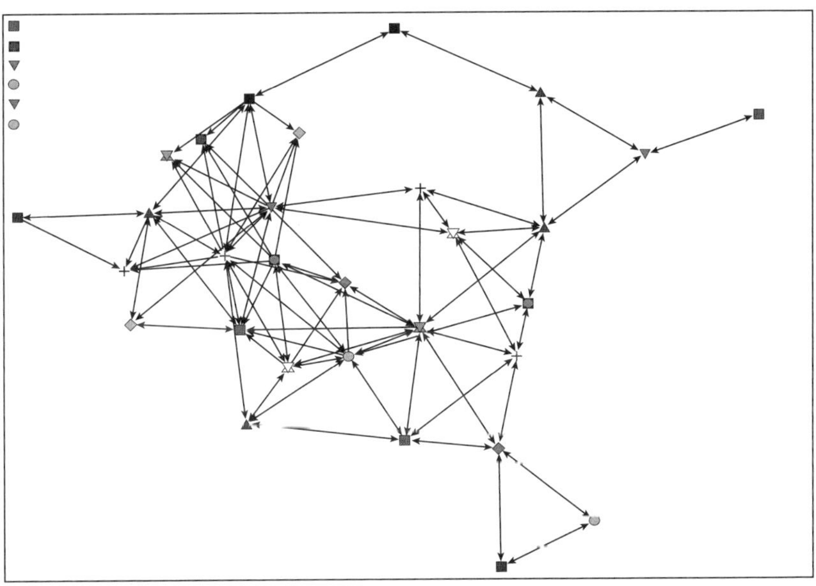

(B) Interconnected Village

Figure 7.6
Family network graphs. The (*upper*) dispersed village and the (*lower*) interconnected village each comprise 36 households, the median village size in the Progresa data. Each node represents a household. Each link between households corresponds to a parent/child link, a child/parent link, or a sibling link. Single-node households that are not linked to any other households are shown at the top left-hand corner of each graph. The figures were generated using UCINET.

Poverty within Families

In this final stage of descriptive analysis we use the information on family networks to shed light on the similarity in characteristics between households within the same family and to show how this differs depending on the type of extended family link between households. In particular, we focus on the poverty index and eligibility status of households within the same family network.

The first row of table 7.5 reports the correlation in the poverty index between various pairs of households. The first column shows that if two households are chosen at random from within the same village, the correlation in their poverty indices is .307. This correlation is higher (.413) for any two families within the same family network. The remaining columns show how this correlation varies across and within generations of the same family.

Focusing first on intergenerational family ties, the correlation in poverty tends to be higher among parent-son links than among parent-daughter links. This may be because marriage is used as a mechanism by which daughters marry into households that have less correlated shocks to those of her family, which allows extended families to diversify their exposure to risk from income and other shocks (Rosenzweig and Stark 1989). This also raises the possibility that net transfers from parents to their sons outside of their household may differ from those to their daughters outside of their household, other things equal.

This intuition is somewhat confirmed when we examine the correlation in households related through same-gender intragenerational family links. The correlation is higher among brothers than sisters. This raises the possibility that any transfers among siblings may in part relate to the gender of the giving and receiving sibling, other things equal.

The second row of table 7.5 provides information on the similarity of eligibility status among families. For two randomly chosen households in the same village, the probability that they are both eligible is .581, and this is only slightly higher (.622) among two households within the same family network. However, when family ties are broken down into inter- and intragenerational links, two important results emerge. First, this probability is lower among households linked through intergenerational family links than would be the case for two randomly chosen households. In contrast, this probability is higher among households tied through intragenerational family links than would be the case for two randomly chosen households. While this may be driven

Table 7.5
Similarity of Characteristics within Families, by Family Link

	Random Matching	Within Family	Adult Child to Parent Intergenerational Links: Son to Parent	Adult Child to Parent Intergenerational Links: Daughter to Parent	Same Gender Intragenerational Links: Brothers	Same Gender Intragenerational Links: Sisters
Poverty index (correlation)	.307	.413	.467	.414	.456	.414
Prob(eligible i = eligible j)	.581	.622	.565	.529	.642	.648
	(.002)	(.006)	(.012)	(.017)	(.007)	(.011)
Prob(eligible $i = 1 \mid$ eligible $j = 0$)	.441	.433	.541	.619	.406	.467
	(.006)	(.009)	(.015)	(.020)	(.011)	(.016)
Prob(eligible $i = 1 \mid$ eligible $j = 1$)	.601	.661	.767	.812	.679	.716
	(.006)	(.011)	(.017)	(.021)	(.011)	(.015)

Notes: Mean, with standard errors in parentheses, clustered by family network. These numbers are calculated using one observation per pair of households in each village.

by the definition of eligibility (partly based on housing assets, which older individuals have had more time to accumulate), these findings open up the possibility that the extent of transfers within families differ significantly between inter- and intragenerational links.

To shed more light on the eligibility status within poor and nonpoor families, the remaining rows of table 7.5 provide information on the probability that household *i* is eligible conditional on the eligibility status of household *j*. Consider a pair of households in the family linked through a head-parent relationship. We see that among nonpoor families, the probability that the household of the head is nonpoor conditional on his parents being nonpoor is 1 – .541 = .459. In contrast, the probability that the household of the head is poor conditional on his parents being poor is .767. The probability of a spouse being nonpoor conditional on her parents being nonpoor is .381, and the probability she is poor conditional on her parents being poor is .812. For each probability, the standard error is always marginally higher among family links involving females than the corresponding male links. This suggests that the economic status of women's households is more diversified than that of male households within the same family network, other things equal. We leave for future work a complete study of the interplay between marriage markets and the intergenerational persistence of poverty

Conclusion

This chapter describes the presence and characteristics of extended families in rural Mexico. Using data from the Progresa social assistance program, we exploit information on the paternal and maternal surnames of household heads and their spouses and the patronymic naming convention to identify the inter- and intragenerational family links of each household to others in the village. We then use the constructed data on family networks to describe (1) whether husbands and wives differ in the extent to which members of their extended family are located in geographic proximity; (2) the characteristics that predict the existence of extended family links; and (3) the similarity of households within the same family network in terms of their poverty, and how this differs within and between generations of the extended family.

We view this as a first step of a broader research agenda in which the challenge lies in understanding whether and how such networks shape household behavior. Before discussing particular issues that the constructed data on extended family networks can be used to explore, it is useful to reiterate two key features of the Progresa research design that should be exploited in any analysis of the effects of extended family networks on household behavior. First, villages in the evaluation data are randomly assigned into treatment and control groups. Hence identification of the causal effect of Progresa on eligible households arises from a comparison of eligible households in treatment villages to eligible households in control villages.

Second, all eligible and noneligible households in each village are surveyed. Hence the causal effect of Progresa on noneligible households can also be identified. Such within-village spillover effects of the program on household behavior are identified from a comparison of noneligible households in treatment villages to noneligible households in control villages.[19]

These features of the data are exploited in Angelucci et al. (2006), who estimated whether households' responses to Progresa in terms of their secondary school enrollment choices, are heterogeneous depending on the existence and characteristics of extended family members in the same village.[20] To reiterate, the Progresa research design allows us to identify these responses both for eligible and noneligible households. This is important because if resources are transferred within family networks, this opens up the possibility of noneligible households benefiting from Progresa if they have extended family links that are eligible for the program.

Angelucci et al. estimated whether households' responses to Progresa differ according to whether any extended family ties are present or not, and conditional on the presence of extended family, whether the precise type of extended family link present influences the response to Progresa. We distinguished between inter- and intragenerational family links in the village, and between the extended family links of the head of household vis-à-vis those of his spouse. Finally, we considered if the eligibility status and other characteristics of extended family links themselves matter, and whether there are similar effects of extended family members that co-reside within the household.[21]

The constructed data on extended family networks can also be used to shed light on the provision of insurance in village economies. In particular, by combining information on family networks with the detailed information on consumption that is collected in the Progresa surveys, one could shed light on whether households within extended families are able to insure each other against idiosyncratic shocks

(Townsend 1994; Dercon and Krishnan 2000). One mechanism through which such insurance may occur is the marriage market. In particular, following Rosenzweig and Stark (1989), the data on extended families can be used to understand how families use the marriage market to insure themselves against risks by marrying daughters into other family networks that face shocks less correlated to their own.

We view this research agenda as helping to clarify the behavior of households in a wider context of being embedded in a family network, and we emphasize the need to collect information on the familial ties between households in future survey data.

Notes

This research was supported by an institution of review board approval from the University of Chicago. The data were obtained from the International Food Policy Research Institute (IFPRI), and the chapter has been screened to ensure no confidential information is revealed. We thank Timothy Besley, Raji Jayaraman, and seminar participants at the BREAD/CESifo workshop on the Microeconomics of Institutions in Venice 2006 for useful comments. All errors remain our own.

1. Evidence that the program had a significant impact on the welfare and human capital investment of poor rural families in Mexico contributed to the decision in 2000 of the Vicente Fox Quesada administration to continue with Progresa and to expand its coverage to urban areas in 2003 under the new name of Oportunidades.

2. The cutoff point in the household poverty index that determines eligibility varies across regions of Mexico.

3. These villages are located in seven out of thirty-one states in Mexico. These states are Guerrero, Hidalgo, Michoacán, Puebla, Querétaro, San Luis Potosí, and Veracruz, and they are mainly located in the southern half of Mexico. Villages were selected on the basis of a marginality index constructed from information on the share of illiterate adults in the village; the share of dwellings without water, drainage systems, electricity, and with floors of dirt; the average number of occupants per room in village households; the share of population working in the primary sector; the distance from other villages; and the health and school infrastructures present in the village.

4. Two concerns arise from the fact that the surname information used to construct family networks is measured in the first wave of postprogram data collection (October 1998, wave 3). First, households may have incentives to endogenously respond to the program by changing the structure of households, in particular, by artificially forming new households in order to increase the number of eligible individuals in the family. This concern is partly ameliorated by the fact that a register of eligible households was drawn up in the baseline wave of data, and only households recorded to be eligible at that point were later entitled to receive transfers. In addition, although there is an increase in the number of households from the baseline survey to wave 3, this increase is proportionately the same in both treatment and control villages. A second concern is that the program may affect the migration of the household head or of his spouse. One piece of evidence against this is that only 0.35 percent (0.50 percent) of households in wave 3 (wave 5) report hav-

ing a migrant head or spouse. Moreover, the share of households with such migrants does not differ across treatment and control villages.

5. The precise wording of the question in Spanish is as follows: "Dígame por favor el nombre completo con todo y apellidos de todas las personas que viven en este hogar, empezando por (jefe del hogar)—(i) nombre; (ii) apellido paterno; (iii) apellido materno."

6. We manually cleaned the names data according to the following criterion. We first removed nonalphabetical characters, replaced "sin apellido" (no surname) with missing values, and corrected some obvious typos based on intrahousehold surname checks. Second, we imputed a small number of missing female surnames from wave 2 (as wave 2 data only contains information on surnames for transfer recipients); and finally, we verified the surnames data using the same information from wave 5. No information on surnames is available in the first wave of data.

7. We use the convention that the head's surnames are written in Roman font and those of his wife in italic font. Paternal surnames are indicated in uppercase and maternal surnames in lowercase. First names are not shown because they are not relevant for the construction of extended family links. Each household in the family tree is assumed to be couple-headed purely to ease the exposition. In Anglo-Saxon countries, F1 would correspond to the family name and *F2* would correspond to the mother's maiden name.

8. Angelucci et al. (2006) provided evidence from the Mexican Family Life Survey (MxFLS), which contains information on the number of family links that exist in any location, to verify that the within-village links that we identify in the Progresa data are indeed no larger than those measured in the MxFLS for a comparable subsample of households.

9. Angelucci et al. (2006) used the MxFLS data to verify the extent to which the Progresa data underestimates the number of links from household i to the parents of the head or spouse because some of those parents will undoubtedly be widowed. However, they noted that female widows above 40 are 37 percent more likely to live as a dependent than as head of an independent household, relative to a similar married woman.

10. These population values are calculated as follows for any given surname type. Let n_i denote the number of households with surname i, and let N denote the number of households that report some surname of the given type. The probability, without replacement, that two randomly chosen households have surname i is then $P_i = (n_i/N).((n_i - 1)/(N - 1))$, and the expected number of households in the population with name i is $E_i = n_i.((N - 1)/N)$. The values reported in table 7.1 are the averages of P_i and E_i over all surnames i.

11. These village values are calculated as follows for any given surname type. Let n_{iv} denote the number of households with surname i in village v, and let n_v denote the number of households that report some surname of the type in village v. The probability, without replacement, that two randomly chosen households in the village have surname i is then $p_{iv} = (n_{iv}/n_v).((n_{iv} - 1)/(n_v - 1))$, and the expected number of households in the village with name i is $e_{iv} = n_{iv}.((n_v - 1)/n_v)$. The values reported in table 7.1 are the weighted averages of p_{iv} and e_{iv} over all villages v, where the weights are n_{iv}/n_v. These weights take account of the fact that the same name may be reported to different extents in different villages.

12. This odds ratio is calculated as follows for any given surname type. We first take the weighted average of p_{iv} over all names i where the weights are n_v/N. These weights take account of the fact that if two households are drawn from the population at random, they

are more likely to come from a larger village. Denote this weighted probability as $\tilde{p}_i$. The reported odds ratio is then given by $\tilde{p}_i/P_i$.

13. For the variance decomposition to sum to the total variance in an unbalanced panel, it is necessary to weight the between component by the number of households in the village, denoted H_v. If N denotes the number of observations in the sample and there are N_v villages, the decomposition of the total variance of the number of family links of household h in village v, L_{iv}, into the within and between components, as reported in table 7.2, is

$$\frac{1}{N}\sum_{v=1}^{N_v}\sum_{i=1}^{H_v}(L_{iv}-\bar{L}) = \frac{1}{N}\sum_{v=1}^{N_v}\sum_{i=1}^{H_v}(L_{iv}-\bar{L}_v) + \frac{1}{N}\sum_{v=1}^{N_v} H_v(\bar{L}_v-\bar{L}).$$

14. We experimented with other specifications before settling on this set of controls. For example, we do not control for years of education because it is highly correlated with literacy; 89 percent (90 percent) of heads (spouses) have no formal schooling if they are illiterate. We focus on temporary rather than permanent migration because the proportion of households that report any members permanently migrating in the five years prior to 1997 is only 3.3 percent.

15. These differential effects of a given control variable across two columns can be easily tested for by using a t-test. This is based on first stacking any two columns of data, say for L_{jh} and $L_{j'h}$, defining the dependent variable to be equal to 1 if either L_{jh} or $L_{j'h}$ are equal to 1, and zero otherwise, and then introducing a complete set of interactions between each control and a dummy variable that is equal to 1 if the observation is from the first column, and zero otherwise. The null hypothesis for the t-test is that the interaction term is zero.

16. Single nodes correspond to three types of household: (1) those in which all family relations are living under the same roof; (2) those for whom there are no children or siblings of the head or spouse heading their own households in the village and for whom the parents of the head and/or spouse are outside the household but are widowed; and (3) those for whom there are no children or siblings of the head or spouse heading their own households in the village and for whom the parents of both head and spouse have either died or do not reside in the same village.

17. There is one observation per family network, so each network has the same weight irrespective of the number of households within it. In the household-level statistics in the lower panel of table 7.4, there is one observation per household, so family networks that are larger will have more weight associated to them.

18. There is a growing theoretical literature on the strategic behavior of agents within network structures. For example, Galeotti et al. (2008) developed a framework to analyze strategic interactions when each agent's underlying network affects their payoffs. Bloch, Genicot, and Ray (2008) developed a model of insurance and information exchange within networks.

19. Earlier studies using Progresa have found evidence of the program's effects on noneligible households (Bobonis and Finan 2006). Progresa's spillover effects are not, however, limited to schooling outcomes. Angelucci and De Giorgi (2006) showed that the program also increases consumption among noneligible households. The mechanism behind this is that the liquidity injection of the program benefits all village residents by improving insurance against risk, thus enabling households to borrow more and reduce their stock of precautionary savings.

20. We thus build on the earlier work of Schultz (2004), Attanasio, Meghir, and Santiago (2005), and Behrman, Sengupta, and Todd (2005), who estimated the effects of Progresa on school enrollment but did not explore whether these effects are heterogeneous according to the presence and characteristics of extended family members.

21. There is evidence from the United States that schooling choices within extended families are correlated. Loury (2006) used data from the National Longitudinal Survey of Youth (NLSY) to show the extent to which the characteristics of extended family networks are correlated to child schooling outcomes. Aunts', uncles', and grandparents' levels of education are significantly correlated to college attendance probabilities and test score results of their younger relatives. In some cases, the sizes of the estimated effects are large enough to substantially narrow the achievement gap between disadvantaged and other youth.

References

Albarran, P., and O. Attanasio. 2004. Do Public Transfers Crowd Out Private Transfers? Evidence from a Randomized Experiment in Mexico. In *Insurance Against Poverty*, ed. S. Dercon. Oxford: Oxford University Press.

Altonji, J. G., F. Hayashi, and L. J. Kotlikoff. 1992. Is the Extended Family Altruistically Linked? Direct Tests Using Micro Data. *American Economic Review* 85: 1177–1198.

———. 1997. Parental Altruism and Inter Vivos Transfers: Theory and Evidence. *Journal of Political Economy* 105: 1121–1166.

Angelucci, M., and G. De Giorgi. 2006. Indirect Effects of an Aid Program: How Do Liquidity Injections Affect Non-eligibles' Consumption? Discussion paper 06-01. Department of Economics, University College London.

Angelucci, M., G. De Giorgi, M. A. Rangel, and I. Rasul. 2006. Family Networks and Schooling Outcomes: Evidence from a Randomized Social Experiment. University College London.

Attanasio, O., and V. Lechene. 2002. Tests of Income Pooling in Household Decisions. *Review of Economic Dynamics* 5: 720–748.

Attanasio, O., C. Meghir, and A. Santiago. 2005. Education Choices in Mexico: Using a Structural Model and a Randomized Experiment to Evaluate Progresa. Working paper EWP05/01. Institute for Fiscal Studies, London.

Bandiera, O., and I. Rasul. 2006. Social Networks and Technology Adoption in Northern Mozambique. *Economic Journal* 116 (514): 869–902.

Becker, G. S. 1981. *A Treatise on the Family*. Cambridge, Mass.: Harvard University Press.

Behrman, J. R., and M. R. Rosenzweig. 2006. Parental Wealth and Adult Children's Welfare in Marriage. *Review of Economics and Statistics* 88: 496–509.

Behrman, J. R., P. Sengupta, and P. Todd. 2005. Progressing through Progresa: An Impact Assessment of a School Subsidy Experiment in Rural Mexico. *Economic Development and Cultural Change* 54: 237–276.

Bernheim, D., A. Shleifer, and L. H. Summers. 1985. The Strategic Bequest Motive. *Journal of Political Economy* 93: 1045–1076.

Bloch, F., G. Genicot, and D. Ray. 2008. Informal Insurance in Social Networks. *Journal of Economic Theory* 143: 36–58.

Bobonis, G., and R. Finan. 2006. Endogenous Peer Effects in School Participation. ⟨http://www.aeaweb.org/annual_mtg_papers/2007/0106_0800_0502.pdf⟩.

Cox, D., and G. Jakubson. 1995. The Connection between Public Transfers and Private Interfamily Transfers: Theory and Evidence. *Journal of Public Economics* 57: 129–167.

Chen, Z., and F. Woolley. 2001. A Cournot-Nash Model of Family Decision Making. *Economic Journal* 111: 722–748.

Chiappori, P. A. 1988. Rational Household Labor Supply. *Econometrica* 56: 63–90.

Conley, T., and C. Udry. 2005. Learning about a New Technology: Pineapple in Ghana. Working paper 817. Economic Growth Center, Yale University.

Dercon, S., and P. Krishnan. 2000. In Sickness and in Health: Risk Sharing within Households in Rural Ethiopia. *Journal of Political Economy* 108: 688–727.

Foster, A. 1993. Household Partition in Rural Bangladesh. *Population Studies* 47: 97–114.

Foster, A., and M. Rosenzweig. 1995. Learning by Doing and Learning from Others: Human Capital and Technical Change in Agriculture. *Journal of Political Economy* 103: 1176–1209.

———. 2002. Household Division and Rural Economic Growth. *Review of Economic Studies* 69: 839–869.

Galeotti, A., S. Goyal, M. O. Jackson, F. Vega-Redondo, and L. Yariv. 2008. Network Games. Working paper ECO2008/07. European University Institute.

Granovetter, M. S. 1985. Economic Action and Social Structure: The Problem of Embeddedness. *American Journal of Sociology* 91: 481–510.

Jensen, R. T. 2003. Do Private Transfers Displace the Benefits of Public Transfers? Evidence from South Africa. *Journal of Public Economics* 88: 89–112.

Loury, L. D. 2006. All in the Extended Family: Effects of Grandparents, Aunts, and Uncles on Educational Attainment. *American Economic Review* 96: 275–278.

Lundberg, S., R. Pollak, and T. Wales. 1997. Do Husbands and Wives Pool Resources? Evidence from the UK Child Benefit. *Journal of Human Resources* 32: 463–480.

Manser, M., and M. Brown. 1980. Marriage and Household Decision Theory: A Bargaining Analysis. *International Economic Review* 21: 21–34.

Manski, C. F. 1993. Identification of Endogenous Social Effects: The Reflection Problem. *Review of Economic Studies* 60: 531–542.

McElroy, M., and M. Horney. 1981. Nash-Bargained Decisions: Toward a Generalization of the Theory of Consumer Demand. *International Economic Review* 22: 333–349.

Munshi, K., and M. Rosenzweig. 2009. Why Is Mobility in India So Low? Social Insurance, Inequality, and Growth. NBER working paper 14850.

Qian, N. 2006. Missing Women and the Price of Tea in China: The Effect of Sex-Specific Earnings on Sex Imbalance. Discussion paper 5986. Center for Economic and Policy Research (CEPR), Washington, D.C.

Rangel, M. A. 2005. Alimony Rights and Intra-household Allocation of Resources: Evidence from Brazil. *Economic Journal* 116 (513): 627–658.

———. 2006. Allocation of Resources within Extended Family Households. Unpublished paper. University of Chicago.

Raut, L. K., and L. H. Tran. 2005. Parental Human Capital Investment and Old-Age Transfers from Children: Is it a Loan Contract or Reciprocity for Indonesian Families? *Journal of Development Economics* 77: 389–414.

Rosenzweig, M., and O. Stark. 1989. Consumption Smoothing, Migration, and Marriage: Evidence from Rural India. *Journal of Political Economy* 97: 905–926.

Rubalcava, L., G. Teruel, and D. Thomas. 2004. Spending, Savings, and Public Transfers Paid to Women. Working paper 024004. California Center for Population Research (CCPR).

Schultz, T. P. 1990. Testing the Neoclassical Model of Family Labor Supply and Fertility. *Journal of Human Resources* 25: 599–634.

———. 2004. School Subsidies for the Poor: Evaluating the Mexican Progresa Poverty Program. *Journal of Development Economics* 74: 199–250.

Skoufias, E. 2005. Progresa and Its Impacts on the Human Capital and Welfare of Households in Rural Mexico: A Synthesis of the Results of an Evaluation by IFPRI. Research report 139. International Food Policy Research Institute (IFPRI), Washington, D.C.

Thomas, D. 1990. Intra-household Resource Allocation: An Inferential Approach. *Journal of Human Resources* 25: 635–664.

Townsend, R. 1994. Risk and Insurance in Village India. *Econometrica* 62: 539–591.

Wasserman, S., and K. Faust. 1994. *Social Network Analysis: Methods and Applications.* Cambridge: Cambridge University Press.

8 Land Rights Revisited

Stefan Dercon and Pramila Krishnan

The role of property rights in development has long been one of the central themes in the economic analysis of institutions. Behind much of this work is a hypothesis that well-defined individual property rights, codified and protected by the state, provide a central precondition for economic growth. Arguments for this view can be found in the work of classical economists such as Adam Smith.[1] More recently, this view was revived in the work of economists such as Coase (1960) or Demsetz (1967) and, within a historical context, North (1981). Macrolevel studies provide suggestive evidence that institutions governing property are an important factor in explaining growth and the lack thereof in parts of the world (North and Weingast 1989; Acemoglu, Johnson, and Robinson 2001). This macroeconomic evidence is mainly based on cross-country growth regressions in which rather crude aggregate data are used to develop highly suggestive narratives. While these narratives receive much attention in policy circles, they converge on the following: institutions, including providing secure and transferable property rights, matter for development.[2]

In this chapter, we briefly revisit some of this literature, focusing on the rights to one crucial asset in most poor developing countries, land. Like the other chapters in this collection, this chapter does not focus on the macrolevel evidence but takes a microeconomic approach. Although many of the issues are generic, our focus in terms of the evidence is on rural land rights in Africa. With poverty persistence most notable in Africa, and with most of the poor still living off the land, this focus remains relevant. We complement the existing evidence by highlighting the case of land rights in Ethiopia. Given its size and persistent poverty, the case of Ethiopia is justifiably highlighted in any debate on the causes of low growth and development. Furthermore, the evolution of its historically feudal land rights system to its more recent system of state-owned land should render its current and historical land institutions of interest to any student of institutions and their implications.

In the next section, we revisit the standard arguments for why secure, individual property rights matter for efficiency. We then discuss some generic methodological issues associated with the empirical exploration of the link between land-related property rights and efficiency. We highlight issues related to the macroeconomic approach and present the case for, and some problems with, a microeconomic analysis. Next, we introduce the Ethiopian case study, describing its recent evolution of land rights and emphasizing its differences with more commonly studied cases in Africa. The final section uses a rural panel data set from Ethiopia with detailed data on land rights perceptions to supplement existing evidence on the impact of the particular land rights context on specific investments in land.

Property Rights and Efficiency

North (1981) provided the standard definition of an economic institution as "a set of rules, compliance procedures and moral and ethical behavioural norms designed to constrain the behaviour of individuals in the interests of maximizing the wealth or utility of principals" (201–202). A property rights system provides such a set of rules, assigning rights to use specific goods or assets from a nonprohibited set of uses. Full private property rights assign and recognize the exclusive use of goods to particular individuals, bounded by some constraints, such as that this use does not violate the rights of someone else. They give an individual access rights to the stream of benefits from these goods and the right to transfer this right to others in whatever way he chooses. These rights are secure and inalienable so that enforcement is never in doubt. However, many property rights are not as complete or individualistic as described here. For example, property rights could be communal, whereby rights are shared, or private but restricted, such as in the context of particular types of customary law whereby rights cannot be wholly ceded by those to whom an asset has been allocated.[3]

Standard results from welfare economics as reflected in the welfare theorems rely on well-defined and enforceable property rights to endowments and commodities to reach conclusions on efficiency of the competitive equilibrium. The rights are private in the sense that control over the use of all endowments and commodities is assigned to specific agents. As developed by Coase (1960), private property rights internalize all incentives, providing a route to efficiency. Two aspects of this need to be emphasized in order to understand the problems related to the inefficiencies caused by incomplete property rights. The first aspect relates to the security of the right to benefit from the use of the endowments and commodities. For example, the stream of benefits from use of endowments in production will accrue to the owner, as will the costs.[4] There is also no uncertainty surrounding whether someone else, another individual or the state, will expropriate these commodities by taking over the right to benefit from them. A second, related aspect addresses the right to trade or exchange the right to the benefits itself; there should be no restrictions to realizing gains from trade. Within the context of otherwise perfect conditions for competitive equilibrium, these related features ensure perfectly aligned incentives for efficient use of resources, with opportunities to realize full gains from trading that are necessary for efficiency.

These efficiency benefits can also be shown to exist in response to marginal improvements in property rights. Besley (1995) provided a simple but comprehensive theoretical exposition of these two basic features of property rights and their implication for incentives to investment in assets, such as land. He showed that marginal improvements in security (expressed as a reduction in the probability of expropriation) or improvements in the ability to trade the asset (modeled as a reduction in the transactions costs of trading) increase investment incentives. He also showed that within the context of imperfect credit markets, for example, due to agency or enforcement of contract problems, there is a third benefit of improved property rights on investment. If land is easier to collateralize because of improved rights, then the bank can lower interest rates, increasing land investment.

However, improving property rights does not occur in a vacuum outside the market; rather, strategic behavior may aim to influence the allocation of rights. Besley (1995) discussed how land rights can be influenced by investment: in particular contexts, such as Ghana in his case, improving the land may result in an increased claim to the land, reducing the risk of expropriation. Deininger and Jin (2006b) presented a related model in which improved security may have ambiguous effects on investment if investment can increase both productivity and future security. More generally, if improving land rights involves actions by the state or another specific agent, then this process may provide incentives for directly unproductive investments, such as corrupt side payments, which may offset any efficiency gains. Improving land rights may also be costly, requiring, for instance, substantial investments in legal institutions. Consequently, a relatively highly efficient, rich economy may be needed to develop such legal institutions, limiting the scope for land rights improvement to stimulate efficiency in poorer contexts.

Furthermore, a multitude of alternative non-market-based coordination mechanisms exist to complement imperfect markets. Examples include informal reciprocal insurance institutions or interlinked credit and other factor markets. The theory of the second best shows that addressing one market failure, such as improving the security of land property rights, will not necessarily lead to an increase in efficiency (Bardhan, chapter 1 in this volume). For example, as Udry and Goldstein (2005) argued, the finding of some inefficiencies in the customary land rights system in the area of Ghana that they were studying does not necessarily prove the case for recommending the introduction of full private land property rights in this context. This was demonstrated by Banerjee, Getler, and Ghatak (2002), who showed that increased land tenure rights may not always lead to efficient outcomes within the context of market imperfections that offer a role for sharecropping contracts. Their model suggests that a landlord's threat to evict a tenant may encourage the tenant to produce greater yields by increasing his effort to an efficient level.

Macroeconomic and Microeconomic Approaches to Studying the Role of Land Rights

In recent years, the main focus of applied empirical work on property rights and their impact has been the exploration of this relationship in the context of cross-country comparisons. In this section, we first briefly revisit the main insights and limitations of this literature. We then explore the opportunities offered by the microeconomic approach as well as the methodological challenges of its application.

An important driving force in the expansion of the cross-country literature on growth and institutions has been the increased availability of data on variables describing institutional quality. A variety of measures have been used, including those related to law enforcement, the operations of formal sector financial markets, democracy, trust, corruption, and bureaucracy (Hall and Jones 1999; Knack and Keefer 1995; Mauro 1995). The most relevant direct measure related to property rights appears to be the measure of protection against expropriation risk, first used by Knack and Keefer (1995) and subsequently in many other studies, such as Acemoglu, Johnson, and Robinson (2001). The measure is defined as a score of the risk of expropriation of foreign private investment by government.

The evidence suggests a close link between protection against expropriation risk and growth. Allowing for the fact that institutions may be the consequence of growth, the most convincing evidence applies an instrumental variable approach with historical data as instruments. Using this strategy, Acemoglu, Johnson, and Robinson (2001) found strong effects of expropriation risk on growth: one standard deviation increase in the protection against expropriation risk increases GDP per worker by 309 percent.[5]

How convincing is this evidence in arguing the case for prioritizing improvement of property rights, more specifically land rights, in developing countries? Clearly, this is highly suggestive evidence that shapes broad policy debates. Nevertheless, much caution needs to be applied. For example, the instruments used are fixed for each country. As a result, the instrumental variable (IV) estimates are purged of the effect of any institutions that change over time. However, this implies that the IV approach cannot identify the consequences of the change in institutions on growth.

More crucially, the nature of the data on institutional quality and the aggregate nature of analysis may well limit its use for policy in particular countries. A number of reasons can be put forward, specifically when considering land issues. First, the measure used when looking at land issues relates to the risk of expropriation for foreign investors. This requires a strong assumption that all investors, domestic or foreign, in all sectors, rural and urban, face the same risks. If anything, the measure may be representative for parts of the urban formal sector but is unlikely to be sufficiently informative for the rural or informal sectors.[6] A related problem is the assumption of macroeconomic analysis that changes in the particular index affect different firms and individuals in different sectors in the same way, even though market failures and variable enforcement of rules are bound to imply that changes in rules and rights in fact have heterogeneous impacts.

Pande and Udry (2006) presented a careful discussion of the weaknesses of the cross-country regression approach for analyzing land issues using this index of risk of expropriation, building on a thorough exposition of evidence from West Africa (Côte d'Ivoire, Gambia,

Congo, Ghana). First, a distinction has to be made in terms of de jure and de facto land rights: customary land law matters in West Africa. Formal codification of the rules governing land allocation is important, but these may not be the full set of rules and norms that guide land rights in practice. In these settings, customary law remains relatively strong and matters in differential ways across countries. Furthermore, land rights are multidimensional, with specific *aspects* of land rights varying between settings. For example, the security of particular land rights within the same country and setting may still differ; land tenure rights are more secure in Ghana than in Côte d'Ivoire in some communities or for some individuals, whereas for others the opposite is true. This heterogeneity also implies that there are likely to be heterogeneous effects from improvements in the overall index of risk of expropriation that are ignored in the cross-country approach.

There are therefore strong arguments in favor of exploring land rights and, more generally, property rights, in the context of microlevel studies in particular countries or regions. A crucial advantage is the relative homogeneity of the institutional and economic contexts, which helps to avoid serious problems of unobserved heterogeneity. Within well-defined contexts, it is more straightforward to find ways of capturing the quality of specific institutions measured by the way in which they affect particular groups and sectors. Average measures of, say, the risk of expropriation, bear little relationship to the actual risks faced by individual cultivators of different areas and plots; using microlevel data, we can allow for these differences in land rights. We may also be able to introduce a more careful analysis of the political economy of rights, that is, the incentives for strategic behavior and the role of political power in shaping rights, which would hardly be possible when investigating rights using average measures. For example, the political economy of land rights, which affects the relative importance of customary versus codified law, can be directly brought into the analysis, as in Udry and Goldstein (2005).

Nevertheless, important challenges remain in this microlevel research program. First, there are serious issues associated with measurement of property rights, such as rights to land. Recognizing that de facto rights may be different from de jure rights requires detailed data on these rights beyond the simple codified rules.[7] If there is heterogeneity in the actual meaning of similar land rights across agents, one must find ways of identifying this heterogeneity in data collection. Furthermore, for investment incentives, local and individual understanding of these rights (perceived rights) are more important than formal legal rights, further affecting the way data may need to be collected or interpreted.

We also need sufficient variation in land or other property rights to be able to identify the effects of these rights in data. Working within a homogeneous institutional, legal, and economic setting may limit this variation. Here, the advantage of the research agenda as applied to developing countries is obvious. Contrary to most rich economies, where there is only limited variation in land institutions within countries, land rights in developing countries display substantial variation. Just listing some examples from Africa, we find customary and formal codified laws both affecting land rights in some settings, such as in Ghana, the Democratic Republic of Congo or Côte d'Ivoire. In recent years, land titling experiments have been taking place in Tanzania or Ethiopia. In many contexts, such as Malawi, communal law still governs the allocation of land rights within communities, although there is increasing pressure for individualization of rights.[8]

The existing variation in land rights within many developing countries provides sources of exogenous variation that allow more credible routes to identifying causal effects. For example, in a number of settings in the developing world, changes to land rights have taken place relatively recently or are in the process of taking place, for example, in the form of introduction of formal land titles. However, while it may be tempting to simply look at the change in efficiency or other outcomes before and after the land rights changes for some households, this general change over time would not necessarily constitute a legitimate source of exogenous variation for identification of the impact of policy change. For instance, it is unlikely that the strategy used during the introduction of formal land titles was entirely random, devoid of any processes of selection, including political ones. The impact may be further contaminated by strategic behavior on the part of households aimed at becoming eligible for the title.

In some settings, it has been possible to exploit features of the implementation of the titling or other land rights programs to convincingly evaluate the impact of land titles. For example, in their work on Peru, Field and Torero (2004) exploited the staggered implementation of the program so that some neighborhoods were reached earlier than others. This neighborhood difference provided the means for comparison of outcomes between those participating in the program and those not. Other studies, such as Banerjee, Getler, and Ghatak (2002) or Do and

Iyer (2008), exploited differences in the way the program was affecting comparable groups in a similar way to identify the impact of the particular forms of land tenure reform that they were studying in India and Vietnam.

Another source of exogenous variation that can be used to identify the impact of land rights and possibly changes in land rights may stem from a proper understanding of the incentives and constraints that a particular land rights system poses for individual households within this land rights system. One may then exploit this information to understand the impact of the institutional setting on outcomes, to the extent that these incentives and constraints vary by the economic, social, or political positions of the households. For example, one may have information on the rules or practice governing implementation of land rights changes. Alternatively, one may have an understanding of the links between actual land rights and the particular social or political position of households. Udry and Goldstein (2005) measured differences in perceived land rights in an area of Ghana and showed that these perceptions were correlated with the political positions of individuals within the community. Holding a political office then becomes the source of exogenous variation linking perceived tenure security to particular outcomes, in their case, yields via the duration of fallow. This allowed them to conclude that there are strong causal effects from land institutions to outcomes.

Such examples demonstrate that this microeconomic approach can convincingly highlight the impact of the institutional settings on outcomes. As mentioned, it nevertheless remains difficult to draw simple policy conclusions from this type of work. For example, showing that institutions cause inefficiencies does not resolve the issue of how to implement change, not least since this process of change will be part of the local political economy as well.

Case Study: Land Rights in Ethiopia

Much work has been done using microlevel data in Africa to explore the impact of land institutions on outcomes and efficiency. Many of these studies have explored land rights in the context of the interaction between customary law and often colonial codified land rights. Besley (1995) provided evidence, for example, showing that in one setting in Ghana (Wassa), having a deed had a positive effect on land rights, whereas in another area (Anloga), customary rules appeared to result in a deed's lowering rights. Overall, he found that land rights increase productivity. A number of studies on Kenya (e.g., Migot-Adholla, Hazell, and Place 1991; Pinckney and Kimuyu 1994) focused on the impact of the land registration policy that had started in the 1960s on farm productivity, finding no impact relative to plots governed by customary law. Brasselle, Gaspart, and Platteau (2002) presented further evidence from other studies, including on Uganda, Burkina Faso, Niger, and Somalia. It is striking that the evidence does not strongly support a positive impact of titles or deeds on land rights and productivity.[9]

Ethiopia presents a different case but not a less interesting one.[10] Traditional customary land rights do not feature here, nor do any private land titles. A land reform in 1976 and subsequent turmoil in rural areas entirely destroyed the previous feudal land institutions. Since then, formal institutions, ultimately controlled by the state, have allocated land to peasants, who only have usufruct rights and face serious limitations on transfer rights.[11] In this section, we introduce the general context of land rights in Ethiopia. In the next section, we discuss evidence on the factors determining land rights perceptions and their impact on investment in perennial crops.

The current land institutions were formed as a consequence of the revolution that removed the emperor from the throne in 1973 and the subsequent establishment of a military government, which is usually referred to as the Dergue (the Committee). This new government implemented a large-scale land reform in 1976. Since then, land has been owned by the state, which offers use rights to farm households. Hiring-out of land, let alone its sale, exchange, or mortgaging, was not allowed, and only under specific and strict conditions could sharecropping take place. Local peasant associations (PAs) were given the task of deciding and distributing user rights to cultivators. These PAs were effectively the local government for an administrative unit consisting of a small number of villages. Legally, land was offered to families based on their household size; this broad correlation is confirmed by all available data. In most areas, cultivators were allowed to retain some of the land that they had been cultivating before the policy change. This group included farmers who had inherited land or were simply tenants for large landlords. Further, under the new system, landless farmers were also accommodated. Nevertheless, it appears that political and local factors played a considerable role as well, suggesting a diverse experience in implementation (Rahmato 1984).

Since the first land reform in 1976, land allocation has been implemented at the local level. Land redistribution decisions are taken at the PA level by a specific committee. Periodic land redistributions were used to reallocate land. Even though land size and need should have been the guiding principles for land redistributions, the process left much room for interpretation and discretion. For instance, whether a newly formed household should be entitled to land was left up to these local decision makers, as were judgments on land quality and, in a country with no codified land measurement units, decisions on the size of the land offered. Suspicions of forms of capture have been well documented (e.g., Rahmato 1984, 43).

As the result of this implementation strategy, there were repeated land reallocations in many areas. For example, the Ethiopian Rural Household Survey (ERHS) showed that more than one-third of households randomly selected from communities in the main regions of the country had lost land at one point or another during the period 1976–1991 through land reallocation. Another study, by Benin and Pender (2001), examined ninety-eight PAs and found that on average they had three land redistributions in this period; one PA even reported fourteen land reallocations, effectively one per year.

The underlying legal framework remained similar until the end of the Dergue government in 1991. After its fall, land reallocations were temporarily halted pending a new constitutional framework. The practice of repeated land redistribution had been already frozen in 1989 as part of the market-oriented reforms undertaken by the Dergue. In practice, at the local level, some occasional land reallocations continued to take place. Politically, land rights again became one of the most hotly debated topics. Expectations were raised for a dramatic reversal toward privatization of land, but in 1996 a new constitution was adopted that consolidated the existing situation with only minor amendments. The constitution states that land is the collective property of the state, and a mandate is given to regional governments for its administration. The constitution offers usufruct rights to land, free of charge, to any farmer who wants to make a livelihood from farming, but strictly prohibits sale, exchange for other property, or mortgage. Land leasing to a third party has now been allowed. Furthermore, transfers within families, specifically toward offspring, are also guaranteed.

On paper, these broader land rights should have provided more stability than before. In practice, land rights remained in turmoil. In

Tigray, it was announced that there would not be any further land redistribution, and in 1998 land registration started tentatively. However, in many parts of the country, any sense of increased stability of rights was undermined by inconsistency in the proceedings. For example, in late 1997 and early 1998, political tensions resulted in the unexpected restart of land reform in one region, the Amhara region, where land was offered to former soldiers and others. This changed the mood about land rights in the country; contrary to the stated policy, compensation was not paid to the former owners of this reallocated land (Holden and Yohannes 2002). In Southern Nations, Nationalities and People's Regional State (SNNP) and Oromia, the other two large regions in Ethiopia, no clear policy statements were made until about 2002. More recently and belatedly, tentative steps have been made toward some registration in all regions.

A number of studies in the period after the new constitution in 1996 have reported that farmers fear that they will be subjected to possible land redistribution without compensation at any time in the near future. In the Amhara region, Benin and Pender (2001) reported, that 80 percent of communities expected further land reform by 2000. Based on a nationally representative survey of farm households, Deininger and Jin (2006b) found that 9 percent of the farmers were affected by land redistribution in the period between 1991 and 1998. In addition, less than one-third of the farmers did not expect land redistribution in the near future. In the data set used in the next section, these results are reasserted: about 7 percent of households in 1999 lost land during land redistribution in the preceding five years; 11 percent of households expected to lose land in the next five years because of land reform; and 10 percent expected to gain land.

Case Study: The Microlevel Determinants of Land Rights and Their Impact in Ethiopia

In this section, we revisit some evidence on the impact of land rights on investment in land and trees in Ethiopia, extending Dercon, Ayalew, and Gautam (2006), in light of the preceding discussion on the problems in analyzing land rights and their impact in microlevel studies. We also draw on evidence from a related study by Deininger and Jin (2006b), who used a large cross-section survey of more than 8,500 farm households conducted in 2001, covering the main agroecological zones. Dercon and co-authors (2006) used the Ethiopian Rural

Household Survey, a panel data set with six rounds collected between 1994 and 2004, covering about 1,450 households with relatively low attrition (about 3 percent per round). Although data on land rights were collected in the last three rounds (1997, 1999 and 2004), Dercon and coauthors (2006) used only data from 1997 and 1999 because some variables required for the analysis were not available in 2004.

Here, we explore and extend the evidence presented in this study on the basis of three questions. First, in principle, microlevel studies can explore the differences in land rights between different groups or individuals. How can we unbundle and measure land rights in this context, and what does the evidence from doing so tell us? We highlight some problems associated with measurement of land rights via surveys and discuss whether the measures reflect the dimensions one would like to capture. Second, what determines land rights and changes therein in the local context? In particular, we explore how local differences in economic, social, and political positions appear to affect the nature of land rights in the experience of different farm households over time. This provides a possible way of identifying the differential impact of land rights on outcomes. Third, what evidence exists on the impact of land rights on land-related investment?[12]

Studying rural land rights and consequences in Ethiopia is difficult for at least one reason: no land is privately owned—it all belongs to the state and is controlled by the local government. As the result, there is no variation in formal land rights across individuals in terms of legal rights. Nevertheless, given the history of recurring land redistribution, there is likely to be variation in the *perception* of land rights among households and plots. Both Deininger and Jin (2006b) and Dercon, Ayalew, and Gautam (2006) collected data on perceptions of different dimensions of land rights based on household surveys. This presents three problems. First, because these are subjective perceptions, they are not necessarily directly related to the actual land rights offered and enforced. But in research on the consequences of land rights in terms of investment and efficiency, it is perceived rights that govern behavior, so this is not a serious problem in our context.[13] Second, collecting subjective data via surveys is vulnerable to framing issues, such as whether the question asked has direct meaning in the context studied. Third, rights have multiple dimensions, and perceptions of rights are rarely in the form of having full rights or no rights. Collecting information on the perceived distribution of rights may be better but is difficult in practice.

Using (broadly) nationally representative data, Deininger and Jin (2006b) collected a data set on a variety of dimensions of land rights, including perceptions of particular transfer rights (rental/sharecropping, mortgage/inheritance, and sales rights) as well as whether the household expected land redistribution in the coming five years. Some data on the recent experience with land redistribution (since 1991) were also collected. The authors found that perception of the right to rent or sharecrop—a right explicitly allowed for in the constitution—was widespread but not complete (91 percent). In contrast, virtually no one (only 4 percent) perceived a right to sell, which is illegal, although there were reports that in some areas people had started engaging in land sales unofficially.[14] About 9 percent of households expected a land redistribution to affect them in the next five years, and 27 percent expected no redistribution. The rest appear to have responded "don't know"—a rather high percentage.

Our own field work experience in collecting the data used in Dercon, Ayalew, and Gautam (2006) highlighted some of the data collection problems related to land. Probing for the perceived risk of expropriation in the next five years proved difficult; a high number of inconsistencies were found during piloting and the actual survey. One reason may have been that phrasing the issue negatively (losing land) made it seem too sensitive within these communities; farmers may have been unwilling to express their fears or confidence. Asking these questions without a time frame of five years also proved difficult. The problems during piloting in probing about these risks of losing land led us to exclude the questions in the 1997 survey, although for comparison we included them again in 1999 and 2004.[15]

Probing for transfer rights in the form of sales or mortgaging rights proved difficult as well, with virtually all farmers offering the official line that these transactions are banned. Similarly, little variation could be detected in perception of rental or sharecropping rights, which by 1997 appear to have been fully established. As a result, after much piloting, a decision was made to focus the survey on probing for perception of the right to benefit from the land and to decide the destiny of the plot of land, leaving the nature of the transaction open (although the primary suggestion was bequests and intrafamily transfers).[16] While these choices were highly dependent on the context in which the research took place, the added advantage of a focus on these control rights is that an open-ended time horizon was used, beyond five years. This appeared helpful in investigating the impact of land rights on perennial crops, such as coffee, which require a long-term perspective, well beyond five years, because any newly planted trees would only offer a full harvest after about eight years and continue to do so for several decades. With low life expectancy and high risk morbidity, an intergenerational perspective would be required for investment. The data revealed that about 59 percent of the land was considered to have land rights defined in this particular way in 1997. In 1999 this proportion decreased to about 52 percent, and by 2004 it was 58 percent. These differences across years are statistically significant.[17]

Both the cross-sectional and time series variation in these measures of land rights are worth exploring further. In principle, there was no formal change in the legal position of land rights during this period. The constitutional change in 1996 largely formalized an existing situation by allowing rental and sharecropping. The only real change was a *commitment* to long-term user rights, including bequest and related interfamily rights.[18] A major change between the first two rounds of the data used (1997–1999) was the unexpected major land reform in parts of one region, Amhara region. If this incident led people to alter their perceptions and see land reform as back on the agenda, it would have provided changing incentives and affected perceptions of land rights. Such an effect would be consistent with the drop in perceived rights between 1997 and 1999 and the subsequent recovery. Without data directly linking these events to the changing perceptions, the link between these shocks and the policy environment is not easily established. Nevertheless, it is possible to explore the correlation between the changes in perceived land rights observed in the data and household characteristics describing the relative economic and political position of the household.

We regressed the perceived rights to transfer land to relatives or others at the plot level on a set of household and plot characteristics, controlling for community fixed effects.[19] The sample size was 9,325 plots. Explanatory plot-level variables included mode of acquisition (whether the land was initially purchased, inherited, or sharecropped, using allocated land as a base group)[20] and how long the plot had been cultivated by the household. Plot-level controls included land quality variables and plot size (not reported). Household-level variables included total household size, total land holdings per capita, and whether the household had ever lost any land up to the particular survey round. To investigate the role of local capture, we included a variable for whether the household held a powerful position on the committee allocating land in the community before 1995, since this is generally seen as a sign of political power in the village (around 10 percent of the sample had held such a position). Table 8.1 shows the results. Column 1 gives the OLS results controlling for community fixed effects, effectively pooling the sample across the three rounds. Column 2 estimates the same specification but with household fixed effects which control for unobserved heterogeneity. Since we are dealing with data on perceptions, controlling for household fixed effects may help to account for systematic household-level pessimism or optimism regarding rights, and other unobservable correlates.

In both regressions, there is a strong negative correlation of land rights with sharecropped plots, relative to allocated plots. Households perceive land rights offered by the state as in any case substantially stronger than those based on simple rental and sharecropping arrangements. However, the difference is well below 1, whereas the expected difference would be 1 if state-allocated land offered full rights and sharecropping none at all (given that this land is offered for sharecropping by another household). In the fixed-effects specification, being a wealthy farmer in terms of land appears to increase perceived rights as well, which is consistent with a hypothesis of capture related to economic positions.

In column 3 of table 8.1, the way the correlates of land rights changed in this period is explored further by interacting the variables describing the mode of acquisition with a year dummy. This enables us to investigate the changes in coefficients for each mode of acquisition over time and relative to land directly allocated by the local government. We also allow for variation over time in the role of the political power variable. In addition, the regression controls for community time-varying fixed effects.

First, it can be noted that non-government-allocated land, such as inherited and purchased land, appears to have lower perceived land rights from 1999; in other words, the level of perceived rights to inherited and purchased land is lower than that to allocated land.[21] By 2004 the perceived rights linked to allocated land also appear to become stronger in relation to those for sharecropped land. Interestingly, this would be consistent with a gradually improved sense of long-term security of land rights to government-allocated land. However, this is only relative to rights to the land that farmers first obtained via purchase and especially inheritance (about 33 percent of all plots), often well before the first land reform in 1976. The time dummy shows that

Table 8.1
Determinants of Perceived Transfer Rights and Threat of Expropriation, 1997–2004

	(1) OLS	(2) Linear Fixed Effects	(3) Linear Fixed Effects	(4) Conditional Logit
Sharecropped plot	−0.451*** (31.01)	−0.471*** (26.43)	−0.416*** (16.24)	−4.394*** (12.07)
Inherited plot	−0.01 (−0.59)	−0.022 (−1.18)	0.107*** (4.60)	0.732*** (3.77)
Purchased plot	0.051 (−1.43)	−0.006 (−0.15)	0.204*** (3.93)	1.975*** (3.58)
Years plot cultivated	0.001* (1.87)	0 (−0.22)	0.001* (1.80)	0.005 (−1.26)
Influential position in PA	0.007 (−.047)			
Whether ever lost land?	0.089*** (5.87)	0.173*** (8.10)	−0.055** (2.19)	−0.472** (2.24)
Household size	−0.003 (−1.59)	−0.002 (−0.34)	0.004 (−0.99)	0.024 (−0.69)
Land per capita	0.013 (−0.95)	0.047*** (2.79)	0.103*** (6.67)	0.697*** (5.43)
1999 sharecropped plot			−0.001 (−0.04)	1.728*** (4.30)
2004 sharecropped plot			−0.329*** (8.06)	−1.834*** (2.64)
1999 inherited plot			−0.149*** (4.50)	−0.996*** (3.68)
2004 inherited plot			−0.192*** (4.79)	−1.437*** (4.35)
1999 purchased plot			−0.406*** (5.94)	−3.825*** (5.53)
2004 purchased plot			−0.326*** (4.12)	−2.701*** (3.87)
1999 influential post			0.054* (1.95)	0.62*** (2.63)
2004 influential post			0.065* (1.91)	0.766** (2.52)
Constant	0.694*** (18.02)	0.591*** (12.65)	0.45*** (10.56)	
Time dummy, 1999			−0.073* (1.69)	−0.552* (1.66)
Time dummy, 2004			−0.286*** (6.12)	−1.825*** (5.06)

Table 8.1
(continued)

	(1) OLS	(2) Linear Fixed Effects	(3) Linear Fixed Effects	(4) Conditional Logit
Plot quality and plot size	yes	yes	yes	yes
Household fixed effects		yes	yes	yes
Community fixed effects	yes		yes	yes
Time-varying community fixed effects			yes	yes
No. of observations	9,833	9,961	9,833	7,702
R-squared	0.16	0.09	0.3	
No. of households		1,140	1,127	736

Notes:
Dependent variable is "perceived rights to transfer land."
Robust *t*-statistics in parentheses.
* significant at 10%; ** significant at 5%; *** significant at 1%.

the constant, which incorporates the land rights of the base group who have land allocated by the government, went down significantly in 1999 and 2004.

Second, there is a striking effect on the political power variable in 1999, persisting up to 2004. The coefficient suggests an increase in the perceived land rights, relative to the base year 1997, by those who have in the past been closely involved in the committees allocating land within the villages studied. This could reflect a simple information issue. Those with local political power may have found the constitutional commitment to long-term land rights more credible after 1999 (after the land reform of 1997–1999 in Amhara), or they may have been expecting land reallocations, which they could have made to count to their advantage, given their influence. Column 4 of table 8.1 repeats this analysis using a fixed-effect conditional logit regression to avoid some of the issues associated with estimating a limited dependent variable model with a linear specification. The findings are even clearer and stronger for the points discussed earlier. First, these results confirm a weakening of perceived land rights for inherited and purchased plots relative to government-allocated plots. Second, they show increasing perceived land rights from 1999 for those with a history in committees related to land reallocation, which persists also in 2004. One effect is somewhat different: in 1999 those cultivating sharecropped plots perceived their land rights as having increased in 1999 relative to 1997 and relative to government-allocated land. This would be consistent with raised expectations for land reform: in 1976 one of the guiding principles of the actual implementation of the land reform was "land to the tiller," with sharecropped land taken away from the owner and allocated by the government to the sharecropper.

While interesting in their own right, these correlations do not answer a more fundamental question: What is the impact of these perceptions of land rights on efficiency and investment? Deininger and Jin (2006b) and Dercon, Ayalew, and Gautam (2006) addressed this issue using their data on land rights perceptions. Deininger and Jin (2006b) investigated the impact focusing on terracing and planting trees as forms of investment, given different measures of perceived land rights. They only observed propensities to invest over a limited period of time, and only for broad categories of investments. They also could not directly control for endogeneity but tried to assign the bias in the theoretical model by exploring the empirical evidence accordingly. Their evidence is suggestive of a significant negative impact of the lack of land rights on investment.

Dercon, Ayalew, and Gautam (2006) used the data in table 8.1 but restricted their analysis to four of nineteen communities and 300 households living in areas suitable for growing perennial crops, such as coffee. The time period considered is limited to two years, 1997 and 1999. Perennial crops require a long-term commitment beyond five years, typically an intergenerational one. In the data, the area allocated to perennials remained at 30 percent in each of the two years, although a significant shift toward coffee and away from other crops, such as eucalyptus and *chat*, can be observed.[22] As in the full sample, on average, perceived land rights decreased significantly in this period. Nevertheless, about 21 percent of households reported improved rights, and 44 percent reported similar rights as in 1997. The rest, 35 percent of the households, reported worse rights than before.[23] The group perceiving worsened rights reduced the land share allocated to perennial crops by 4.4 percent, and those reporting improved rights increased land allocated to these crops by 4.5 percent. These changes are significant and constitute suggestive evidence for the hypothesis that land areas allocated to perennial crops are affected by changes in perceived land rights.

The underlying regression in Dercon, Ayalew, and Gautam (2006) used a household fixed-effects model with share of land allocated to tree crops by the household as the left-hand-side variable. However, it may well be that trees (such as coffee trees) are planted to affect land rights; in this case there is a problem of endogeneity. For example, as noted by Besley (1995) and others, trees may be planted to increase the claim to land rights, which subsequently improves perceived transfer rights. There are other good reasons to suspect endogeneity, including that the same unobservable factors that may induce a change in land allocated to particular perennial crops may alter perceived transfer rights. For example, particular farmers may simply develop a more pessimistic outlook, which is totally unrelated to the changing and confusing land policy environment. In this case, the change in perceptions has little to do with the change in land allocation to perennial crops, in a causal sense. To deal with the problem of potential endogeneity, the household average of the plot-level transfer right-hand variable was treated as endogenous. In view of the results reported in table 8.1, we used two variables as identifying instruments: whether the household head had in the past (before 1995) an influential position in the committee for land allocation in the village, and the share of cultivated land sharecropped for more than two years.

The specification by Dercon and co-authors (2006) further includes household fixed effects control for all sources of unobserved and observed heterogeneity at the household and farm levels, including controls for factors that may affect allocation to specific crops, such as knowledge, risk preferences, and wealth or farmland quality. There are also controls for some household-level time-varying variables, such as changing household characteristics (number of adults, livestock wealth, land owned). A large number of different household characteristics were tried; none affected the findings and are therefore not reported. Time-varying community fixed effects are used to capture relative price changes and other communitywide factors that may affect land allocation.

Table 8.2 reports the results. Column 1 contains the OLS estimates, which show that full perceived land rights, as defined previously, increase the land allocated to perennial crops by 4.5 percent. Column 2 shows the effect of land rights in a 2SLS specification, treating land rights as endogneous, when the share of land sharecropped for at least two years and the village power variable are used as identifying instruments.[24] The first-stage IV regression passes the usual tests for instruments, which appear relatively strong, although the Sargan overidentification test is only rejected at 9 percent. In Dercon, Ayalew, and

Table 8.2
Impact of Perceived Land Rights on Land Allocation to Perennial Crops, 1997–1999

	(1) OLS		(2) 2SLS	
	Coefficient	*p*-value	Coefficient	*p*-value
Land rights?	0.045	0.02	0.115	0.04
Cragg-Donald identification chi-square			41.54	0
Sargan overidentification chi-square			7.93	0.09
Joint significance *F*-test for identifying instruments			8.09	

Notes:
n = 300.
Dependent variable is "share of land allocated to perennial crops."
All models control for household fixed effects and time-varying community fixed effects.
p-values report significance levels for two-sided tests of equality of the coefficient to zero.
Column 1 is linear fixed effects model assuming transfer rights exogenous; column 2 is 2SLS fixed effects regression based on a first-stage regression with instruments. The identifying instruments include the share of land sharecropped for at least two years and whether the household has a powerful position in peasant association (PA), with time interactions and land size interactions.

Gautam (2006), the instruments and the robustness of the results were further explored. They showed that dropping sharecropped land as an excluded instrument does not significantly change the results. The evidence suggests a significant effect of perceived land rights on land allocation to perennial crops. One cause of the decline in land allocated to coffee by some farmers in the sample is the changes in the perceived land rights in this period. Dercon and co-authors (2006) calculated that if one improved land rights perceptions for government-allocated, purchased or inherited land fully, then this could be expected to raise the share of land allocated to perennial crops by 16 percent (from just under 30 percent to about 35 percent of land allocated to these crops). Coffee is the dominant perennial crop in these areas. It is also the main source of export earnings for Ethiopia, suggesting substantial economic benefits from improving farmers' perception of land rights.

Conclusion

This chapter revisited the analysis of property rights in a developing context, with an emphasis on land rights. A review of the macroeconomic evidence pointed to a number of econometric problems as well as issues of interpretation and policy relevance. In the context of land rights, the difference between codified legal rights and customary rights or local practices for implementation and enforcement makes the use of simple indicators, such as whether a title for the land exists, unlikely to be sufficient to describe variation in rights across countries. Furthermore, within countries, a set of existing land rights may have differential impact on different households, a point lost when using aggregate analysis but necessary for understanding the policy implications. Furthermore, any change in land rights, such as via titling programs, are themselves affected by the local political economy and strategic behavior.

A microeconomic approach to the study of land rights and its implications is then warranted because context-specific information can be used to understand differential rights and their implications within countries, to address the problems associated with the macroeconomic approach. However, this does not mean that all methodological and analytical problems are easily resolved. In particular, the fact that land rights may have different meaning and implications for different households poses a challenge for the measurement of these rights. Furthermore, to link land rights to outcomes such as efficiency and investment requires that rights variables represent exogenous variation in the data. This chapter discussed a number of possible approaches to dealing with these problems. One approach is to exploit a situation in which there is variation between otherwise similar households resulting from some households and not others getting particular rights. Such a situation may, for instance, occur because of a gradual rolling out of a program. Another route is to include information that reflects the political and economic position of households because, in the context of particular land rights systems, it affects the incentives and constraints faced by households.

This chapter discussed some of these issues in a case study of Ethiopia. In this country, land is state-owned and farmers only obtain user rights for the land. Land redistributions have been a regular occurrence, although a recent constitutional change includes a commitment to more secure long-term land rights. The chapter used a panel data set on perceptions of land rights, focusing on a right to control who can get the land, for example, in the form of a bequest or a gift to a relative, which appears to be offered in the altered 1996 constitution. This right is relevant in the context of long-term investments such as coffee, which require a horizon of more than a decade, as well as high mortality and morbidity. We also discussed some of the problems of measuring land rights in this setting, which led us to focus exclusively on land rights defined in this way.

The data showed that between 1997 and 2004 there was some variation in these rights, with on average a decline in perceived land rights in 1999, possibly linked to renewed fear of land reform in the wake of an unexpected redistribution in part of one region. The correlates of the factors determining these changes showed that they are consistent with a loss in perceived land rights in absolute terms between 1997 and 1999 and in relative terms for government-allocated land compared to originally inherited and purchased land. Those with a history of political influence at the local level also appeared to improve their perceived land rights in this period; this trend was consistent with expectations that they might benefit from any new land redistributions. There is also evidence that those with sharecropped land appeared to have perceived land rights to these plots that are higher than they would have been in a setting of well-defined ownership rights, possibly consistent with expectations that these sharecroppers may be able to obtain these plots from the government for long-term use during a new redistribution of land.

The variable describing the history of political influence in land allocations before 1997 was found to be a helpful identifying instrument to address the endogeneity of land rights in a regression that explored the impact of land rights on land allocated to perennial crops (mainly coffee) in 1997 and 1999. The results showed that land rights as defined in this chapter matter for land allocation. Offering full and credible long-term rights to inherited, historically purchased, and government-allocated land would increase the proportion of land allocated to perennial crops by 16 percent. Given the importance of coffee in the Ethiopian economy, this is likely to have strong effects for overall growth.

Notes

1. Adam Smith ([1776] 1978) started his first lecture in the first series of lectures on jurisprudence with "The first and chief design of government is to maintain justice: to prevent the members of society from encroaching on one another's property, or seizing what is not their own. The design here is to give each one the secure and peaceable possession of his own property" (5). He appears to have found this a self-evident statement, as relatively little further discussion on this point appears in his work.

2. For example, see tables 1 and 2 in Pande and Udry (2006).

3. Bruce and Migot-Adholla (1994) documented forms of customary land laws in Africa with this feature.

4. In contrast, such arrangements as communal land may invite free-rider problems, resulting in underinvestment in the land.

5. Acemoglu, Johnson, and Robinson (2001) used settler mortality as their instrument. They used mortality rates among European-born soldiers, sailors, and bishops while stationed in colonies to measure the effects of local diseases on people without inherited or acquired immunities. The argument is that in places Europeans could not easily settle because of high mortality they were more likely to set up extractive institutions. These extractive institutions affected current institutions, with the causality going from potential settler mortality to current performance only via institutions.

6. For example, many countries have established different types of export-processing zones and other schemes to stimulate investment by foreign investors. These schemes offer specific rights, incentives, and safeguards that are well above what investors in the nontradable or rural sector would receive.

7. Codified rules may provide useful instruments in statistical analysis, but if the way the formal legal structure maps onto actual rights is heterogeneous, the meaning of the average effect is limited for policy purposes, as this heterogeneity has been purged out of the analysis.

8. Pande and Udry (2006, table 4) showed the wide variety of land rights exploited in microlevel studies in the developing world.

9. One reason may be that many of these works assume property rights variation to be exogenous, potentially causing biased inference. Only Brasselle, Gaspart, and Platteau (2002) and Besley (1995) tried to account for this problem using variables such as mode of acquisition and tenure history.

10. This section draws on Dercon, Ayalew, and Gautam (2006).

11. This land rights system has more in common with, for example, China or Vietnam than with other African countries. A number of works by Rozelle and co-authors (Rozelle and Li 1998; Jacoby, Li, and Rozelle 2002; Brandt, Rozelle, and Turner 2004) explored the effects of land reallocation in northeastern China by village administrators. The dismantling of agricultural cooperatives in the late 1970s ushered in a household responsibility system whereby households were granted user rights to land in return for meeting particular tax and quota obligations. Ownership remained vested with the village, and despite calls for tenure security, a series of land reallocations followed in which land was taken away from households and redistributed to others. However, the data display substantial heterogeneity in the security of tenure displayed across villages; in some security is high, and apart from the right to sell land, households seem to be able to deploy the land as they choose. Since there is variation in both the timing of reallocation and where it occurs, the data can be exploited to evaluate the effect of expropriation risk on investment.

12. A number of other studies explored the impact of land rights on long-term investments in Ethiopia. Holden and Yohannes (2002) investigated the planting of perennial crops using data from fifteen different sites in southern Ethiopia. They found that tenure insecurity has little effect on the decision of farmers to plant perennials. Gebremedhin and Swinton (2003) suggested that farmers' perceived land tenure security in Tigray was significantly and positively associated with long-term durable soil conservation

investments such as stone terraces. Gebremedhin, Pender, and Ehui (2003) argued, using village-level data, that perceived tenure security increases land investments. Despite their suggestive evidence, these studies do not appear to address endogeneity and other identification problems sufficiently.

13. The reverse, constructing "objective" land rights without considering the perception of these rights independently, is possibly more problematic. For example, in a study on the impact of land rights in China, a context rather similar to the Ethiopian case, Jacoby, Li, and Rozelle (2002) focused exclusively on calibrating "objective" risks of expropriation based on past history of expropriation and linked these to land-specific investments.

14. They also reported perceived mortgage and inheritance rights (table 2), but as a joint category. Note, however, that while inheritance would seem to be possible now with the altered constitution, mortgaging land is still explicitly banned, making this category unfortunate and hard to interpret.

15. It is possible to link the data from 1999 on the risk of losing land in the next five years to whether land was actually lost in 2004. In 1999, 14 percent of households expected to lose land. Overall, only 2.2 actually lost land in 2004. There is some correlation between those expecting to lose land and actual land losses: of those that lost land in 2004, 16.6 percent expected to lose land five years earlier, compared to 13.9 percent of those that did not lose land. The difference is not significant. By 2004 the percentage of people expecting to lose land in the subsequent five years went down to 6.3 percent.

16. The question asked was, "Are you able to pass on the plot to a family member or someone else?"

17. There is some correlation between losing land in 2004 and limited control rights in 1999: 47 percent of the land held by those who lost land in 2004 was classed as land that could be passed on to relatives and others (i.e., land with land rights), whereas among those who did not lose land, this proportion was 52 percent. This difference is not significantly different from zero.

18. The period considered is too early for the more recent initiatives, which have resulted in offers of land registration.

19. It would have been interesting to unpack the differences across regions and communities, but with only fifteen villages this could not be done in a robust way.

20. Purchased land refers largely to land purchased before the land reform. It accounts for less than 3 percent of the plots in the sample. About 30 percent of the plots were inherited, and 9 percent are sharecropped plots. Approximately 68 percent of the plots are allocated; this is used as the base group in the regressions.

21. For example, the sum of the coefficient on the level variable plus the interaction term for 1999 for purchased land is now -0.20, implying that relative to land allocated, this type of plot had on average 20 percent lower perceived land rights in 1999.

22. *Chat* is a mild drug with effects similar to amphetamine. It is increasingly widely grown and used in Ethiopia and exported to neighboring countries.

23. The analysis is conducted at the household level, using plot sizes to weight the contribution of plot-specific land rights in a household measure of land rights.

24. The "power" variable is also interacted with land size to allow for different effects for those with a large amount of land and those without. It was found that those on the land

allocation committees with smaller land parcels had significantly lower predicted land rights than those with more land. We used land sharecropped for at least two years, and not just any land sharecropped, so that any land acquired via sharecropping as part of a strategic decision in response to the changing land rights situation would be excluded. For example, it could be that people tried to engage in sharecropping in 1998 so as to benefit from possible land reform in favor of those not owning the land they cultivate. Only the share of land sharecropped before 1997 is included as an instrument to deal with this issue.

References

Acemoglu, D., and S. Johnson. 2005. Unbundling Institutions. *Journal of Political Economy* 113 (5): 949–995.

Acemoglu, D., S. Johnson, and J. A. Robinson. 2001. The Colonial Origins of Comparative Development: An Empirical Investigation. *American Economic Review* 91 (5): 1369–1401.

Adal, Y. 2001. Some Queries about the Debate on Land Tenure in Ethiopia. In *Proceedings of the Tenth Annual Conference on the Ethiopian Economy.* Ethiopian Economics Association.

Alston, L. J., G. D. Libecap, and R. Schneider. 1995. Property Rights and the Preconditions for Markets: The Case of the Amazon Frontier. *Journal of Institutional and Theoretical Economics* 151 (1): 89–107.

Atwood, D. A. 1990. Land Registration in Africa: The Impact on Agricultural Production. *World Development* 18 (5): 659–671.

Banerjee, A. V., P. J. Getler, and M. Ghatak. 2002. Empowerment and Efficiency: Tenancy Reform in West Bengal. *Journal of Political Economy* 110 (2): 239–280.

Benin, S., and J. Pender. 2001. Impacts of Land Redistribution on Land Management and Productivity in the Ethiopian Highlands. *Land Degradation and Development* 12: 555–568.

Besley, T. 1995. Property Rights and Investment Incentives: Theory and Evidence from Ghana. *Journal of Political Economy* 103 (5): 903–937.

Binswanger, H. P., K. Deininger, and G. Feder. 1995. Power, Distortions, Revolt and Reform in Agricultural Land Relations. In *Handbook of Development Economics*, vol. 3, ed. J. R. Behrman and T. N. Srinivasan. Amsterdam: Elsevier.

Brandt, L., S. Rozelle, and M. A. Turner. 2004. Local Government Behavior and Property Rights Formation in Rural China. *Journal of Institutional and Theoretical Economics* 127 (4): 627+.

Brasselle, A. S., F. Gaspart, and J.-P. Platteau. 2002. Land Tenure Security and Investment Incentives: Puzzling Evidence from Burkina Faso. *Journal of Development Economics* 67: 373–418.

Bruce, J. W., and S. E. Migot-Adholla, eds. 1994. *Searching for Land Tenure Security in Africa.* Washington, D.C.: World Bank.

Carter, M. R., and P. Olinto. 2003. Getting Institutions Right for Whom? Credit Constraints and the Impact of Property Rights on the Quantity and Composition of Investment. *American Journal of Agricultural Economics* 85: 173–186.

Coase, R. M. 1960. The Problem of Social Cost. *Journal of Law and Economics* 3: 1–44.

Collier, P., and J. W. Gunning. 1999. Explaining African Economic Performance. *Journal of Economic Literature* 37 (1): 64–111.

Deininger, K., and J. S. Chamorro. 2004. Investment and Income Effects of Land Regularization: The Case of Nicaragua. *Agricultural Economics* 30 (2): 101–116.

Deininger, K., and S. Jin. 2006a. Land Rental Markets in the Process of Structural Transformation: Productivity and Equity Impacts in China. WPS 4454. World Bank.

———. 2006b. Tenure Security and Land-Related Investment: Evidence from Ethiopia. *European Economic Review* 50 (5): 1245–1277.

Demsetz, H. 1967. Toward a Theory of Property Rights. *American Economic Review* 57 (2): 347–359.

Dercon, S., D. Ayalew, and M. Gautam. 2006. Land Rights and Investment in Rural Ethiopia. Unpublished paper.

Do, Q., and L. Iyer. 2008. Land Titling and Rural Transition in Vietnam. *Economic Development and Cultural Change* 56: 531–579.

Feder, G., and D. Feeny. 1991. Land Tenure and Property Rights: Theory and Implications for Development Policy. *World Bank Economic Review* 5: 135–153.

Feder, G., and T. Onchan. 1987. Land Ownership Security and Farm Investment in Thailand. *American Journal of Agricultural Economics* 69 (2): 311–320.

Feder, G., T. Onchan, Y. Chalamwong, and C. Hongladarom. 1988. *Land Policies and Farm Productivity in Thailand.* Baltimore: Johns Hopkins University Press.

Federal Republic of Ethiopia. 2002. Poverty Reduction Strategy Paper. World Bank and International Monetary Fund.

Field, E., and M. Torero. 2004. Do Property Titles Increase Credit Access among the Urban Poor? Evidence from a Nationwide Titling Program. Unpublished paper.

Gavian, S., and S. Ehui. 1999. Measuring the Production Efficiency of Alternative Land Tenure Contracts in a Mixed Crop–Livestock System in Ethiopia. *Agricultural Economics* 20: 37–49.

Gebremedhin, B., J. Pender, and S. Ehui. 2003. Land Tenure and Land Management in the Highlands of Northern Ethiopia. Unpublished paper.

Gebremedhin, B., and S. Swinton. 2003. Investment in Soil Conservation in Northern Ethiopia: The Role of Land Tenure Security and Public Programs. *Agricultural Economics* 29 (1): 69–84

Glaeser, E. L., R. La Porta, F. Lopez-de-Silanes, and A. Shleifer. 2004. Do Institutions Cause Growth? *Journal of Economic Growth* 9 (3): 271–303.

Greene, W. 2003. Fixed Effects and Bias Due to the Incidental Parameters Problem in the Tobit Model. Working paper. Department of Economics, Stern School of Business, New York University.

Hall, R., and C. Jones. 1999. Why Do Some Countries Produce So Much More Output per Worker than Others? *Quarterly Journal of Economics* 114: 83–116.

Hoben, A. 2000. Ethiopian Rural Land Tenure Policy Revisited. Paper presented at the Symposium for Reviewing Ethiopia's Economic Performance 1991–1999. Inter-Africa Group, Addis Ababa.

Holden, S., and H. Yohannes. 2002. Land Redistribution, Tenure Insecurity, and Intensity of Production: A Study of Farm Households in Southern Ethiopia. *Land Economics* 78 (4): 573–590.

Jacoby, H., G. Li, and S. D. Rozelle. 2002. Hazards of Expropriation: Tenure Insecurity and Investment in Rural China. *American Economic Review* 92 (5): 1420–1447.

Jagger, P., and J. Pender. 2000. The Role of Trees for Sustainable Management of Less-Favored Lands: The Case of Eucalyptus in Ethiopia. Discussion paper 65. International Food Policy Research Institute (IFPRI), Washington, D.C.

Knack, S., and P. Keefer. 1995. Institutions and Economic Performance: Cross-Country Tests Using Alternative Institutional Measures. *Economics and Politics* 7: 207–227.

Lanjouw, J. O., and P. I. Levy. 1998. Untitled: A Study of Formal and Informal Property Rights in Urban Ecuador. Discussion paper 788. Economic Growth Center, Yale University.

Mauro, P. 1995. Corruption and Growth. *Quarterly Journal of Economics* 110 (3): 681–712.

Migot-Adholla, S., P. Hazell, and F. Place. 1991. Indigenous Land Rights Systems in sub-Saharan Africa: A Constraint on Productivity? *World Bank Economic Review* 5 (1): 155–175.

North, D. C. 1981. *Structure and Change in Economic History*. New York: W.W. Norton.

North, D. C., and B. Weingast. 1989. Constitutions and Commitment: Evolution of Institutions Governing Public Choice. *Journal of Economic History* 49 (4): 803–832.

Pande, R., and C. Udry. 2006. Institutions and Development: A View from Below. Discussion paper 928. Economic Growth Center, Yale University.

Pender, J., and M. Fafchamps. 2006. Land Lease Markets and Agricultural Efficiency in Ethiopia. *Journal of African Economies* 15 (2): 251–284.

Pinckney, T. C., and P. K. Kimuyu. 1994. Land Tenure Reform in East Africa: Good, Bad or Unimportant? *Journal of African Economies* 3 (1): 1–28.

Place, F., and K. Otsuka. 2001. Population, Tenure, and Natural Resource Management: The Case of Customary Land Area in Malawi. *Journal of Environmental Economics and Management* 41 (1): 13–32.

———. 2002. Land Tenure Systems and Their Impacts on Agricultural Investments and Productivity in Uganda. *Journal of Development Studies* 38 (6): 105–128.

Platteau, J.-P. 1996. The Evolutionary Theory of Land Rights as Applied to sub-Saharan Africa: A Critical Assessment. *Development and Change* 27 (1): 29–86.

Rahmato, D. 1984. *Agrarian Reform in Ethiopia*. Uppsala, Sweden: Nordic Africa Institute.

———. 2004. A Review of Ethiopia's Land Tenure System and New Policy Initiatives. Report prepared for the World Bank, Addis Ababa, 2002.

Rozelle, S., and G. Li. 1998. Village Leaders and Land-Rights Formation in China. *American Economic Review* 88 (2): 433–438.

Shiferaw, B., and S. Holden. 1999. Soil Erosion and Smallholders' Conservation Decisions in the Highlands of Ethiopia. *World Development* 27 (4): 739–752.

Sjaastad, E., and D. W. Bromley. 1997. Indigenous Land Rights in sub-Saharan Africa: Appropriation, Security, and Investment Demand. *World Development* 25 (4): 549–562.

Smith, A. [1776] 1978. *Lectures on Jurisprudence.* Oxford: Oxford University Press.

Udry, C., and M. Goldstein. 2005. The Profits of Power: Land Rights and Agricultural Investment in Ghana. Discussion paper 929. Economic Growth Center, Yale University.

Weder, B. 1998. Africa's Trade Gap: What Should Africa Do to Promote Exports? ⟨http://www.unu.edu/hq/academic/Pg_area4/Weder.html⟩.

World Bank. 2001. *Attacking Poverty. World Development Report 2000/2001.* Washington, D.C.

Name Index

Subject Index